Springer

Berlin
Heidelberg
New York
Barcelona
Hong Kong
London
Milan
Paris
Singapore
Tokyo

Klaus Doppler · Christoph Lauterburg

Managing Corporate Change

Terminology checked by Prof. Dr. Klaus Hinst

Springer

Klaus Doppler
Ammergaustr. 15
81377 München

Christoph Lauterburg
Birkenstr. 243
8454 Buchberg, Switzerland

ISBN 3-540-67903-0 Springer-Verlag Berlin Heidelberg New York

Cataloging-in-Publication Data applied for

Die Deutsche Bibliothek – CIP-Einheitsaufnahme

Doppler, Klaus:
Managing corporate change / Klaus Doppler ; Christoph Lauterburg. –
Berlin ; Heidelberg ; New York ; Barcelona ; Hongkong ; London ;
Mailand ; Paris ; Singapur ; Tokio : Springer, 2000
   ISBN 3-540-67903-0

Springer-Verlag Berlin Heidelberg New York
a member of BertelsmannSpringer Science+Business Media GmbH

© Springer-Verlag Berlin Heidelberg 2001
Printed in Germany

Cover desig design & production, Heidelberg
Typesetting: otosatz-Service Köhler GmbH, Wü zburg
Printed on a d-free paper   SPIN: 107796 1   07/3020 ra – 5 4 3 2 1 0

Contents

List of Illustrations

Foreword

Whoever starts to write a book, ought to address three questions that arise. First, what sort of book is it meant to be? Secondly, who is it intended to help? And thirdly, has it not been written before by someone else – possibly several times, in fact, and much better?

Our answers to these questions, for the reader of this book and for ourselves, are: first, this book is intended as a kind of "cookbook" on how to manage change in companies and institutions – a book that will give you the courage to roll up your sleeves and get on with carrying out the changes that are needed. A book which highlights the most important ideas for taking action and gives a methodological guide to practical activities in specific projects. In other words, a "do-it-yourself" handbook on how to develop companies and organizations.

Secondly, our hope is that the book can be of use to people who are directing, or are involved in, processes of change and development within organizations: by employers and executives, organizational and personnel experts, trainers, and consultants. Or by people who have had bad experiences with organizational changes in their own professional environment – and who want to know whether there are better ways of approaching change than the ones they have seen in the past.

Thirdly: yes, unfortunately the book has indeed been written several times before – so far as its subject-matter is concerned, anyway. It was quite impossible for us to find a title that we could be absolutely certain had not been published already somewhere else. But most books on change management that we know of deal mainly with the basic principles of change and its prospects of success. What we wanted to do was to write from the basis of our practical experience, aiming the practitioner. With specific items for you to pick up and put to good use.

In part I   We deal with the question of why change has come to be necessary, how it should take place, and what the results should be.

In part II   We describe the laws that govern processes of change, and the principles that need to be followed to implement changes effectively and with tolerable social effects.

In part III The methodological tools are described: how to proceed in specific projects, as well as in the specific situations that can arise during processes of development and change. This is where you'll find the essential information you need about various methods and procedures, summed up in a few pages. However, with these "recipes," the same applies as in cooking: on its own, a recipe is no guarantee of success. To be sure of an enjoyable evening, you need to know the guests you're going to entertain, show a certain amount of tact, and add your own ideas – and above all: *create a good atmosphere!*

You can use this book like a cookbook and immerse yourself in it, or flick through it, or just pick out whatever you happen to need at the moment.

If somebody were to come up to us one day and say, "I read your book – and it helped me successfully carry out the changes needed in my area of responsibility" – then we would be able to say, "Mission accomplished!"

Part I
Scenario for the Future

Today's Situation, Tomorrow's Prospects

Warning signals

Wherever you go nowadays in the business world, and sometimes even in public institutions and government bodies, managers at all levels are under increasing pressure and stress – often, they are already at breaking point. Twelve hours a day in the office is a good average in many cases. The whole day is just one meeting after another. Business meetings over lunch, and in the evening dinner with clients. Time to read files and documents – at the weekend. Time to talk to staff: rarely. Time for quiet thought: on vacation – if ever.

Mergers, bankruptcies, and mass redundancies are the order of the day, with companies reorganizing left, right, and center. Plans are going out of date before they have even been implemented. And if a manager ever succeeds in keeping to his budget, he is liable to be subjected to an investigation because there must be something suspicious behind it.

Top managers are becoming more and more anxious about the future. Doctors are always pointing out that the health of many of the top people in business is being affected by way they have to work. Some have problems with their circulation, others with their digestive system; others again have problems with their blood alcohol levels. Insomnia and headaches, tranquilizers and antidepressive drugs: these are where the big growth is in today's business.

What's going on?

The world has changed totally. Entrepreneurship and company management are being conducted today in conditions completely different from what they were only a few years ago. There are three new structural conditions determining success or failure today: *reduced time resources, reduced financial resources,* and a *dramatic increase in complexity.*

Structural condition no. 1: reduced time resources

The whole business world is under massive pressure to achieve performance and change. This is primarily due to technological developments – mainly in the field of microelectronics, computer science, and telecommunications. It is largely computers and television that have brought about this upheaval. They make it possible to channel information in any way you want, and transport it almost instantaneously. This has led to an unimaginable acceleration of every single process involved in business.

It used to be that a retail store only found out once a year, after careful stocktaking, how many products of which types it had sold across the counter. Today, top managers in retail chains start a normal day's work by studying exact figures for nationwide sales the day before, broken down in any way they wish into hundreds or thousands of individual products or by each individual sales point, with all the useful comparative data added – and that very same day, targeted adjustments can be made on the sales front itself if they are needed. The good old days are long gone when you could drop a five-page or ten-page report into the mailbox and expect weeks to go by before a response or an edited version landed back on your desk. Today, in the era of remote data transmission, you are lucky to get one or two days' peace if the addressee happens to be away, or does not have time to go through the report immediately. And if you are not lucky, it will be only an hour before the corrected paper is back in your mailbox or churning out of the fax machine – and then the ball will be back in your court again.

At the same time, people's attitudes and behavior are changing in practically every area of life. Everything happening anywhere in the world is transmitted with live pictures and sound straight into the living-room of every single citizen and consumer. The shooting of President Kennedy, the first astronauts landing on the moon, starvation in Bangladesh, the Exxon Valdez pollution disaster on the coast of Alaska, the view from the cockpit of an American fighter-bomber at the moment the latest air-to-ground missiles were hitting their targets in Iraq, day turning to night in the desert when Saddam Hussein set all the oil wells on fire. On top of it all, every possible type of expert commentary is available to you in your own home – and sooner or later people form their own opinions as well.

And, in addition to all that, everyone is mobile nowadays – the individual's physical range of activity is many times larger than it used to be. Living in the country and working in town; a quick one-day business trip of a thousand miles; heli-skiing in the Rocky Mountains; snorkeling in the Maldives or on the Great Barrier Reef; going for a walk on the Great Wall of China or steeping oneself in legend in the Inca city of Machu Picchu in the Andes. It is the development of electronic media and modern transport that makes all these things possible.

The influence of the mass media and their effects on people's mobility are massive. Values that remained stable for decades or even centuries in earlier days are now being questioned. New lifestyles and customs are constantly emerging in society. Consumers' wishes and needs are changing from one day to the next.

Entire markets are collapsing, entire professions are disappearing – with new ones taking their place. At the same time, national boundaries are breaking down. International economic spheres are emerging. Even for small companies, world-wide business activities are now perfectly normal. And depending on the political and economic conditions, one country or another suddenly becomes attractive or unattractive as an export market or production base.

In other words: the economic, political, and social environment is becoming extremely unstable. While this means fresh opportunities, it also means fresh risks. A company that wants to survive in these turbulent conditions has to react quickly and be able to adapt to changing conditions quickly. That means: fast product innovation, shorter and shorter product life-cycles, and – both before and after – the internal company changes needed to make these possible. The pressure for innovation is massive, and the cycles of changes being introduced into organizational and personnel structures are breathtakingly fast. Speed has become a strategic factor for success. One smart observer of the scene has used this to calculate a new Einsteinian formula for success in business:

$$S = Qc^2$$
(Success equals quality times the speed of light squared)

Time-based management is one new recipe for success: a consistent effort to reduce processing time. A substitute for total quality management? By no means. Today, quality is still just as important as it used to be – but it is no longer sufficient. Only the ones who are fast as well as producing top quality are going to get ahead in the market.

Structural condition no. 2: reduced financial resources

Everyone has noticed that financial resources have recently been short everywhere. But even the so-called experts are not really sure what the reasons for this are. The most peculiar theories about business cycles are in circulation. The consequence is that many people still believe only a momentary whim of the world economy is involved, a transitory economic fluctuation of the type there has always been. This is a surprising attitude to take, since anyone who reads the newspaper is confronted with several fundamental facts every day.

- *Natural resources are being exhausted.* In earlier times, riches were harvested from the soil or from the sea. But those times are gone. There is an increasing shortage of wood. The oceans have been fished out. Drinking water is becoming a precious commodity. The American midwest, the world's granary, is threatening to turn into a desert as its water-table drops due to excessive irrigation. In short: raw materials are becoming more and more expensive.
- *Massive costs resulting from social distortions.* The aging of the population, progressive damage to the human immune defense system, and accelerating rates

of physical and nervous diseases associated with modern civilization, are leading to an exponential growth in the need for medical care – and at the same time, technological developments in medicine, mistakes made in the health-care system, and mismanagement in hospitals have meant that medical costs have exploded. Drug abuse is ruining the lives of increasing numbers of young people, causing immeasurable suffering to countless families and bringing crime in its wake, of a type that none of the world's security services are capable of fighting any more. And organized crime, eating away countries' economic life from the inside out, has now developed into the most important sector of the world's economy.

- *Increasing range of tasks the state is responsible for.* The security services are already unable to manage, there are hopelessly long delays in court procedures, the prisons are overcrowded, hospitals, retirement homes, schools, and universities are overstretched. Street cleaning and garbage disposal can no longer be carried out regularly. At the same time, due to technological and social developments, new legislation is constantly being passed – and bodies responsible for upholding the new laws are being created along with them. In spite of increasing cutbacks in many areas, these state activities can only be sustained by higher and higher taxes. And it is by no means rare for the same people who complain about "state intrusion" in one area to loudly demand more state intervention somewhere else – when it is something that affects their own pocket-book.

- *Threatening ecological catastrophe.* We are not going to defend the view here that environmental protection is in principle uneconomical and hostile to business. On the contrary, new, lucrative markets are opening up in this field. But the environmentally friendly production methods that are now required mean massive investment costs for industry. Above all, disposing of older harmful waste materials that have been incorrectly dumped – the deadly sins of the past – can consume unimaginable quantities of money. And our only choice is to pay up – or go under.

- *Living on credit.* Millions of consumers are living on credit nowadays. Most of the cars we see driving around the streets are not paid for. Most companies are living on credit as well – with quite a few financing their entire activities using outside capital. Their existence is under threat whenever the slightest cash-flow problems appear, and more and more bankruptcies are the result. The great majority of local authorities, states, and nations are deeply in debt – and many are not even able to pay back their interest any more. Both on the small scale and the large one, the moment of truth comes round sooner or later. "Credits" that are completely incapable of being repaid have to be written off. Corrective movements in values take place, and – in a world living entirely on credit – these can cause chain reactions in which industrial corporations, banking empires, and state budgets all collapse together. Small-scale and large-scale crashes become everyday events.

- *Balancing out rich and poor.* A balancing out of the world's wealth is imminent, both between east and west and between north and south. And in fact it has already started: masses of economic migrants are becoming a severe social and political problem in Europe. Here again, the only choice we have is between two equally costly alternatives: either we help developing countries and emerging economies to build their own powerful economies – or we will be hopelessly flooded with impoverished people in our own countries.

- *Ruinous competition for markets.* This is a home-made problem. Unbelievable overcapacities have accumulated in recent years throughout the industrial sector. Everyone has been carrying out their planning on the principle "it's a big world – and it all belongs to me." If only half of the cars were built that the various manufacturers had the capacity to make today, the roads would be so full that everything would grind to a halt. Hundreds of airplanes have already been mothballed, with no prospect of ever flying again since overcrowded airspace and limited runway and airport capacity make it impossible. The same applies to the printing trade, the construction sector, the computer industry – and many other sectors too. Too many large-capacity suppliers are treading on one another's toes in sharply restricted markets. This means: *everyone is getting less and less money for doing more and more.* Only the toughest are going to be able to survive this knockout competition. And every time a company goes bust, hundreds or thousands of people lose their jobs.

- *Ever smaller numbers of jobs.* This is probably the most serious long term problem. Mass unemployment on an as yet undreamed-of scale is more or less foreordained. It is fashionable nowadays to talk about "structural adjustments" and "healthy reductions" in the economy. The idea is encouraged that the main problem is how to retrain the unemployed. In fact, however, in practically every single market, many companies with no chance of long-term survival are still happily going about their business. Massive numbers of jobs are going to be lost in the coming years due to bankruptcies. But even when this big clean-up is over with and the survivors have gone through the most rigorous downsizing, the gradual reduction in jobs will still continue, without nearly being compensated for by new jobs. There are two reasons for this. First, more and more tasks – not only in manufacturing goods, but also in the service area – can be carried out faster, with more precision, and at lower cost today without any need for human activity. And if you want to survive, you have to make full use of these opportunities for rationalization and automation. Secondly, even jobs that cannot be automated are vanishing – they are being exported. More and more companies in Europe are closing down and moving to low-wage countries, for example in the Far East. And as long as there are countries with much lower standards of living and wage levels, European companies will be forced to export jobs.

All in all, it can be assumed that closures, rationalizations, and job exports will be threatening 30–40 % of existing jobs over the medium term. However, there are three processes connected with each individual new unemployed person in the economic cycle. First, there are massive costs to the state. Secondly, the state loses a taxpayer. Thirdly – and this is often overlooked – the market loses the spending power of a potential consumer. And without consumption the economy can never be healthy. At the time of writing, the politicians neither have any real awareness of this problem nor any scenario for what it means – and certainly no solutions for dealing with it. On the contrary, a perfectly astounding process of collective mental suppression of the problem is going on.

Each of the developments mentioned above is a serious factor restricting economic growth. But the combination of all these factors represents a powerfully explosive force (Figure 1). One has to ask, "Who is going to pay for it all?" Where is all the money going to come from that will be required and consumed by all of this?

The answer is simple, but unpleasant: it is going to come from all of us. Every single citizen and every single company. We will receive less and less money for the same amount of work – and at the same time we will have to pay higher and higher taxes. So the shortage of cash is not just going to be temporary. Money is going to continue to be short, and it will even get worse. In plain language: it will only be possible to absorb the profound shifts in the world economy mentioned above by suffering a significant *reduction in our living standards.*

This does not necessarily mean that we will be leading less healthy or less happy lives in the future. It is a well known fact that it is not money that makes people happy. But the age of affluence is definitely over. Optimizing performance and optimizing costs are going to be the factors determining entrepreneurial thinking and action.

Structural condition no. 3: dramatic increase in complexity

Everyone has the same impression – nowadays, there are just far too many things going on simultaneously. Politicians, managers, top officials: no one has an overall grasp any more of everything that is happening at any one moment. We are no longer always able to grasp why it is that things happen when they happen. We simply do not have a reliable grip on everything any more. We cannot always steer things when we think they need to be steered. And quite often, we find we are exposed to developments whose outcome we cannot predict at all.

But above all: everything is becoming increasingly "networked" with everything else. What you do in one place can have unpredictable effects somewhere else completely. Technical, economic, political, and social processes all influence each other interactively and develop their own dynamics. "Tip-over" effects happen, and from one day to the next what used to be a realistic scenario turns into its opposite. What this means is: it is not only a shortage of resources that we are facing, but also an increasing level of complexity. The business of management has become generally more difficult.

This is mainly due to rapid structural and social changes. Practically nothing today is the way it used to be – and if there is anything that can be reliably predicted, it is: *things are never going to be the way they used to be any more.* For many

Figure 1. Anatomy of the economic crisis

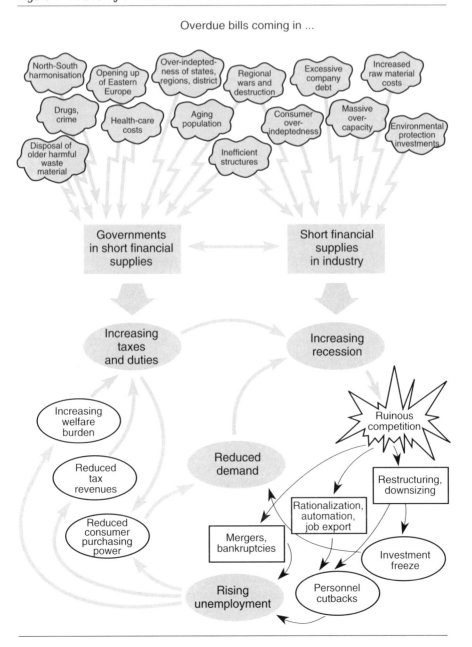

Overdue bills coming in ...

North-South harmonisation

Opening up of Eastern Europe

Over-indepted-ness of states, regions, district

Regional wars and destruction

Excessive company debt

Increased raw material costs

Drugs, crime

Health-care costs

Aging population

Consumer over-indeptedness

Massive over-capacity

Environmental protection investments

Disposal of older harmful waste material

Inefficient structures

Governments in short financial supplies

Short financial supplies in industry

Increasing taxes and duties

Increasing recession

Increasing welfare burden

Reduced demand

Ruinous competition

Reduced tax revenues

Rationalization, automation, job export

Restructuring, downsizing

Reduced consumer purchasing power

Mergers, bankruptcies

Investment freeze

Rising unemployment

Personnel cutbacks

Figure 2. Challenges that will shape everyday management work in the future

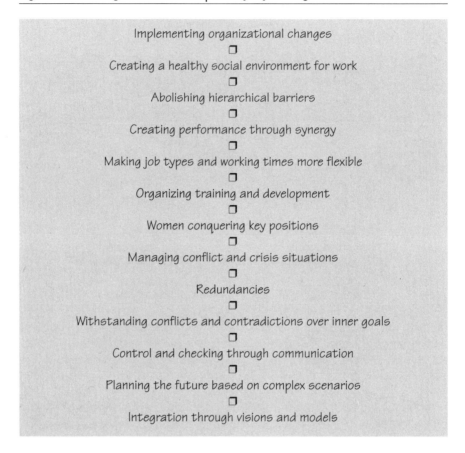

Implementing organizational changes

❒

Creating a healthy social environment for work

❒

Abolishing hierarchical barriers

❒

Creating performance through synergy

❒

Making job types and working times more flexible

❒

Organizing training and development

❒

Women conquering key positions

❒

Managing conflict and crisis situations

❒

Redundancies

❒

Withstanding conflicts and contradictions over inner goals

❒

Control and checking through communication

❒

Planning the future based on complex scenarios

❒

Integration through visions and models

people, however – and not only in business – this change has taken place too fast. Managers and executives are suddenly, often quite unexpectedly, faced with completely new tasks – tasks that sometimes require completely new forms of expertise and ability.

Based on a few of the important trends that can be recognized today, the following outline describes the ways in which the functions and tasks of managers are changing in everyday business life; the complexity this is introducing into their working lives; and what types of management ability will be needed in the future (Figure 2).

The new challenges

Implementing organizational changes

In the next few years, decisions will be taken on strategy and company policy to secure the future, shifting around duties and leading to new interfaces within organizations – often cutting through individual firms right down to the grass roots. These will include redesigning the product range; cutting administrative costs; planing down the hierarchy; creating results-oriented business areas; decentralizing to move closer to markets and customers; mergers, collaboration agreements, joint ventures; moving business activities to different countries.

Each of these decisions means that, for six months or the whole year, masses of management staff at every level will have to meet two challenges simultaneously: sustaining normal operations – and restructuring their organizational unit. In most cases, people are more or less capable of managing normal business operations, although even here not everyone is entirely in top form. But many people are today, for the first time in their lives, facing the need to reorganize their own area of responsibility as well. A project of this type requires special mechanisms for planning, control, communications, and leadership – and in personnel matters, the greatest possible prudence and care are needed to ensure that everyday business is able to carry on as usual without the atmosphere being ruined. And it all has to be done under extreme time pressure and pressure for results. This is all beyond the ability of some people – both as human beings and as managers.

Creating a healthy social environment for work

Enjoyable social conditions and collaboration in the immediate working environment – in addition to other factors such as adequate pay, interesting tasks, and freedom in the workplace – become all the more important the bigger a company is, the more technology it uses, the larger the number of changes that need to be made, and the greater the pressure is to produce results. Nowadays, people are no longer cocooned by life in their villages and extended families in the way they used to be. Often, they have not been brought up even with a minimum of human acceptance, security, attention, and warmth. As a result, they tend to seek an emotional "home" in their working life, in order to be able to identify with the company and unfold their full capacities for achievement.

Some of those who complain that workers today behave as if they were just doing odd jobs, without showing any interest in the business, should first take a good look at the state of human relations within their own area of responsibility. But this aspect of management work involves special requirements: enjoying contact with people; empathy; and also a certain amount of calm and a willingness to provide enough of one's time, since constantly looking at stopwatches and ticking off points on checklists does not always produce the best results in human communications.

Abolishing hierarchical barriers

Today it becomes more and more obvious that organizations with deep echelons of hierarchy are too slow-moving and inefficient for the fast speeds now required. Paths have to be shortened, and the number of levels has to be reduced. The slogan is "flat hierarchy." But a flat hierarchy means a wider span of control: each individual manager has a larger number of employees directly reporting to him or her. This in turn means a massive increase in the complexity of the management process: more employees requesting individual discussions, larger numbers of people at management meetings, greater efforts required for coordination, a wider variety of technical problems needing to be solved in everyday operations. And all of this, as mentioned above, at a generally much higher speed.

But even flat hierarchies cannot by themselves ensure that the top and bottom levels will never become divorced from one another. The cascade-like delegation of clearly delimited tasks from level to level leads to a fatal dilution of relevant information both from top to bottom and from bottom to top. The grass roots no longer know what "the people up there" really do, not to mention why they are doing it – and management no longer knows what people at the grass roots are concerned about, what it is that motivates them, and what it is they need in order to work at their best and produce results.

The system of official channels has not been superseded as a method of taking operational decisions and coordinating tasks. But quality management in a company requires that managers at every level should be able to communicate across several levels. Direct contact with the next level but one is needed in order to know what information is reaching them and what is not. Direct contact with the grass roots and a good ability to listen are needed in order to gain a sense of what is going on in the company. "Management by wandering around" is quite capable of becoming the most important management tool. And this when you already have an appointments book in which there is barely room to slip a razor-blade between one meeting and the next.

Creating performance through synergy

Today, the art of management is more and more becoming a matter of exploiting the same resources as are available to competitors in order to achieve better overall results through synergy effects. This partly depends on the structures involved – tasks need to be logically linked. It also depends, in fact it depends decisively, on people's behavior – on who communicates and collaborates with whom in what way. This applies to the interplay involved in the organizational context of a large group of companies in exactly the same way that it does to the interplay involved between employees and work groups within a business unit. Influencing this is one of the core functions of management.

But this means that specific capabilities become important in everyday management work: the art of chairing meetings skillfully; organizing meetings and conferences; acting as a facilitator in the processes involved in originating ideas and solving problems; forming and developing teams; project management; conflict resolution. There is nothing fundamentally new in that. But the significance of these activities is becoming much greater in the changed conditions for business and entrepreneurial management. Forms of expertise and ability that used to be the preserve of educational and organizational specialists who were called out on a case-by-case basis are now increasingly becoming indispensable tools of regular management.

In larger corporations, and in particularly in multinationals, synergy mainly means the networking of distinct cultures. Intercultural management has become a hot topic. But even in one country, cultural-relations work may become necessary when different companies have to be integrated into a single corporation when one is bought up by another, or when companies merge. There are some captains of industry who have bought up vast empires on the principle of "exploiting synergy" – but who have achieved nothing except for mere volume. If intensive work is not carried out on the culture of the individual companies involved, and if the willingness to work together is not developed in a meaningful way, a corporation can never become more than the sum of its individual parts.

Making jobs types and working times more flexible

Making yourself an attractive employer and winning company loyalty from qualified staff continue to be success factors guaranteeing a future – and these require flexible forms of working: part-time work, outwork, job sharing, job rotation. The potential of women – in many areas possibly the decisive source of future talent for demanding specialist and management jobs – can only be widely tapped if flexible working arrangements are available, not only for women who need suitable facilities for taking maternity leave or going part-time and then returning to work, but also for their partners. More and more men nowadays are becoming willing to share as full partners in running the home and looking after children – and for the children, who have not come into the best of all possible worlds anyway, parents' efforts in this direction are only to be welcomed. But in this case the father, too, is going to need flexible paternity-leave arrangements so that the mother can stay at work instead.

With regard to making working hours more flexible on a much more consistent basis, particularly with management jobs, a great deal of rethinking is needed in business and administrative bodies. Admittedly, the chairmanship of the board of directors is not a job that should be done at home or part-time, and perhaps not even with job sharing. But in most companies and administrative bodies, there are other jobs apart from the top management ones. It is surprising how many opportunities for flexible working turn up in practice when you go through the organization chart and look at it with fresh eyes. However, all this does not come free. It means higher training costs per job. And above all: flexible forms of working make everyday business management more complex. People are not all there at the same time any more. You need suitable electronic media. Increased coordination costs are involved.

Organizing training and development

For more and more people, particularly in the younger generation, training is becoming the decisive aspect of an attractive workplace. Targeted encouragement of individual development – both in relation to specialist expertise and as part of personal development – is becoming an important element in successful personnel policy. Training used to take place in courses and seminars, while work took place at the company, but the two are becoming more and more integrated nowadays. Training is being carried out more and more "on the job," based on problems and experience. This means that an employee's boss is becoming the main person encouraging and following his or her individual development, usefully delegating tasks, agreeing goals on a basis of partnership, and offering open discussion of achievements, results, and cooperation based on mutually constructive criticism – as well as presenting prospects for the employee's future professional career. Nothing rouses people's enthusiasm more than seeing their own progress. A boss who does his best to ensure such progress is going to have staff who give of their best.

But it remains true that progress reviews discussions demand time. Each employee has to have his or her individual capabilities and personal learning curve encouraged appropriately. Asking too much of people is just as much of a hindrance to achievement as asking too little of them. But above all, you never have fully trained employees. Anyone who has a reasonable command of his current duties is actually ready for the next step of development.

Women conquering key positions

This is a pre-programmed trend: more and more women are succeeding in reaching management positions – in politics just as much as in business and administration. The significance of this development for the qualitative growth of our society is still widely underestimated.

Wherever women are involved, the climate becomes more open, discussions grow more lively, you tend to reach the core of the matter much more quickly in complex problem situations. This is not always pleasant, but it is definitely efficient. In addition to being no less intelligent than men, women have more immediate access to the emotions – both their own and those of others around them. And feelings require fewer detours than analytical thinking. They often provide the shortest route between two points – such as a symptom and its cause. It might be debatable whether women are braver on average, whether they have more courage in their convictions than men – but in practice that is the impression one has. However, this may be connected with the fact that women are far less often the sole breadwinners in their families, so that they are able to take greater risks in their professional lives. In any case, there is no doubt that formal power, tactics, and career considerations are not as important for women as they are for men. This leads to different ways of balancing one's energies.

And one thing is certain: it is not only for women that it is difficult to assert oneself in a man's world. Men, for their part, often find it difficult to adjust to having women as equal partners at work. For example, a capable female colleague who spurns all the requirements of competition rituals and puts all her energies into the task facing her and in cooperating with others. And for some men, suddenly finding oneself with a capable woman as one's boss is not a bed of roses. In addition, if she happens to be not entirely unattractive, one or two people may need to fundamentally rearrange their behavioral repertoire before they can get on with their work again.

Managing conflict and crisis situations

Differences of opinion and conflicts of interest between individual people, groups of employees, or organizational units are perfectly normal parts of everyday business life: target conflicts between two departments; differences of opinion between colleagues; troublespots in individual departments; the occasional conflict with a labor union or a dispute with a government office. In an age in which technologies are racing out of control and uncontrollable floods of data are pouring forth, there are no companies that are magically protected against serious breakdowns, accidents, or failures that suddenly set them in conflict with outside interests, or place them in the public limelight.

Consequently, managers are now increasingly being confronted with critical situations – be it as *conflict partners,* e.g., as representatives of the interests of a specific function within a company or as representatives of the company's interests on higher-level bodies; or as *conflict managers,* e.g., when individual employees are not cooperating within one's own area of responsibility, or whole departments go into trench warfare with one another. These tasks require both toughness and resilience, as well as sensitivity, expertise in managing crisis situations, and a highly developed capacity for dialogue. It is hard to believe how many managers retreat behind their desks in the face of smoldering conflicts. Their behavior is the result of the urge to take flight. They are afraid of their own employees.

Redundancies

One of the worst things that can happen to a manager is having to dismiss employees for economic reasons. Only one thing is worse – being dismissed oneself. But unfortunately there is no doubt that in the future, occasional dismissals are still going to be part of the business of management. What matters is the way in which it is done.

If you take your management responsibilities seriously and want to avoid damaging your company's reputation, you cannot afford to carry out dismissals in a bureaucratic way. You need to deal personally with those concerned and discuss the matter with them – and if your heart is not made of stone, this will affect you deeply, particularly in a period in which many people have little chance of finding another job. If there is any situation in management in which you face a choice between running for cover or standing fast, it is here.

Withstanding conflicts and contradictions over inner goals

In the future, managers are more and more going to be exposed to situations in which their own interests, needs, or values are found to be in conflict with one another. For one thing, there are contradictions between one's own emotional needs and external constraints – as in the case of dismissals for economic reasons. Then there are constant contradictions that have to be coped with in everyday professional life between one's own opinion – if one has one – and the need to make official statements as a representative of the company's interests. You can't always say what you personally think and feel in such situations. The fact that many managers prostitute themselves more than might be absolutely necessary to preserve life is another matter.

Last, but not least: contradictions are constantly arising between personal opinions and the views generally predominant in the context. Pressure from the hierarchy from one's superiors, and group pressure from colleagues or employees, are probably among the most common and at the same time most difficult burdens in managers' working lives. Many people with official capacities in business and administrative bodies have had the ability to think and act independently trained out of them over the course of the years. Inner conflicts and contradictions are simply suppressed, and sometimes habitual optimists no longer even notice any more what they are really feeling. And then you're suddenly faced with a generation of critical young people who question everything and treat nothing as sacred – and who are only willing to cooperate if the questions that are in the air are taken seriously and if the problems that exist are genuinely addressed.

Control and checking through communication

Managers, even at the middle level, are being asked more and more often to appear in the political field as opinion-formers. Companies and the public are becoming more and more interwo en. Informat' on is spreading faster both internally and externally. Rumors, situat onal ad-hoc i ports, and opinion trends are developing a dynamic of their own. A d on top of a that, the whole basis of our existence is in danger – technological a d political co trol systems are proving to be flawed more and more often. People are therefore less and less willing to leave politics to the politicians, research to the scientists, and business to the corporations. People feel they have to interfere, and as a manager you are forced into disputes. "Image" is becoming a central aspect of power, both inside companies and in their external relations. Trusting in one person – whether this is justified or not – is capable of mobilizing the masses, and wide acceptance of an idea is capable of moving mountains.

"He who loses public approval is no longer king," as Aristotle said so long ago. Dealing with large groups, the public and the media is becoming an increasingly important area of work for managers. But it also means that new capabilities and characteristics are becoming important: credibility in statements and expression; spontaneity; quick-wittedness; sensitivity. Every television viewer knows how quickly a politician loses sympathy when he spouts empty phrases, avoids discussion, or always somehow manages to be somewhere else when critical questions are being put.

Planning the future based on complex scenarios

When you look at it in the cold light of day, most branches of industry nowadays are having to cope with the unplannability of the future. Economic trends, the dollar, interest rates, energy costs, markets, competition, the political situation in the various regions of the world – none of the fluctuations in these areas can just be extrapolated from one planning period to the next in the way that they used to be. Long-term strategic planning, and even medium-term planning, is increasingly being based on scenarios. You are always dealing with several possible futures. In this kind of turbulent, high-risk situation, there are basically two things that matter.

First: *flexibility and adaptability*. Instead of planning the unplannable, the company has to concentrate all its energies on being able to react quickly to new conditions in the market. "Design for change" is what is needed. Flexible structures and processes, and mobility and polyvalency in employees, are strategic factors for success.

Secondly: *returning to core competences*. What is it we are particularly good at? Where are we better than our competitors? Instead of planning every possible activity that might be of interest, you concentrate all your energies on what you're really good at – and make sure that you continue to be better than others in that area in the future. This means that qualified workers become the decisive resource.

But flexibility requires a completely different kind of organization. Shifting boxes in the organization chart is not enough. In addition, having qualified staff in flexible structures means using people-oriented and process-focussed management styles.

Integration through vision and models

The most efficient organizations, the largest political and social forces in the world – religions, reform movements and revolutions – are based on a few central "messages" that are addressed to the individual's important emotional needs and offer meaning and comprehensible goals, and which direct his behavior in a specific direction – whether to the benefit of others or not. An industrial company is certainly not a religious organization. But even in business, management by providing meaning has also proved to be the only possible way of guiding large numbers of people toward a common goal in large and complex organizations. A "philosophy you can touch" is what is needed. Abstract strategy papers filling three ring binders and written in scientific jargon stored away in the cupboards in top management, plus a few specialists in the planning department, are no use for this. What matters is having a few simple ideas and principles that can be communicated to the grass roots and understood there, supported by practical management measures, and made credible through modelling behaviour – ideas and principles enabling every employee to see the company's value to the customer and the importance of his or her individual contribution to shared success.

The growing importance of identification is the common thread running through every best-selling book in the literature about management – from Drucker and Peters/Waterman to Carlzon and Iacocca. But creating identification requires intellectual leadership, an ability to communicate on the emotional level, and personal commitment on the part of management. That means carrying out a critical analysis of trendy issues and values – and saying what you think openly. Colorless and nondescript characters, technocrats, breakfast-table directors are the last thing you need. As Antoine de Saint-Exupéry wrote, "If you want to build a ship, don't start by collecting wood, sawing planks and assigning jobs; start by arousing men's yearning for the vast expanses of the ocean."

Darwin rules

At the time of writing, all hell has broken loose in the business world. To understand what is going on, and what it is all leading to, you have to see developments along a time axis. Over the longer term – in very simplified form – three phases can be distinguished:

1 Boom

Uncontrolled growth is a thing of the past. The period in which money seemed to be just lying about. The period in which there were amateurs and gamblers everywhere in the market who could literally earn a fortune. The occasionally overheated economy; the consequent affluence syndrome; the disproportionate expectations that were aroused; the expectations of maintained living standards that raised these attitudes to the status of legitimate claims and entrenched them there. Speculation, profiteering, running up debts, and the environmental destruction that went with it.

At that time, a strategy was not really needed in order to be able to do business. Neither high productivity nor high quality were required to produce sales. You could afford to have overcomplex product ranges and organizational structures, elaborate hierarchies, masses of incompetent managers in key positions, and unbelievable communication gaps in management. And if capacity caused bottlenecks, it was not the organization and the processes involved that were optimized; you simply hired more people. Costs – it seemed – were completely unimportant.

Whether we want to believe it nowadays or not: uncontrolled growth did not at that time simply fall from heaven onto business like so much manna. Growth was raised to the status of a philosophy by business itself, and was literally conjured up organizationally. Every self-respecting head of accounting went about calculating for everyone down to the third decimal place how many percentage points of growth were absolutely necessary even just to compensate for inflation. No growth, the argument ran, meant running backwards, even mortal danger.

The following statement comes from the field of biocybernetics: "The functioning of a system has to be independent of its growth." This is nothing new. We always knew that. And another thing that industry has always known: forced growth is deadly. The most efficient weed-killers are growth hormones. They make the plants grow too fast – so fast that they die. But the people caught up in the euphoria of growth never wanted to believe all that. "Nothing will work without growth," was the motto.

Nowadays, no one will admit that they ever said anything of the sort. It is astonishing how many people who have lost their short-term memories can survive in top positions.

2 Recession

This is the present state: economic decline – and not just as a matter of cyclical variation of the sort that has always been seen. On the contrary, what is now going on is a crisis phase of deep structural adjustment. Resources are short, markets are tight, competition is ferocious. The deeper reasons for this are described at the beginning of this chapter.

In addition to companies whose sales have collapsed and who are fighting for sheer survival, there are others taking advantage of the moment to carry out restructuring measures that have been overdue for years. This only accentuates the crisis that is already there. Widespread cutbacks in investment and staff mean reduced demand – and when demand drops, more and more companies start having to struggle for their existence. It is as simple as that. And this is the time when the wheat is separated from the chaff: a process of selection takes place, on the good old Darwinian pattern. The principle is: survival of the fittest.

Quantitative growth is no longer possible during this phase. Qualitative growth is what would be needed. But many of those in top positions in companies today have not even the faintest idea of what that means. When your market and your customer base are shrinking, you have to shrink with them. One down-sizing follows the other. But shrinking alone is not a survival strategy. In many companies, profound restructuring measures are needed that will only make sense if they are based on intelligent, long-term strategic considerations – i.e., you have to have a convincing answer to the question, "What are the core activities that can make us successful in the future on the basis of our specific expertise, the activities on which we need to focus?" It is by no means sufficient just to adjust the structures. It is even more important to optimize management, communications, and co-operation. You have to successfully bring entrepreneurial thinking and action to the front-line, grass-roots troops. This is one of the most demanding processes involved in development.

If you go on losing weight instead of just slimming down to get fit, then as time goes on you will stop being able to find food, and sooner or later die of malnutrition. And this is exactly what is happening to many companies at the moment. Ultimately, they have no ideas for the future, and are simply reacting defensively to market conditions that are hostile to them. When the great spring-cleaning falls due, they will simply be shaken out of the market.

The extent of the fall in prices, however, is making life difficult even for companies that are basically healthy. They, too, are no longer in a position to bring in adequate profits. The reason: practically everyone who is fighting for his existence tries before his final downfall – which he never believes in until it happens – if not to bring in profits from the market, then at least to cover costs. There are companies who slash their prices right down to the level of their variable costs. All this accomplishes is to delay the end, while at the same time it fouls the market for everyone else. Ultimately, the question is simply who will be able to hold out longest and who will be left over at the end.

Some have made so much easy money during the boom years that it is a long time before their reserves are exhausted. And while every company that files for bankruptcy does leave open a larger share of the market to others, since the market as a whole is shrinking, only a fraction of that share can be "inherited" by the survivors. Even for strong, healthy companies, the period of famine can therefore be long and difficult.

But one thing should also be mentioned: the crisis would be much easier to master if everyone did not behave as if the comforts they used to know had been acquired on the basis of magnificent achievements – and as if hard-earned rights were now suddenly being disputed. We are suffering from a mass disease syndrome of affluence and indulgence. Many people even regard it as a piece of affrontery if they are merely asked to switch to a different task. People who during the boom years would switch jobs at the drop of a hat to earn just a little bit more money somewhere else regard it as the greatest possible social injustice when they are given notice today because of restructuring measures that are required. Managers who are responsible for massive redundancies don't think twice about continuing to receive their usual annual bonus. And some entrepreneurs who have made their fortunes in the past without any particular effort are now claiming that it is the state or the labor unions who are responsible for the difficulties in their businesses. The only response to that is: we do not *have* a crisis – we *are* the crisis.

3 The normal market

This is the future: the cleaned-up, healthy, normalized market. If you want to know what that is, the best thing to do is to go to a little provincial town in a Mediterranean country and take a look at the weekly market – so long as it is still supplying a genuine demand and has not been turned into a mere tourist attraction. Practically everyone in this local market has a competitor, but they all get along quite peacefully together. Customers examine what is on offer very critically. Low prices are the main priority, because every penny counts. Quality makes a name for itself: one supplier has a lot of regular customers – and another does not. But in spite of all the variety, the range of goods on offer is still manageable. There are no luxury goods, because no one here can afford them. But there is everything you need to live and work. People are shabbily dressed, many of them are unkempt. But very few of them look unhappy. The scene is not marked by rush, turbulence, and conflict, but by extremely lively human contacts, joy in life, talk. The goods on sale are one thing; contacting other people, exchanging information, meeting up and getting together is another. Sales are pretty modest. Nobody gets rich. But everyone has enough to live on.

This image cannot be transferred to future business markets in every detail. But this much is certain: there will be fewer suppliers on the market than there are today. Competition will continue to be tough, but those who are able to participate will be able to bring in satisfactory profits once again. Customer orientation, quality and innovative energy, and – in connection with that – flexibility will be the decisive factors for success. It is not the broadest possible diversification that will ensure survival, but top technical expertise and a high degree of professionalism in market operations. A return to core competences is what is needed – and creating a working environment in which qualified specialists and managers can show personal commitment to the customer and to the company's success.

In view of the sometimes devastating factors that can have a fundamental influence on a company, one might fear that stabilization of the economy – even at a lower level – is no longer possible in principle, and that a total crash – which has been predicted by so many analysts – is unavoidable. But there are positive trends too. The most important one: the automation of working processes leads to gigantic increases in productivity, which the lay-person can barely imagine. Products and services of unprecedented quality can be offered at comparatively low prices. Slim organizations and qualified management in the companies that survive will complement and enhance this trend. But new markets will also constantly be emerging, creating new jobs – even if only to a limited extent. The increasing global networking of national economies, the opening up of Eastern Europe, an increasing awareness of the environment, and the new demands arising in a changing society are associated not just with risks, but also with opportunities. All of this should not be exaggerated, particularly in view of the extremely critical state of the world economy overall. But the positive energies also have to be included in calculations when we are investigating the future.

And last, but not least: in contrast to the grotesque scenarios according to which "every sector of industry will have only two or three giant corporations left", there will continue to be lots of interesting areas of activity, as well as fresh challenges, for genuinely dynamic and innovative small and medium-sized companies. It will still be the case that nobody has everything their own way all of the time. The market will settle down at a level much lower than today's. However, at a generally much lower standard of living, there will be a normally functioning market once again – and therefore opportunities for healthy entrepreneurship.

Organization: Design for Change

New tasks – new structures

When time and money are short, while at the same time everything is becoming more and more complex every day, it is simply not possible any longer to carry on business in the same way as in the past. The challenge for each company is to find:

*Faster, more economical ways of completing
an increasing variety of quickly changing tasks.*

And this has implications for the organization. Every wisecrack here in the West has always thought that the centrally controlled planned economy in the Soviet Union, with its extremely hierarchical organizational forms based on the division of labor, was inefficient and led to bureaucracy and a loss of motivation in enterprises. But not everybody has noticed that we in the West have similar structural problems in large organizations as well.

The trend in most large enterprises today is away from the classic functional divisional structure, which is a highly centralistic concept based on the division of labor. The prerequisites for survival today are:

- *Staying close to the market and the customer*
  by reducing distances.
- *Ensuring fast reaction times and high flexibility*
  by shifting responsibility for operational decision-making to the front line and the grass roots.
- *Increasing productivity and quality*
  through motivation, communication, and cooperation.
- *Optimizing costs*
  by tightening up the product range, reducing the administrative superstructure, and simplifying procedures.

It is not question of cosmetic retouching here, but one of fundamental *re-engineering of business processes.* And these are the organizational conclusions that are being drawn today all over the world:

Decentralization
Regionalization
Profit-center organization
Holding-company structure
Lean production
Lean management
Project organization
Total quality management

The perfect model: the network

One thing is truly remarkable: taken to their logical conclusion, all of these concepts imply a single, quite specific form of organization: the *network structure*. The characteristics of a network structure are: its flat hierarchy, the high degree of independence enjoyed by individual organizational units; the wide variety of local differences between the organizational forms; and the way in which overall control is achieved via common targets and strategies. These are characteristics both of the organization as a whole – for example, a company structure with a differentiated network of daughter companies and profit centers – and of the detailed structure of individual enterprises, with today's trend toward project organization, production islands, autonomous work groups, and similar forms of flexible working organization (Figure 3).

It is no accident that the network structure is so widespread in nature, due to millions of years of evolution. It is clearly superior to all other forms of organization in the following ways: it is capable of managing by far the highest degree of complexity; it allows fast reaction to changes in its surroundings; the organization is capable of adapting itself very flexibly to new conditions; and all in all, it is less prone to disruption and crisis. Breakdowns and accidents can put part of the system out of action – but it is almost impossible for the whole organization to be crippled by the failure of only one central function. And since all of the important subfunctions are integrated into the individual subsystems, failures at one point can be compensated for fairly easily at another point. This increases the organization's overall productivity, its capacity for regeneration, and thus its capacity for survival.

Structural principle: process chains

The principle "structure follows function" was developed by the architects at the Bauhaus. In the beginning, there is the idea, the vision – and the formulation of a model. The organization's aims are derived from this – as well as the strategies needed to achieve those aims. Concrete tasks are then derived from these basic principles – and the processes required to complete these tasks. The design of an

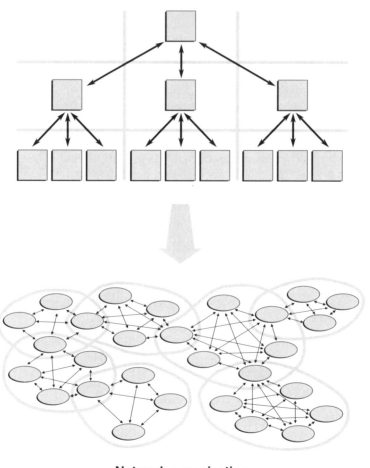

Hierarchical organization based on division of labor

Network organization

organization today has to be based on *processes capable of functioning* and on *effective process chains* – nothing else.

In times of stability and continuity, when tasks were able to remain unchanged over long periods, it was customary to think in terms of the boxes in an organization chart – or, if you were extremely progressive, in terms of job descriptions. When the environment is unstable, however, the tasks that face an organization, and the processes required to meet them, are subject to constant change. Thinking in organizational categories needs to be replaced by thinking in terms of quickly-changing process chains. Flexible project organization for limited periods – which was earlier only used sporadically to carry out specialized tasks in research and development – is becoming more and more important in comparison with linear organization. In many areas, long-term organizational arrangements are now already the exceptions that need to be justified.

When everything is in flux, fast and reliable communication is a matter of survival. Information flows have to be connected to the process chains. Established hierarchies, where they still exist, are not porous enough to let information through. Each intermediate layer alters the message, if it passes it on at all – since people are reluctant to pass on information that might damage them, while the individuals handling the information each want to leave their own mark in the hope that it might be personally advantageous.

Achieving effectiveness and productiveness in a situation of non-stop change requires that when information is available, it can be sent by the most direct route to the point at which it is needed – and this direct route passes along the process sequence. What this means is that hierarchical positions are more and more being pushed to the sides of the flow of relevant information. A creeping redistribution of power is taking place. And more: the hierarchy has lost its own legitimacy. Each level in the hierarchy is finding that it needs to justify itself. If it wants to survive, it has to justify its existence by the added value it creates in the context of defined process chains. In the massive pyramids of established hierarchies, this is not always possible. The hierarchies begin to level out. Routes become shorter.

Quantum leap to the third millenium

It is seldom realized that this concept involves more than a normal organizational adjustment. Instead, we are dealing with a *radical structural transformation*. The new concepts are based on a completely different organizational model. We are moving away from the classic organization based on the division of labor and on hierarchy, toward a network of independent, highly integrated enterprise groups capable of managing themselves in the operational field.

For this type of organization to be able to function properly, it is not enough to smash or split up centralized functions and shift them to the periphery. It is not a matter of arranging tasks slightly differently by shifting around a couple of boxes in the organization chart. Instead, what is involved here is a fundamentally different way of approaching tasks altogether. There are two factors that represent vital preconditions for this.

First: self-management demands a *high degree of communication and cooperation* within the individual groups and organizational units. A capacity for genuine teamwork at every level is central to success. As the authors of *The*

Wisdom of Teams have written, "Real teams are the most common characteristic of successful change efforts at all levels."

Secondly: effective coordination within an overall association presupposes *entrepreneurial thinking and a readiness to act in the general interest* at all levels. Specifically, there has to be communication and cooperation at all points, across responsibilities, departments, and individual enterprises – independently and on each individual's own responsibility, of course, because there is no longer any central control. As the boss of a Swiss mechanical engineering firm advised his staff, "Act on an order, act without an order, act against an order – but act in the interest of the company!"

So what we're talking about is a network organization as a highly *interactive organism*. Open and lively communication is the whole basis of its system of management and self-regulation. Ultimately, this is the only suitable alternative to a management system based on a tight hierarchical structure. Or, to put it more simply: *communication is the alternative to hierarchy.*

It is a quantum leap not unlike switching from an old VW Beetle to a highly sophisticated Ferrari Testarossa. But twelve-cylinder power and twenty-four valve technology alone are not enough to guarantee a pleasant trip. If the car is not going to smash into the first wall it encounters, it needs to be properly steered. There is a critical bottleneck factor involved – human nature. And exactly the same applies to a highly differentiated and sensitive organizational model like a network organization. Three things are needed from employees and management: personal commitment, a capacity to communicate, and a willingness to cooperate.

The last point is the hardest. For real cooperation to take place, good cooperation needs to be consistently rewarded and inadequate cooperation needs to be just as consistently punished. But our entire existing range of management tools is aimed at encouraging and rewarding individual achievement and individual responsibility. Consequently, we have produced hordes of individual warriors and loners who – especially once they have risen to become directors – are impossible to retrain and can only be replaced.

Wanted: motivation and identification

In spite of adverse conditions in the environment, it is usually possible to obtain commitment, communication, and cooperation from most members of staff and management – on two conditions: first, there has to be a high degree of job motivation; and secondly, a high degree of identification with the company. Motivation results from having interesting work, responsible tasks, and sufficient scope for action and initiative. The conditions required to provide all of these are still relatively easy to create, i.e., to organize in a purposeful way by introducing new forms of work. But with identification, matters are a little trickier. Identification with the company presupposes something management cannot just conjure up organizationally from one day to the next – something that can only be built up by a careful process of development: a strong and lively corporate culture based on openness and trust.

Some people may find it confusing to read about "culture" in a chapter which is supposed to be about "organization." But this is precisely where the fundamental breach with past thinking lies that is taking place in today's management. The future-oriented structural models referred to are based on a new, wholistic conception of organization. Just as data processing systems consist not just of hardware but also of specific software, so too an organization is characterized not just by its "hard factors" – technical and administrative structures and processes – but also by various types of "soft factors": staff motivation, for example; the working atmosphere; management style; information flow; the way

Figure 4. Culture

Culture is the sum total of the convictions that a group, a nation, or a society has developed during the course of its history to cope with the problems of internal integration (cohesion) and external adaptation (survival).

It is the sum total of the rules (dos and don'ts) that function so well that they become "unwritten laws" and are passed on to each successive generation as the "right" way of thinking, feeling, and acting.

Figure 5. Interdependent dimensions of a corporation

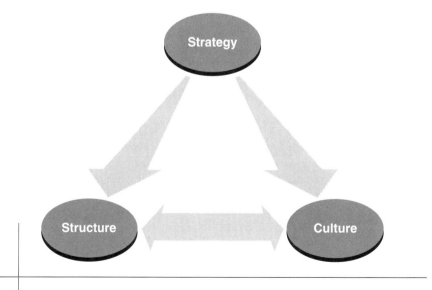

Organization: Design for Change

in which decision-making is carried out in the company; and the ease or difficulty of implementing necessary changes.

Just as software has proved over the years to be the real bottleneck in computing systems, it can be seen today that in a modern organization aiming at productivity and achievement, the trick lies not so much in its structural conception as in the design of the "soft factors," i.e., in the development of an appropriate corporate culture. And in exactly the same way as with technological systems, the hardware and software have to be carefully coordinated with one another in social systems too. Every self-respecting manager today pays lip-service to the principle "structure follows strategy." But most of them still have to learn a second, equally vital principle: "culture follows strategy" (Figures 4 and 5).

Corporate culture: five key factors

The essential elements of a corporate culture that welcomes change (cf. Part III, Chapter 11 on "Changing the Corporate Culture") have been summed up particularly well in a book by Clifford and Cavanaugh called *The Winning Performance – in a Changing Environment*. The book is based on empirical studies. The authors looked at a large number of companies that had survived exceptionally well in international competition in particularly turbulent markets.

Five factors emerged, and these are in fact the decisive requirements for the dynamic management of change:

- *Creative disruption*
  Changes in the environment, in company strategy, in the structures and processes needed to meet the company's future tasks, and in the skills required, not only *cause* disruption in the system – it is precisely disruption in the system that these factors *require*. A pioneering spirit, creative disruption, and experimentation at all levels are absolutely indispensable ingredients of the culture of change. Every bureaucratic ossification needs to be uncompromisingly resisted from the very start, and new ideas, mobility, and willingness to readjust have to be consistently rewarded. Those who have always tried to avoid every "staff disturbance," seeing it as threatening the company's existence, are going to have to radically rethink their position.
- *Capacity for conflict*
  Structures and processes, game rules and forms of behavior, information channels and decision paths, all have to be changed; traditional and familiar features need to be replaced by new and unfamiliar ones. None of this can be achieved without tension and conflict. Different opinions, vested interests, and individual needs are bound to collide. A constructive culture of argumentation will become a factor in success: the capacity to identify fields of tension at an early stage and not to suppress conflict, but to lay it on the table and have it out constructively.

- *Sense of belonging*
  A sense of belonging to the company and having a share in it. "Us" instead of "the people over there," "the people down there," and "the people up top." A sense of community based on openness, trust, and mutual acceptance. Of course, all that is easily said, but attractive phrases and pious wishes are not enough here. Someone who has no influence at all on decisions in everyday operations, and who risks landing in the street at the first sign of recession, is never going to dream of saying "us." Companies in which there is a strong sense of identification with "us" explicitly guarantee their employees no *job security*, but a high degree of *employment security*. And when it comes to the crunch, financial sacrifices have to be asked for on the basis of solidarity: salary cuts can increase progressively toward the top, and extend into company management – so that no one has to be dismissed.

- *Conveying a sense of meaning*
  The art of making understandable to each member of staff – right down to the grass roots – the company's philosophy and goals, the meaning of each person's activity in serving the customer and society as a whole, and the value of each individual's own contribution to the common good. It is easier to achieve this in a company involved in third-world development aid, or in a convalescent hospital, than in a cigarette factory or an arms factory. But the clearer it is to people what the overall significance of each person's everyday work is, the more willing they will be to give their personal commitment to the company they work for – and, if necessary, to accept additional burdens.

- *Communication*
  It is particularly important to recognize that you can never communicate too much. The worst that can happen is that you will communicate wrongly. In addition: the formal type of organization is fundamentally incapable of ensuring the amount of direct, personal communication that is needed in a period of fast-moving changes in the company. Informal communication has to be consistently encouraged and exploited. Information meetings and conferences transcending specific levels have to be arranged. Talking together instead of producing paper is what matters. And "management by wandering around" has proved to be the only way of staying adequately informed and ensuring some degree of overall control over the complexity of business operations today.

Every company has its own unmistakable identity, which expresses itself in lots of specific characteristics – both in its structure and in its culture. As with the structure, however, there are also fundamental principles involved in its culture, and these can be more successful under some specific conditions than under others. In today's times of change, the five factors listed above are a clear standard that no company can afford to ignore if it wants to survive tough competition.

Survival strategy and safeguarding the future

Time pressure, a tendency to take on too much work, the danger of overstraining oneself and at the same time the necessity to take on new tasks and acquire new abilities – juggling all of these factors is only possible, both for employees and management, in an environment in which the atmosphere is comparatively relaxed and people can talk to each other about their personal experiences and about their own insecurities and professional difficulties: in an open, lively, partnership-oriented and team-oriented management culture.

Unfortunately, "corporate culture" is still sometimes seen as being just a passing fashion or a luxury. In fact, however, it is not just about the individual's quality of life in the workplace. Instead, the questions involved are of decisive significance to the company's future, i.e.:

- Whether the company's problems are recognized and solved early enough. An open, lively enterprise culture in which people think and speak critically is the best *early warning system* there is.
- Whether members of staff and management identify with the company or not and are personally committed to its success, or whether they are simply "doing a job" and are likely to wander off at the first opportunity – a question that is relevant to *creating and maintaining expertise* in the company.
- And above all: whether, how quickly, and how consistently management decisions and organizational changes can be implemented in the enterprise – the crunch question when faced with rapid change.

The demographic developments that are taking place are clear. Clearly, the supply of younger staff is noticeably declining. There will be tough competition to win each well-qualified employee. The question then is which company is going to be best at building up, developing, and making the most of qualified staff capacity.

In technology, administration, and also in market approach, all the well-known companies today share more or less the same standards – a high level of professionalism. It requires considerable mental gymnastics to find a way of marking oneself out from the competition. Corporate culture will increasingly be seen as an ever more important distinguishing characteristic – and one day it may well turn out to offer a decisive competitive advantage.

Leadership:
the Manager's New Role

Management yesterday – management tomorrow

There are several reasons for the trend toward decentralized self direction among employees. First, people are better qualified professionally than they used to be, and are therefore capable of accepting duties in which they can use their own discretion. Secondly, the younger generation in particular have a different attitude to work. Independence is one of the most important motivating factors. Freedom to act on one's own initiative has become one of the decisive aspects of an attractive job. Thirdly, most bosses are in any case so overworked that they are no longer able to take care of every detailed task personally in the way that they used to.

But that is not all. The trend is also being affected by technological developments.

In the past, a fundamental aspect of management activity at the middle levels was acquiring information, processing it, channeling it, and passing it on. Today, information technology makes it possible to package the "management information" needed for independent on-the-spot activity into suitable portions and pass it on much faster than before to the people who need it at the front. Modern data processing is what is really making independent activity at the grass roots possible at all – and competitive pressures are forcing us to take advantage of the potential.

This does not mean that middle management is not going to be needed in the future. But the total numbers of managers working at the various levels will be substantially reduced. And above all, supervisors and superiors will in the future have a different function.

Changing the emphasis

Management's tasks are undergoing a shift in three main directions.

1. Securing the future. Looking ahead: What has to be done today in order to ensure that tomorrow's tasks can be fulfilled? Ensuring the necessary infrastructure as well as resources for current work – at the lowest possible cost in time and effort.

2. Leadership. Training and looking after employees; developing capable teams; agreeing goals and checking that they can be met; providing advice and support on specialized problems.

3. Managing constant organizational change. Coordinating everyday business and project work; managing staff allocation; clearing up differences of opinion and conflict situations; ensuring internal and external communications; and – careful handling of awkward personnel cases.

Looked at closely, this is actually a completely different job. Masses of managers have arrived at it overnight, quite unexpectedly. They have not sought out these duties, they have not been trained for them – and, basically, they have no idea of how to tackle them either.

It is sometimes claimed that most managers use up a substantial part of their time and energy in securing their own positions. That they use information from a tactical point of view, and not in the company's general interests. And that they do more to obstruct their employees in carrying out their tasks than to support them. And when you look into this question on the spot in a large number of companies, by discussing their everyday work personally with the men and women concerned, and by taking part in solving organizational problems, the conclusion you are forced to draw is: yes, that is indeed precisely the case.

A great many management capacities could be fused – and every third or fourth position could be abolished without being replaced. Although it sounds unbelievable, the disappearance of the top manager from one day to the next would in many cases not only not leave a gap, but on the contrary would release employees' suppressed energies to a considerable degree. Many lower and middle managers, particularly of the older generation, are nowadays like the fireman on the American electric railroad locomotives years ago. They have been trained to carry out a task that is no longer needed – and the task that would be required today requires a completely different range of inclinations, attitudes, knowledge, and abilities. Between the two lies an unbridgeable gap.

Management redefined

When you sum up the changes that are taking place today, it can be said that the task of management today no longer consists basically in planning work, distributing jobs, and coordinating everyday business, but instead in:

Creating the structural conditions
that will allow employees of normal intelligence
to fulfill their tasks independently and efficiently.

To do this the first thing needed is a different view of one's own tasks as a manager. Someone who treats the organizational unit he is in charge of as *his* turf, the people working there as *his* people, the output as *his* performance, and meeting targets as *his own* personal responsibility, is in fact behaving in his department like a dog patrolling its territory – and in an organization based on networks, he is letting himself in for nothing but trouble in advance.

In a system as highly networked as the modern high-performance organization, the superior's function is no longer that of being a dynamic doer and chief controller, but rather that of a trainer, coach, and consultant – which basically means: a highly qualified service provider. Some managers of the old school may not like this, since to them consultants and service providers are "eunuchs" – people who have no power to give orders and therefore carry no responsibility. But this only shows how enormous the transformation needs to be that we are dealing with.

The core questions management must face are:

▶ *What kind of qualifications do employees need? Who needs to learn what in order to reach the required level of performance?*
▶ *What information, resources, and personal support do employees need in order to carry out the tasks facing them independently and successfully?*
▶ *What can or must be changed in terms of optimizing costs and benefits in the company?*

Peter Drucker offers the following advice here: *"If you want to know what can be improved in your company, ask your staff!"* To that we might add, *"And ask your customers, too!"*

The constant process of optimizing performance and costs in a systemic and controlled way – this is one of the central functions of modern management.

A profession: manager of change

Masses of managers are suffering today because they failed to recognize and grasp the transition from specialist to manager. Just as many will be suffering tomorrow – and causing others to suffer – because they are failing to recognize and grasp the next stage required in professional reorientation: the transition from classical manager to "change agent."

At the root of this problem lies fear. Change always seems threatening – and all the more so, the more you are affected by it yourself. However, those whose main professional focus is on change, particularly in leading positions, should be capable of overcoming their fear of change. The first thing needed to be able to do this is to understand the nature of "change" and "development" – and to be able to assess realistically both the potential and the limitations of your own ability to influence change. Once you know what you are dealing with, a great deal has been gained.

With regard to the nature of "change" and "development," it is salutary to work on the following assumptions:

1. *Everything is always in movement.*
   Ultimately, there is nothing that is really stable. Everything is always in a state of flux. The only thing that remains the same is change. Basically, change is the normal condition. What we perceive as being "stable" are states whose changes we are not capable of observing. Once you have understood and accepted this, there is much less danger of wanting to make desperate efforts to preserve the status quo.

2. *Changes are effects of force fields.*
   Nothing changes just for the sake of it. Every change in a state is a consequence of corresponding forces or energy fields. And if there is ever anything approaching a stable state for a short time, it is a consequence of opposing forces canceling each other out – an exceptional situation that never persists for very long. This means that, if you recognize the force fields and energy flows, you can intervene in the process to guide it.

3. *Changes in a social structure are the result of divergent interests and needs.*
   Emotions – expressions of individual and collective interests and needs – are what move things in human organizations. Love or hate, money or power, recognition or self-fulfillment. These are the forces pulling the strings to create what happens on the stage: the forces of persistence and change. Those who recognize this and take it seriously early enough can influence it.

4. *Necessary changes are always taking place – the only question is, in what way.*
   The fatal mistake would be to believe that one could carry out or prevent any specific change simply by acting adroitly enough. If a development is due, it will come into effect by itself. Those who expend their energy in trying to prevent it will at best only be able to delay it slightly. But as time goes on, the pressure increases – and with it the price that ultimately has to be paid. Sooner or later, no one can afford the effort that would be required to prevent the change any more – and the shift in opinion, the market breakthrough, or the bankruptcy that were needed finally take place. Those who can keep their hand on the pulse of what is going on will be able to apply their energies at the right time in the right place.

5. *Usefully exerting influence means recognizing necessary developments at an early stage, encouraging them consistently, and making them socially acceptable.*
   This is the task of the "change agent": recognizing necessary developments, encouraging them consistently, and making them as constructive as possible for all involved. That only sounds like a modest affair if you look at it superficially. Managing changes means ensuring that a company in which a large number of people work remains healthy as a living organism, and is capable of surviving in turbulent environment. It is a task that is both interesting and challenging - and in addition it is a socially beneficial profession that makes sense and is capable of bringing satisfaction (Figure 6).

Figure 6. A story of four people

This is a story about four people
named Everybody, Somebody, Anybody and Nobody.
There was an important job to be done
and Everybody was asked to do it.
Everybody was sure Somebody would do it.
Anybody could have done it
but Nobody did it.
Somebody got angry about that
because it was Everybody's job.
Everybody thought Anybody could do it
but Nobody realized
that Everybody wouldn't do it.
It ended up
that Everybody blamed Somebody
when Nobody did
what Everybody could have done.

Does this new role for the manager mean saying good-bye to the exercise of power and influence, good-bye to the role of displaying personal commitment and serving as a model? Is the leader going to degenerate into being a mere mediator and consultant? A comment in *Fortune* magazine stated, "Forget your old tired ideas about leadership. The most successful corporation of the Nineties will be something called a learning organization."

It is true: the successful company of the future is indeed a learning organization. But so far as "leadership" is concerned, our own view is completely different. Do not forget your previous ideas too soon, for heaven's sake! The management of the future will not be able to survive without vision, strong momentum, and personal commitment. On the contrary: without personal acceptance and persuasiveness on the part of management, nothing will work at all in the future. In a period of automation and of large, anonymous organizations, personal qualities in management will take on fresh significance as a fundamental precondition for individual identification with the organization's goals. The colorless, nondescript figures on the top floors of old-fashioned bureaucracies have had their day.

The keys to exercising a guiding influence, the keys to genuine economic viability in turbulent times are credibility and confidence. The flood of information is so large, the interactions within a company are so complex, that in the end they can no longer be processed by individual employees. Either employees can believe what they are told – or the ensuing alienation on their part is predictable. But in today's complex organizations, no one can any longer afford the effort and expense needed for control and steering mechanisms ensuring behavior appropriate to goals and regulations at every level. Management is simply being forced to delegate responsibility. Genuine leadership will be required in the coming years more than ever before.

Profiling what's needed for the future

Until quite recently, it was basically sufficient to be a good specialist, to carry out administrative work effectively, and to display one's official authority as a superior, in order to establish oneself and make one's career – often right up to the very top levels. Three additional factors have now emerged that will be of decisive significance in the future (Figure 7).

First: *strategic competence* – understood as an ability to understand complex interactions and dynamic processes, and draw practical conclusions.

Secondly: *social competence* – understood in its broadest sense as the ability to deal with people, not only with individuals in one-to-one discussions (probably with a big mahogany desk between you and the employee); nor simply with small groups of directly dependent and loyal followers. What is needed is an ability to deal with lots of people through all the tensions and turbulences that can arise on the business front, in management conferences, in complex projects, or

Figure 7. Job requirements – yesterday and tomorrow

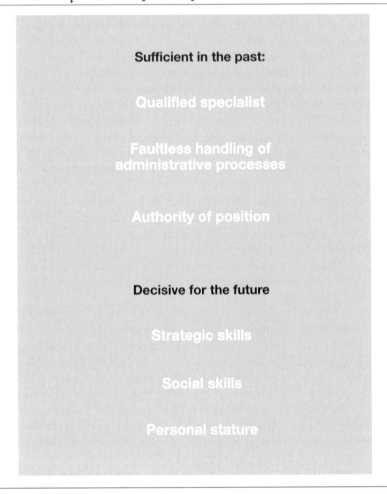

Sufficient in the past:

Qualified specialist

Faultless handling of
administrative processes

Authority of position

Decisive for the future

Strategic skills

Social skills

Personal stature

at a workforce meeting. Only those who understand group dynamics will be able to take advantage of teamwork to help the company develop.

In connection with social competence, there are two terms that have become particularly important recently. The first is what is called *process competence* – an ability to coordinate information processes, decision-making processes, and working operations carefully with people's capacity to learn, with their learning curve. On the other hand, there is what is called *chaos competence* – the ability to keep a cool head and an ability to act appropriately during acute conflict and crisis situations when everything is in turmoil. Chaos competence is not just a question of an ability to work under pressure. It is closely related to the ability to listen well and respond to people. And it has to do with a basic trust in the ability of people and groups to organize themselves – or, to put it differently, with an intuitive awareness that a "chaotic" situation does not represent meaningless and irretrievable confusion, but merely a degree of complexity that it is not currently in our power to control.

Thirdly: *personality.* You don't have to be a Churchill to hold your own at middle management level in business. But there is one thing that cannot be denied: there are qualities becoming important now that cannot be freshly learned from scratch as an adult – a few apparently simple things: openness, honesty, self-confidence, and having the courage of one's convictions. Those who have these qualities can win the hearts of their employees – and mobilize all their available energies. Those who do not have these qualities keep making mistakes – and thereby create resistance so great that nothing can be done about it any more.

This was the response that Peter F. Drucker gave to a journalist who asked him what management work in postcapitalist society would involve: "*You have to learn to cope with situations in which you cannot give any orders, in which you are neither controlled by someone else yourself nor capable of exercising control over others. That is the elementary change. Where it used to be a question of combined rank and power, in the future there will be relationships of mutual agreement and responsibility.*"

One aspect that is frequently underestimated in its significance for success or failure in management capacities is the manager's attitude to his work. In a high-velocity age of scarce resources and bewildering complexity, it is no longer possible for anyone in middle management to oversee everything in detail anyway, and it is certainly not possible for him to have everything "under control." The successful ones are those who are lucky enough to get the most important things done properly. The main thing is to set priorities. And it is intuition that is needed. Drucker continued, "*Good instincts for what is going on are more important nowadays than analytical ability.*" Because those who analyze too long get there too late.

As the proverb has it, "*A manager does things right – a leader does the right things.*" Those who have fully grasped this will be able to enjoy their professional work in management even in today's turbulent and conflict-ridden times.

From dignitary to players' coach

No one can claim that managers do not have enough work to do – particularly those at the top levels. On the contrary, there is often almost no limit to the hectic rush that their working lives consist of. Nor can it be said that they are ignoring the signs of the times. On the contrary, wherever you look, studies are being commissioned, project groups are being established, specialists are being invited to management meetings when important decisions are being taken. Companies are invested with armies of consultants and officials.

But the top men themselves remain invisible, shut away from what is actually happening in the company. Their places of work are the desk, the conference room – and the airplane. Because their activities are becoming more and more like those of jet-setting shuttle diplomats. The top bosses remain inaccessible to their staff. They have an "open door," of course – but there is no one in the office. If they are in the building at all, they will be at a meeting. Busy developing strategies, adjusting budgets, initiating cost-cutting measures, deciding on re-organizations. The company and the changes taking place in it – if the importance of these has been recognized – are administered to perfection from within the Holy of Holies. And the result is often the terse diagnosis: "Management is out of touch."

Misunderstandings of the tasks of management very often begin right at the top – and continue downward: the image of the manager as a highly qualified but desk-bound director of operations. Particularly in periods of turbulent change, however, what is needed is something completely different: a human being of flesh and blood, someone who knows what is going on in the company, who is close to people and can listen to their questions, pass on guidance, provide the stimulus for change – and who can give people the courage to overcome difficulties. Management by persuasion is what is needed – and it needs to be done not by sending out circulars, not by giving interviews to the newspapers and not by deputies, but in direct contacts between people. It is one thing to decide on "decentralization" and "staff cuts" in meetings in an academic way, and quite another to justify these steps to the employees and managers actually affected and to help them to understand their necessity and motivate them to carry them through.

Many restructuring measures often founder at the initial stages; rationalization projects fizzle out, mergers have still often not been completed ten years after being announced – not because the decisions were basically wrong, but simply because there were technocrats at work who thought that taking a carefully balanced, objectively justified decision at company level was all that was required of them. On the contrary – that is precisely the point at which real management work starts: when a difficult decision has been taken and what matters is to implement it.

Some of those who complain about how difficult it is to run a company nowadays should first take a critical look at where they spend most of their working time. It is a bitter pill for comfortably established managers to swallow – but changes cannot be dictated *ex cathedra* and administered from the desk. Anyone who believes that as a director or member of company management one is "only responsible for strategy" is on the wrong track. The boss is part of what goes on. Particularly in difficult times, his place is at the front – as one part of his duties, at least. He must either expose himself to the changes as well – or they will not take place.

The strategic bottleneck in management capacity

It may seem paradoxical, but the future is going to see further increases in the unemployment figures – while at the same time, skilled workers are going to become even scarcer than they are today. The same apparently contradictory picture applies to managers. Their total numbers are going to be drastically reduced. Many of them, particularly those of the older generation, are superfluous. Early retirement and outplacement consultancies are boom industries, and unemployment is affecting the managing class for the first time. Simultaneously, qualified management abilities are becoming a scarce resource, even to the extent of causing a strategic bottleneck.

Today, companies can simply no longer afford to leave managers in key positions in which they can continue to wreak havoc. The just deserts for good or bad management are received nowadays four times faster than they were even a few years ago. Time is short on the market, and belts have to be tightened even more. Managers who do not or cannot fulfill their tasks in accordance with the goals are becoming risk factors themselves. This is why much more attention is given to a candidate's management talents today than used to be the case when making appointments to important jobs. Management talents are unfortunately also much thinner on the ground than they used to be, since in the past the outstanding specialists were usually always promoted to become boss.

In almost every respectable company nowadays, tremendous attention is being given to training and promoting young managers. Assessment centers, which were often scorned not so long ago, are being set up in practice everywhere. Many companies have a well-established training system with a wide-ranging and demand-oriented program offering seminars and programs aiming to alert tomorrow's generation of managers to the complex tasks of the future and provide them with the qualifications to meet these. In progressive companies, questions that some have hardly dared to ask yet are being worked through in a targeted way with expert assistance: the ecological impact of company activities; cooperation between men and women in everyday management work; interactions between professional life and family life; long-term and integrated life planning and lifestyle design; drug and alcohol dependence among employees – or management. Behavioral training in group dynamics and personality development are being widely included in programs for giving managers the qualifications they require.

But all of these measures only take effect over the long term. Capable managers are needed right now. Those who know how to manage people and how to cope with processes of change are therefore going to be at a premium on the market (Figure 8).

Figure 8. Change – a developmental process

Part II
Designing Change:
Basic Principles

The (Psycho)Logical Basis
for Failure

Change is what is needed – in many areas of life. There is hardly anyone who does not feel affected by changes, either as "perpetrator" or as "victim." The fact that there is a need for change seems to have been basically recognized, therefore, and in principle there is plenty of willingness to act accordingly. So why does everything take so long when time is so short? Why is there so much commotion about it? Why is there so much conflict? What are the real problems?

When we have recognized the need for change, but are having so little success in putting it into effect, there must be reasons for it. We will attempt here to identify what these reasons are. Based on practical everyday change management, we will demonstrate the typical procedures which, in our experience, cause these difficulties and failures. The important aspect here is that these mistakes do not happen accidentally. On the contrary – they are already implicit in the program of change. In a way, they are systematic. To put it more bluntly: *they are intentional.* There is meaning in them. They are produced (psycho)logically, consistently, by clearly identifiable patterns of thinking and acting on the part of the "perpetrators" and by equally typical reaction patterns on the part of the "victims."

However, the fact that these patterns – which are common and familiar to everyone from practical experience – can be located and diagnosed also provides some hope that the malady can be treated, as well as an opportunity to do so. As Einstein put it, "Once a problem has been recognized, the way to solve it is obvious." Some hope, certainly, but no assurance – particularly since Einstein was probably thinking here more about scientific problems than interpersonal processes, the laws governing which appear to us humans particularly complex.

We will describe here the most important patterns, so that we can track down better what it is we are actually up to during these processes subconsciously, whether we are initiating them or simply being affected by them passively.

Cold start

Goethe wrote, "*Wouldst thou rejoice in the world, a meaning for it must thou mold.*" To give their lives meaning, people make a multiplicity of arrangements, use all sorts of psychological tricks, and if necessary invest vast amounts of energy. Not only to give meaning to life as a whole, but also to give meaning to the specific individual activities and duties they carry out, the roles they have to fulfill and need to cope with.

Someone initiating change is disrupting many of these delicately wrought, extremely complex networks of personal meaning. The more drastic and radical the potential effects of the changes on working and living conditions, the more brutal the disruption is felt to be. From a cold start, people are confronted with things they cannot see the point of. People are "content" with the existing situation, or have at least come to terms with it. They see no reason to alter it, and even less likelihood of genuinely being able to do so.

As long as it is not clear, has not yet been made clear and therefore cannot possibly be clear, what the point of the whole operation is, who is supposed to benefit from the changes, what the point of them is, and what their attraction might be to the individuals concerned, *anxiety and resistance* will be a perfectly natural reaction. *Resistance* to the planned changes develops as a natural response mechanism *to protect the threatened context of meaning*.

It is difficult to introduce changes in a situation like this. It is like being a salesman going from door to door offering products no one really wants, or like a farmer casting seed on frozen ground, or a radio station broadcasting its message when nobody has their set turned on. Or like an angler who happens to enjoy oranges who uses them as bait to catch fish – ignoring the rule that the bait needs to be tasty to the fish, not to the angler.

What is it that makes this procedure "meaningful" from the point of view of the person initiating it? What is the attraction of driving things forward without sensitivity, giving no consideration to the feelings of the people involved in what is happening? Is it stupidity? Insolence? Sadism? It might appear so at first sight. But when you look at it more closely, the picture becomes more complex. Typical management problems can be recognized: time pressure that is one's own fault due to bad planning; concentrating on short-term results instead of long-term success; a need to flaunt managerial authority; an incapacity to respond to others; a fear of having to correct one's own ideas if one gets involved in any discussion. And also the primordial fear many managers have that the authority to act might slip away if they do not apply constant pressure. The manager's most deeply concealed secret is exposed: fear as the mainspring for action.

We know from dealing with machines how much strain a cold start can put on the system. This is all the more true with human beings – particularly complex creatures who have a long-term memory, especially about occasions when they are shown insufficient personal respect. Because precisely this is the common denominator to which everything is reduced if one does not take the time to discuss planned changes with the people who are going to be affected by them.

All things good come from above

In some companies, the motto of top management is "nothing can be done without us." It is not leadership that is looked for, but high-quality office work. When
a company like this hits a crisis, these people reserve to themselves the right to
deal with it. The so-called managers rush from one meeting to the next. Frantic
activity goes on – but only behind closed doors. Everyone puts on theatrical airs
of importance, proud to belong to an elite group of initiates, the heroes who are
going to save the situation. An aura of mystery envelops them. They savor the
power of keeping those who are actually affected at a distance by merely drop-
ping hints, and keeping the solution hidden from them until it has been finally
decided. The announcement of the solution is turned into a large-scale event, a
proclamation. At this solemn celebration, the roles involved are clearly defined:
managers as the active rescuers, employees as the implementing auxiliary
organs. Gratefulness is expected, because everything has been sorted out from
"the top." Just like the politicians who think that discussions behind closed doors
can solve the problems of people "out in the country." This form of role-play has
various effects:

- When top management takes exclusive responsibility from the outset, it is forced to act quickly. Managing means solving problems, being effective, displaying a command of affairs. Everything has to be done by yesterday at the
  latest. These dynamic go-getting types cut through natural periods of growth
  and development in order to demonstrate their own strength. "There is no
  time to develop consensus," is the catchword. Doing things slowly might give
  others the impression that one is not in control of the situation, or – even
  worse – that one is dependent on people lower down in the hierarchy for
  solving problems.
- This purposeful, skillfully stage-managed hectic operational rush automatically creates an atmosphere of competitive self-glorification. At last people
  have a chance to show off what they can do – to an admiring audience of
  governors and staff – and to stand out from their colleagues.
- This emphasis on the rescuers' speed, aloofness, and elite quality means that
  they have to be constantly on their guard. It is prudence rather than courage
  that is needed here. A distinctive image, yes, but not so distinctive that your
  colleagues, also struggling for self-glorification, might turn against you. This
  means: never being either completely against something or someone – you
  have to mark yourself out, but at the same time keep all your options open.
  "Yes, but _" is the typical pattern. Being both for and against something
  simultaneously is the supreme skill in opportunism. Anything but clarity –
  except when it is guaranteed to be secure and watertight through a thousand
  compromises and "trade-offs."
- This type of provocative, theatrical staging of management as the great prob-
  lem-solver logically casts employees in the subordinate roles of drudges,
  servants, and marveling admirers. How "attractive" this *spectator role* is like-

ly to be to them – particularly when they know that it may well cost them their shirts – requires no further comment.

The "not invented here" syndrome

The more brutal the cold start is, and the more mysterious and enigmatic bosses try to make themselves as exclusive solvers of all conceivable problems, the more likely it is that any proposed solution will suffer the same fate as children offered for adoption: the older they are, the more difficult it is to find someone to accept them. After all, one would prefer to be involved in the planning and conception oneself. The whole natural sense of one's own worth, as well as the basic need to mark oneself out and have a share in arranging matters, operate against simple acceptance of a "ready-made product."

In situations like this, there is no choice but to let those who are going to be affected "work through" the pre-established solution for themselves. In the worst case, they will demonstrate that it could never have worked – because things one would prefer not to happen are bound to be impossible. In the best case, you will get away with those affected adding their own elaborate touches to the proposed solution. Both of these processes cost time, which was what you were actually hoping to save by selecting this approach – quite apart from the extra annoyance, disappointment, and waste of energy you have let yourself in for.

The wrong question

Try an experiment. Ask any colleague for some advice, and observe closely what happens. You will find you hardly get enough time to explain your starting-point in any detail. Hardly anyone will ask more detailed questions that would let them even begin to understand you and your problem. Instead, they will quickly pick out an appropriate keyword and then eloquently explain to you how familiar they are with the problem (which you have not even had time to describe properly) from their own experience. And they will not have the slightest hesitation in offering you, in a couple of sentences, a ready-made patent solution to *your* problem based on *their* experience. In other words, you will get the correct solution – only for the wrong problem.

Most people are *fixated on solutions*. They are not really interested in understanding problems and their context. They immediately ask, "*What needs to be done?*" But the decisive question, "*What is actually going on?*" is never asked.

There may be two reasons for this. The natural desire to mark oneself out and achieve personal recognition is apparently easier to satisfy by offering solutions than by making any attempt to understand things first. Someone who can offer solutions creates an image of himself characterized by energy, drive, and ultimate success – in contrast to someone who is still searching and does not yet know what the result will be. A hero is defined by deeds, not by thinking. The second motive for offering quick solutions is the hope of getting a troublesome inquirer off one's back. Like the young Lieutenant Hofmiller in Stefan Zweig's novel *Beware of Pity*, who only *too* soon – although too late to prevent catastrophe – recognizes that what he had thought was sympathy, which led him to become engaged to Edith, a girl suffering from paralysis, was nothing but "impatience of the heart": an attempt "to release himself as quickly as possible from embarrassed sympathy for another's misfortune."

The solution is part of the problem

"I need a new custom, one we should start up at once – the custom of thinking afresh in each new situation."   Bertolt Brecht

Example no. 1: people complain about traffic jams. To prevent these, they build more roads – attracting even more traffic. The increased traffic in turn causes new traffic jams. So even more roads are built – it's a vicious circle.

Example no. 2: employees ask for better recognition through special job titles and other ways of marking themselves out. As a result, the number of levels in the hierarchy and the numbers of job titles are increased. But this in turn weakens the incentive system more and more – until in the end the absurdity of this collective behavior draws the inflation in hierarchy and titles to people's attention in the company.

In both cases, the solution is part of the problem. It is stuck in the same basic pattern, with "more of the same" (as Paul Watzlawick put it) creating or reinforcing the very problem that was supposed to be solved.

The human image and the organizational model

In secret meetings, strategies are discussed, schemes for carrying out changes are developed, implementation plans are hatched. The employees affected are treated as chessmen that can be set up and moved about just as the game requires.

Of course, even today there are still employees who are happy to have no "entrepreneurial" responsibilities in the workplace. Employees like this never complain when they are moved from one job to another. They can be enterprising and show initiative in their own leisure time, at home or at their clubs. People who want employees of this type are behaving entirely consistently if they follow the pattern described above. But if what you want is "on-the-spot entrepreneurs," you will ruin all your chances if you start with that approach.

"Form follows function" is a fundamental guideline in modern organizations. The decisive factors are the goals that have to be reached and the tasks that need to be carried out. The form that allows this to be achieved in the best possible way has to be subordinate to the function and must derive from it: organization as a constantly open-ended experiment, constantly under the microscope.

But most organizations only succeed in meeting this requirement once – when they are founded. Once they are successfully established, an inertia mechanism comes into force that leads to the guideline being turned on its head to become "function follows form." The organizational form – above all for those who created it – becomes an element offering stability and guidance in times of uncertainty and change. Something to hold on to. The organization becomes a kind of cathedral or palace – stable, sublime, and completely unalterable. And the catchphrase for the organization's members becomes "Let's just try and make the best of it."

Outlining what's needed and appealing for behavior to match

When tasks change and developments are needed, personnel development officers are in their element. Eagerly, they formulate new job descriptions, as laden with importance as they could possibly be. You would think they were looking for a candidate for President: the candidate identifies with the job, is enthusiastic, friendly, good at making contacts, good at cooperating with others, communicates well, is flexible, creative. Plus: must be reliable, show initiative, be independent, ambitious, responsible, results-oriented, must get things done – in short, the perfect entrepreneur. More recently added to the above requirements: must have a capacity for networked and systemic thinking, self-organization and integration. A capacity to accept criticism and feedback is taken for granted, as is the capacity for lifelong learning. Undoubtedly most important are the qualities of credibility, ability to set an example, having a positive image and personal charisma. These specifications are then rounded off with general "basics of leadership and cooperation."

The above is a description of a mythological creature that is not mentioned even in Grimm's fairy tales – an egg-laying woolly milk-yielding sow. The crossbar for the high jump has been set so high that all you can do is pass below, waving respectful greetings into the air without a trace of bad conscience.

Most of these appeals are well-meant and quite unobjectionable. But they are completely divorced from reality. They lead to an absolute dead end. On the one hand, they require behavioral patterns that simply do not exist in this combination – and even if they did exist, the first thing to do would be to investigate the organization's existing structures and regulations to check whether it would be able to accommodate behavior of that sort. But usually the real situation is in complete contradiction to the specified requirements: collaboration is expected, but management is actually being conducted on a "divide and rule" basis. Thinking for oneself and being enterprising are expected, but checks are carried out on the assumption that everyone is a potential shirker and cheat. Cooperation and communication are demanded, but competitiveness and individual achievement are rewarded. The managerial model invokes enterprise and having the courage of one's convictions, but the people who make successful careers are conformists and skillful tacticians. In short, anyone who did exactly what was required in these job descriptions would be "irrational" and ineffective, and would actually have to be fired. And this is exactly what happens again and again in practice.

Playing it down – or the truth by installments

"No one will be worse off than before, and many will be better off."
Helmut Kohl to the East Germans after the fall of the Berlin Wall

Communicating "bad news" in such a way that in spite of it, or precisely because of it, the employees affected feel particularly motivated and committed, is a skill that is as valuable as it is rare. Particularly at the beginning, there is a temptation to choose the path of least resistance, for tactical reasons. You try to use mollifying words of the "no one will be worse off than before" sort, just to get by – knowing perfectly well that the claim is a false one.

What is the point of this strategy? It is a fear of what in psychology is termed "withdrawal of love," or a loss of acceptance, that might follow if the problems were openly discussed in public. But it is also a lack of confidence – or rather a lack of experience – in the ability of "bad news", emergency situations, and approaching danger to release self-healing energies on an undreamed-of scale. One does not have the confidence to go the whole way, and one behaves as if what is required – a leap over a yawning chasm – could be divided into several steps.

Not only does this underestimate the resilience of the system, but in addition piecemeal tactics also prevent these self-healing energies from being activated – potentially threatening the entire company's existence. Any feeling for the "state of the nation" which those who are affected might have, any awareness of shared responsibility, is nipped in the bud.

Dramatizing – or the business of fear

The two strategies of operating a cold start and playing things down both consciously attempt not to cause alarm, in order to avoid turmoil and resistance. Change is smuggled in through the back door. The system is literally circumvented. The strategy of the purposeful scare is the direct opposite. People are alarmed and frightened to such an extent that they naturally start to fear for their own jobs. Once they have been prepared for the worst, things can only get better. This method of dramatizing events for concealed motives manipulates those affected into releasing every energy resource they have. But woe betide you if they see through the strategy! Then it's like the tale of the man who set off the fire alarm a few times for fun. When there was a real fire everyone thought it was just a joke – and no one came to the rescue. If you tell a lie once …

The strategy of fear can also cause *paralysis of the entire system.* Everyone takes cover and stiffens into rigidity, hoping no one will notice them until the danger has passed. This is an age-old form of human behavior, the reflex of playing dead and hoping for a miracle. Every kind of individual creativity and responsibility in searching for a solution to the approaching threat is thereby obstructed. The thinking behind it is: "Must avoid making the slightest mistake _ best thing is to do nothing at all ... at all costs never take the slightest risk." But without risks, without questioning conventional ways of doing things, there can be no innovation, no solution to a problem, and no change.

Another potential reaction to the strategy of fear is *escape.* Solidarity and collaboration, built up and developed over many years, can be destroyed at a single stroke. Then all that counts is "every man for himself" and looking after one's own skin.

Those who intentionally inject fear, without real necessity, in order to threaten the indispensable foundations of human well-being – safety, security, and recognition – are directly creating problems that they will have to cope with later on. At the very beginning, they are burdening the program for change with debts so great that it may be impossible to pay them off during the whole period in which the changes are carried out. Because those who are unable to predict what is about to happen to them need to safeguard themselves, protect themselves, and defend themselves. Those who have absolutely no idea what the future holds, and who do not even know whether they personally will have any place in that future, are hardly going to be willing to summon the energies needed to shape it in a creative way.

This is perhaps the most difficult, and at the same time most important aspect, of process-oriented work: *dealing with fear* – one's own and that of others. If people have no fear at all, they become complacent. They become immobile, and grow fat. But if people have too much fear, they become paralyzed – and equally immobile. *Controlling the level of fear* is therefore one of the advanced skills in leadership – in management just as much as in teaching or psychotherapy. And the following are the sources that will always tell you what the "right" level of fear is: healthy common sense, a sense of reality, a good conscience – and trust in one's own employees.

Isolated solutions

Organizations and companies differ from one another not only in the goals they have, the products they create, and the equipment they use, but also in terms of culture. The culture of a corporation is the totality of the written and unwritten traditions, laws, and values that influence the thoughts, feelings, and actions of the organization's members.

There are companies in which there is an almost palpable sense that every employee enjoys having individual responsibility, exercising a personal entrepreneurial will, taking the kind of decisions that always involve risk. The catchphrase is: "Too many questions means too many mistakes." Within their own areas of responsibility, people think and act in the same way as an entrepreneur. In companies like this, the customer is always able to contact someone, there is always someone available to provide a service that cannot be postponed – or to take a decision, even if it does not lie in his own field of responsibility. Fast reactions are guaranteed.

In stark contrast to this are company cultures that are based on playing safe. Everyone is quite happy for the "people up top" to keep all the decision-making to themselves. The advantage is that you can always complain about the "hierarchy," without ever needing to be afraid of exposure to any responsibility yourself. In cultures such as this, what is known as "anticipatory obedience" is top of the agenda – and this can stretch to the level of embarrassing obsequiousness. Consequently, even in companies in the West, there is still a considerable "Eastern-bloc" mentality: lots of committees, lots of interfaces, interference at every level – but no clearly designated responsibility for results; large, immobile head offices mainly preoccupied with themselves; no time for the customer; a deathly hush falling in the entire building at the precise moment official working hours end; fear of competition and the open market; and many people doing nothing but criticizing others – not in order to solve problems, but simply to create a distraction from their own contribution to these appalling conditions.

Between these two extremes lies a culture in which precisely delimited areas of responsibility demand and encourage independence, but prevent any thinking that extends beyond the boundaries of the existing framework. Each person is orientated toward the profits of his or her own department, even when this is at the expense of neighboring departments and the overall results turn out to be negative.

The greater the contrast between a project for introducing changes and the overall corporate culture that predominates beforehand, the poorer are its prospects of success. Trying to introduce changes that demand a new way of thinking and require behavior that was previously neither normal nor desired, far less rewarded, and which has therefore never been "learned," is like trying to catch the wind. People who have for years been trained to conform, obey, and show obsequiousness have already had years of experience in acquiring a "survival strategy" that involves not taking on any responsibility themselves without getting firm approval beforehand. It is almost as difficult as making someone who has once had full responsibility become submissive again. Emancipation cannot be reversed. At best, you can make it more difficult to implement it, or try to prevent it.

In other words: someone trying to plant something alien in an environment that has not been prepared is building a palace in a desert, where there is no infrastructure to support it. It requires vast, and in the long run unaffordable, maintenance costs.

Juggling with names – or the "hidden agenda"

Someone who wants to change things has a purpose. Usually, the purpose involves asserting one's own interests, or the interests one believes one serves. However, this does not happen in a completely unoccupied "no man's land," but in a field of tension between various competing interests. The more attention one party receives, the more another is likely to feel disadvantaged. It may suit the spirit of the times to talk about "win–win models" everywhere all the time – everyone wins, no one loses, no one has to sacrifice anything. These clichés are attempts to "sell" to employees programs for cost-cutting, increased productivity, and performance enhancement that are quite obviously biased in favor of shareholders' interests – and sometimes go as far as requesting employees to rationalize themselves away. But when there is no confidence that employees are going to see reason, no attempt is made, and there is no opportunity for employees to confront hard reality. Quite the contrary: under the careful camouflage of "modernization" – which no one can possibly object to – a radical strategy of cuts and waste reduction is pursued. And the victims of this policy are unlikely to be the ones actually responsible for creating the appalling state to begin with.

Those who want to avoid this "dirty work" themselves usually pass the job on to specialized consultancy companies only too eagerly – in the not unjustified expectation of being able to hide behind the consultants' proposals in implementing the always unpopular measures that are needed. The loss of personal competency involved and the lack of confidence in one's own firm that this shows are accepted as the lesser evil. The captain who leaves the bridge in the midst of the storm thus reveals himself to be a fair-weather strategist.

It is quite astonishing how much energy can be invested by masses of employees in opposing this type of hidden strategy. There is a kind of silent unity in resistance: a truly admirable degree of creativity is developed underground in developing models for subverting the officially set procedures. The most promising models are traded on a regular "black market." All this energy, which could have moved mountains, is lost to the company. It is wasted in applying brake-power and resistance. People who have been deceived know how to take their own revenge.

The credibility gap

The future always involves a risky wager. In a wager, there are only two possibilities: you can either accept the wager, or try to avoid it. Which of these two choices you select basically depends on how much you think you can trust the people you depend on in each of them.

However, trust does not develop as an isolated factor in empty space. The way in which people deal with one another, the degree of openness and directness people expect and think others can accept, the extent to which they are allowed to be involved in developments affecting them – all of this creates trust, or else arouses distrust. All of these aspects create an instinctive sense of who deserves trust and who one should be wary of. And the degree of credibility and trust ultimately determines whether there is any willingness to accompany someone into uncharted territory.

Depending on each individual's personal background and disposition, it may take varying amounts of time to develop a good basis of trust. If it is ever undermined – and this can happen very quickly – it takes a long, long time for the damage to be repaired, if it ever can be.

With regard to management, therefore, it is worth carrying out a kind of parallel book-keeping system, constantly keeping accounts for oneself of the extent to which one's own actions are building confidence and credibility – or threatening them. In crisis situations, it is confidence in management that determines success or failure – and this confidence cannot be simply conjured up from one minute to the next when you happen to need it.

Key Factors
for Successful Action

2

Rousing energies and building trust

We have shown above that certain specific approaches are virtually bound to lead to failure. Particularly dangerous is the temptation to simply overwhelm those affected, taking them to the cleaners, serving them up a ready-made menu they never ordered, not letting them take part in shaping a future that is, after all, going to be their *own* future. This undermines both their trust and one's own credibility and, paradoxically, forces precisely the people whose support one needs most in order to make the plans work onto the defensive, provoking their resistance.

To avoid falling victim to this temptation to make things all too easy for yourself, an effort has to be made to win over to your plans the people who are going to be affected by them. However, this presupposes that you have given careful attention to their initial situation.

Picking up those affected from where they actually are

Those who are going to be affected by changes will probably be distanced from the problem in various ways to begin with. And it is fairly likely that they will also have a variety of different responses to it:

▶ *Why can't everything just stay the way it is?*
▶ *What do other people do in a similar situation?*
▶ *What is actually the concrete aim of what's being planned?*
▶ *Are there any alternatives?*
▶ *Why proceed in precisely this way and not another way?*
▶ *What are the risks we're going to be exposed to? What are we likely to lose?*
▶ *What are we going to have to do differently, or in a completely new way in the future?*
▶ *Is there any future at all for us – for me?*
▶ *What part are we supposed to play in these changes?*
▶ *Will we really be capable of carrying out these steps?*

▶ *Can we trust the people who want us to take these steps?*
▶ *Could we not just have a bit more time?*

Anyone being confronted for the first time with a specific plan for change is bound to ask himself these or similar questions inwardly.

If there is already at least a minimum basic awareness of the problem, and in principle therefore some degree of willingness to face up to inevitable changes, it will be enough to take a look at individual aspects of the plan in peace and quiet together with the people it affects. Things will be more difficult if those affected are still in a state of unperturbed contentment. As long as staff are thoroughly satisfied and contented, as long as they take their situation for granted and consider it as unalterable, the preconditions for change are fundamentally absent. In this case, what has to be done is to *destabilize* people's peace and quiet, to "thaw" them out and make them uneasy and restless – in the first place using scenarios for future development. The amount of motivation with which staff will be prepared to commit themselves will depend on the extent of their awareness of the problem.

To select the "correct" procedure for this process of sensitization, you have to be aware of the initial situation. There's an old rule in public speaking that says, "Pick your listeners up from where they actually are" – if what matters is getting your message across to them.

The essential points

To get more details about the initial situation, the following points need to be checked:

- *Being clear about the goals*: How clear is it to those affected what the concrete aims of the changes are? This does not mean, "How clear are the aims to the person trying to introduce them?" It means: "How clear, how specific, and how understandable are the objectives to those affected – from their point of view, and from where they stand?" Can they concretely picture to themselves how things are going to be different afterward? Or do they feel they're just being showered with empty phrases?
- *State of information*: How much information about the subject can you assume that the people who are going to be affected have? Are there any serious differences in the amount of information that various people have? What do those affected know about the way in which the project has developed, whose idea it originally was, and what else or who else is behind it?
- *Awareness of the problem*: Do those affected see the situation as being a problem at all? Is it causing enough mental trauma to force them to change it? How widespread is such trauma? Have people maybe long since come to terms with the situation, even seeing advantages in it? How openly do they talk about it?

- *Credibility of the plan and its initiators*: How seriously are the initiators taken when they say they are genuinely only concerned with the facts of the matter? To what extent do people suspect them of having hidden, possibly self-interested motives? Do people believe them when they say they're only interested in getting everyone to act together to retrieve a bad situation? How widespread are suspicions that the whole thing is just an alibi for some other plot, or an attempt to manipulate people?
- *Energy and commitment*: The amount of energy that those affected will commit to analyzing the problem and its solution, or whether they will baulk at it, depends on all these factors.

It is only once you have the feeling that those affected have recognized the problem, and that there is an urge to engage in creative cooperation, that there is any point in continuing to the next step, i.e., to the phase of concretely discussing the problem.

Of course, all of this can only succeed on the basis of open and sensitive dialogue with those concerned. It is also clear that, depending on where those concerned are "located" to begin with and how different their positions are, more or less time is going to have to be included in the calculations in order to put people in touch both with each other and with the topic, to get them ready to take part in the dialogue and make the subject discussable.

Thinking in processes, not structures

> Dans la vie, il n'y a pas de solutions.
> Il n'y a que des forces en marche;
> il faut les créer et les solutions suivent.
>
> [*There are no solutions in life.*
> *There are only forces in motion.*
> *You have to create them – and the solutions will follow.*]
> Saint-Exupéry

If you want to orientate your organization to the market's ever more quickly changing requirements, constant adaptation and change can never be the exception for you; they have to be the rule. The simpler and more flexible the organization is, the easier it is to make changes. And this is precisely where a problem arises: most organizations are built on the model of vast, immovable palaces and cathedrals. Imposing structures, clear forms, regulated processes – all in all, a solid, substantial framework – are the nature of an organization. Managers, in this model, provide guidance. They ensure order, and guarantee some degree of security to those they lead. They claim, and create the impression, that they are able to genuinely guide people's fates, that they have everything under control. And it is this guiding, controlling function that legitimizes their specially privileged position.

By contrast, it is rare to find organizations that are consistently oriented on the principle of "structure follows function" – organizations that work on a flexible and short-term basis on the principle of project organization, and in which it is matters needing longer-term preparation that are the exception that needs to be justified.

And it is even more rare to find people thinking in terms of force-fields, energy streams, and open processes. Normally, everything with effects that are not unequivocally quantifiable, and with a trajectory that is not precisely controllable, is dismissed as dubious and chaotic. "Chaos" has the negative connotation of "mess" – "not properly planned," a sense of something "disordered" and "incalculable"; in short, it means something any responsible person and every manager ought to avoid. The fact that the phenomenon concerned may only have been described as an unquantifiable mess because its internal patterns of organization are not known, is not an insight that is very widespread. It is even more rare for managers or advisers to feel comfortable in chaotic situations, where they could just as easily see themselves as having a new and important function. In today's turbulent times, the important role of the "chaos pilot," a person who seeks out his path more by instinct than by knowing what he is doing, is still not very respectable. Most managers still behave as if they were capable of controlling developments in a completely deliberate way, and as if they could simply halt or ban anything that happens to annoy them whenever they want. But they pay a double price for this misjudgment. In the first place, they are deluding themselves; they are manipulating a steering wheel that is not connected to the guidance system (or as Goethe put it, "You think you're pushing, but it's you who are being pushed"). Secondly, they are wasting a lot of energy – the longer they try to steer back and forth, and the more the effort they put into it, the more energy they are wasting.

The modes of action in dynamic systems always remain more or less obscure to an observer who is at the same time trying to control them forcibly, because this deluded activity distracts the observer's attention. Almost inevitably, therefore, incorrectly guided systems suddenly go off course – to the complete surprise of the managers directing them. They "slip" out of a control that was in any case only illusory, and take on their own independent life – like a ball filled with air that you push underwater by force, and which suddenly jumps out of your hands as soon as your attention is distracted.

The method of thinking in open processes and networked systems has been described in detail by Frederic Vester, among others. It involves using the judo principle to recognize and redirect existing forces, instead of destroying them: *moving with the force, not against it.* The challenge of submitting to this dynamic approach to thought and action is one that everyone has to face if they want to survive and take up a leading position in a world that is turbulent and fundamentally incapable of being governed by regulatory intervention. Dynamic systems, whose existence is *a priori* constantly threatened, can only ensure their own survival by using intelligent strategies for adaptation and development. Everyone wanting to provide successful leadership in such times has to meet these challenges – whether they are business managers, heads of non-profit organizations, politicians, teachers, or parents.

Everything today is in flux. This is just as true in business as it is for the state and for society as a whole. In principle, we have two choices: either we can try and shut our eyes to this threatening dynamism and take refuge in the arms of those who promise us order, security, and guidance – at the expense of our freedom and personal responsibility. Or we can accept the existence of incalculable factors and learn how to move with them and survive. To do this, we need to practice the art of

- investigating the inherent pattern of systems; discovering when and why they go into motion and how they can be set in motion – while accepting that much (even perhaps most) of what there is to know about them will remain hidden;
- learning to "lock into" what is happening, smoothly working ourselves into the thread of it and skillfully, from the inside out, encouraging and supporting what serves our purposes;
- and above all: learning to sense developments and trends intuitively – and act early enough, with the right amount of risk, without having to wait for any ultimate certainties.

Matching the business to its environment

The development of every business is influenced by a wide variety of factors and surrounding conditions: customers, markets, the competition, legal regulations, the economic situation, etc. For factors that have a decisive influence on the business and thus determine its success or failure, we will use the term "relevant environments" (stakeholder).

If you are not autonomous, or not powerful enough to be able to determine your own environment just as you wish, you need to take account of it early enough and see yourself as forming part of a larger network in your interplay with it. You need to be able to perceive what is going on, analyze it, and adapt yourself in order to survive.

What follows is a practical exercise that can help you make yourself aware of where your business is situated within the effective structures of its relevant environments:

Exercise: Business–environment interactions

Step no. 1:
Make a list of the specific environments (stakeholders) that are important for the success and continuation of the business. Make a "map" showing the business within its network – set in relation to everything that can decisively influence its condition and its success, e.g.: specific markets, special target

customers and particularly important market segments, competition, legal framework, general economic and social trends, staff expectations, etc. For the sake of clarity, external and internal relationships and influential structures can be presented separately.

Step no. 2:
Make a list of the communication channels, sensors, and feedback loops that the business uses to maintain contact with its defined environments. Examine the quality of the individual links: is the business able to identify soon enough what is happening and what developments are taking place? Are the individual messages reaching the right people fast enough and without distortion?

Networking through communicating

Many companies are not basically suffering from a lack of the information that is vital for their successful survival. It is just that the information is not in the right place. It gets lost somewhere in the jungle of internal vertical or horizontal shielding strategies that operations managers and departments develop. The information is not assimilated quickly enough, it is not called up when it is needed, and it is not processed coherently and consistently. The best and fastest information supply systems are useless if the information is not immediately processed – without loss of time or content – and converted into appropriate action.

Ensuring internal networking within a company through communications, permeating the company with communication channels, is one of the most important tasks for management. The goal must be to turn the company into a *learning system*. A wide variety of sensors can supply the information from all the environments that are important for successful survival. The external environments (market, customers, competition, government influences, or social trends) are just as important as internal ones (staff motivation and attitudes, expertise and core abilities, availability of resources).

With this equipment, the company should be able to guide and regulate itself by and large. There will no longer be a need for special management authorization for every action or reaction. This saves time and management costs. Processing speeds increase, as do the company's chances of being able to reposition itself quickly enough to meet current demands and requirements even in unstable environments.

As far as communications are concerned, a company is like the human body, with a highly differentiated system of arteries and nerves that extend to the very last corner and supply it with information. As with the human body, however, companies also need to ensure continuous circulation of information, based on feedback. It is not individual, isolated pieces of information that are needed, but communication. In management practice, this means: not just giving orders or explaining things from behind one's desk – but going out to people and talking to them; listening to their views and getting a sense of how they feel about things. Their questions, doubts, and objections need to be noted, and the background to these has to be understood – building up a basis of trust which in turn makes it possible to clarify to them one's own concerns. Only people who are themselves good sensors, capable of pointing their antennae in the right direction, are going to get the information that will make it possible for them to influence and guide matters usefully within a social system.

The more sensitive the topic and the more people's own interests are affected, the more time they need to be given to feel their way forward to the trickiest questions. One of the most important concerns of those who are going to be affected by changes is to test the credibility of the main actors and build up a basis of trust.

Specific methods and ways of professionally designing these communication processes, both external contacts with the outside world and internal ones, are described in a separate chapter ("Handling Communication").

Organizing from the outside in

What needs to be done now is to link up two insights: "A company can only be defined in the interplay between its relevant environments" and "Structure should be oriented to requirements and function – not the other way round." There are three groups that have corresponding claims on the company: customers, staff, and shareholders. It might be desirable, but it is not always possible, to balance the interests of all three groups perfectly. Priorities therefore have to be set, and the effects of these for the organization need to be assessed.

- Giving priority to staff requirements means that the internal scope for action, the feelings of staff members and their prospects, have to be made into the measure of all things – with the danger that the company will then only concern itself with its own internal needs. The consequence is that one organizes from the inside out – a risky approach at a time when there are serious threats looming from the outside.
- Giving priority to expectations of short-term returns on the part of shareholders can mean – depending on the profit situation – splitting the company up, merging it, or even possibly closing it and investing the capital on the financial markets. Customers and staff are clearly of secondary importance – a view that can quickly start to undermine the company's foundations.
- Giving priority to customers and the market means consistently organizing the company in the form of a chain of processes: the starting-point for all considerations will always be the market and the customer's needs. Strategies, goals, and operational measures are derived from these needs, on the basis of available resources, in order to supply the market and meet recognized

customer needs, providing suitable products or services and supplying them to the market and the customer on favorable terms with regard to time and quality. Here we are *thinking and organizing from the outside in.* Each step in this chain of processes needs to be legitimated by the proven *added productive value* that it contributes. Everything that stands in the way of the process chain, distorts it, unnecessarily extends it, or slows it down, must be radically opposed.

In this model, the short-term requirements of both staff and shareholders will always take second priority. But the one thing that is in the long-term interest of everyone concerned is safeguarded: the company's existence.

Facilitating learning

Are living systems not "rational" in trying to manage with as little energy expenditure as possible? Is a yearning for stillness and inertia, as well as speedy satisfaction of one's needs, not a law of nature? How much insecurity can a human being bear beyond the basic need for safety and security? A great deal of vigilance and a lot of energy are needed to promptly and successfully resist the natural tendency toward sluggishness and paralysis, and to prevent an organization from falling victim to internal growths and degenerating to become an end in itself.

What specific ways are there in which this apparently natural flow can be redirected?

- In the case of machines, we have long since become accustomed to having them inspected and serviced at regular intervals. Exactly the same procedure is needed to keep social systems working efficiently. It has to become a matter of course for management to check at short and regular intervals its strategy, the operational measures deriving from it, and the organizational and procedural structures established to take such measures, as well as the forms of communication and cooperation that are being practiced – in order to see whether they still meet current requirements. A lot of fairy-tales have been spread about the inimitable, highly specific qualities of Oriental cultures that have enabled the Japanese to force their way into our market with such innovative and inexpensive products. Few people have bothered to examine how the Japanese have radically shortened their planning cycles and kept their internal structures in a state of almost constant flux.
- The rigidifying tendency, which in practice leads to vital checking procedures being allowed to "go under" in the hectic rush of everyday business, can be countered using a simple technique: nothing should be arranged for an indefinite period. As soon as a rule or an organizational form comes into force, a point in time is set at which it will automatically lose its force – if it does not stand up to a fresh examination. This is the reverse of the usual practice. The principle "Everything will stay in force until changes become

necessary" is turned upside down to become "Nothing will remain in force unless a check-up has justified trying it out for a further period."

- Building up a sensitive, multidimensional "early warning system" is particularly important: the current state of things, as well as developmental trends, can be reliably assessed by systematic "management by wandering around," by constant evaluation of all the information coming in via institutionalized communication channels, and also by targeted surveys of the market, customers, and staff. Prompt action can then be taken if need be on any of these fronts.

- Another method is to set up a "sensor team" and commission it to carry out probes. The company's management can appoint a special task force consisting of people recognized as having sharp, analytical minds, people who are known for bluntly discussing things that have gone wrong and who are impatient to push things forward in their own areas. The members of the team can be given the additional task of listening in on the company, the market, or specific target groups of customers, and evaluating all the information that is important for the company's development. This kind of team can carry out as its official duty what many people always want to do anyway – showing no respect for persons or taboos and confronting management with the critical questions, worrying trends, and apparent weaknesses that inevitably emerge as soon as you start looking for them. As well as intelligence and sensitivity, the task demands a great deal of uninhibitedness and courage. If the team is to have the "cheek" it will need to do its job properly, it needs to report directly to management.

- If you need to collect ideas from as many members of staff as possible within a short time, and quickly get a feeling for important opinion trends among staff, it is also possible (even on a short-term basis if necessary) to carry out a series of workshops with groups of employees, groups that can be fairly large and have alternating membership. This extremely lively way of gathering data requires an open, team-oriented culture, or the availability of experienced moderators for the meetings.

Phases of the Process and Their Pitfalls

Development processes and change projects always run in typical, clearly distinct phases and steps, each of which builds on the preceding one. Each of these phases can be seen from two different standpoints: the objective logical procedure, i.e., the purely *organizational methodology,* on the one hand; and the emotional processes, i.e. the *psychological structuring of processes,* on the other. Both of these are important for success.

The typical phases and steps are all briefly sketched out below (see Figure 9). However, in this chapter, the emphasis is distinctly on the *psychological structuring of processes,* mainly concerning the psychological pitfalls that are involved in the individual phases and steps. How each of these steps is to be structured, which specific questions need to be asked, and which matters need to be regulated, are described in a separate chapter ("Process-Oriented Project Management").

First thoughts

Everything has to start somewhere. You may be wondering whether it might be useful to analyze a specific situation in more detail, and perhaps change it. You air this idea to a few selected people in the office – staff, colleagues, bosses – think about whether a consultant's support might be needed, and perhaps make initial, non-committal contacts with a consultant. At this point, it is often by no means clear yet whether a definite project will develop out of the idea, far less how it might be structured in detail, whether a consultant will really be needed, and whether the person contacted would be at all suitable. It is even less clear what forms this outside support might take in detail. All of this really needs to be clarified to begin with.

Risks: often, however, there are already problems implicit in the fact that the process does not begin in a "virgin" fashion. You have not started by examining the symptoms more closely, analyzing them, and clarifying the preconditions and framework for a development process in an impartial way. Instead, there is a *ready-made solution* that you have had in mind – perhaps even for a long time

Figure 9. Steps in the process of change, and their pitfalls

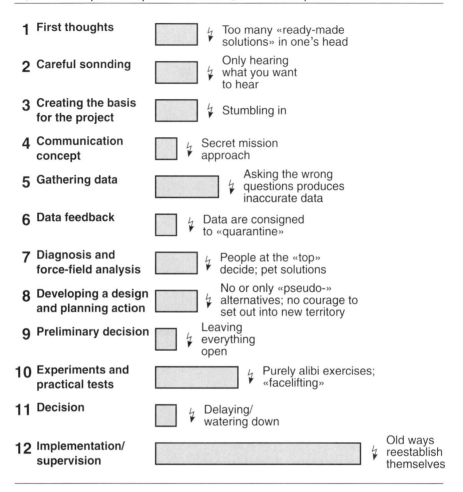

already. In this case, the potential consultant is not presented with an open starting point, and his insight into the situation is obstructed from the outset by one potential solution.

The conclusion to be drawn from this is that anyone giving preliminary consideration to possible changes is well advised to check whether the "starting-point" is a genuine one or not – or whether his mind is not already set on a specific solution, prejudicing all the subsequent "research."

Careful sounding

A prejudiced narrowing of the point of view leads to equally prejudiced restrictions on the range of action. Making an effort to carry out a preliminary investigation and "test the water" can expose this danger at an early stage.

Who should be included in this sounding phase? Since it is initially only a preliminary investigation, the numbers of people and groups included can easily be kept to a minimum. However, the decisive factor is that every aspect that is relevant to the subject concerned should be taken into account. Depending on the issue, various criteria can be relevant, e.g., departments, professional and operational groups, hierarchical levels, age, length of service with the company, degree to which the person is affected by the problem. Impressions "from outside," from internal or external clients, can also be revealing.

If the right people are asked about the right topics without prejudice, a good impression can be acquired concerning the urgency of the intended project, its contents, its probable cost, and its practicability.

Risks: The person initiating the project may feel driven by a kind of "mission," and may succeed in casting a spell on others – even consultants. Everything suddenly looks to be in favor of the project, and a feeling develops that there is no time to lose and that it should be started as quickly as possible. Enthusiasm distorts the view of things. Differing opinions are no longer required, and if they are voiced in spite of this, you simply pretend you have not heard them. A vicious circle develops: your own prejudices cause a narrowing of perspective, and you only see what you believe in; and in turn, this narrower view merely serves to confirm the existing prejudices.

Still, to avoid the accusation that you are behaving in a blindly activist fashion, the sounding phase is still carried through to serve as an alibi, although a biased selection of participants is included in it – people directly dependent on you, or like-minded friends who have been tried and tested in previous struggles – and suitably biased questions are used.

Creating the basis for the project

Once the idea has survived these first shaky steps, and if it still appears to be useful to start the project up, an initial project design has to be established based on the current information provided by the preliminary investigation.

This project design serves internally to provide guidelines and a framework for everyone involved. At the same time, it can provide the basis for the agreement with the external consultant. Obviously, this type of project design is a "living" process, which has to be regularly checked and flexibly adapted to changes in the context and in the project's state of development.

Whether the basis for the project should just be discussed verbally, or whether it should also be recorded in writing, is in our view a secondary matter. What is decisive is that the points involved should be discussed carefully enough to ensure that everyone involved understands them in the same way.

Risks: Agreements of this type may be regarded as unnecessary, because one knows the people who are involved well enough, or will get to know them while working with them. This omission leads to the following dilemma: an absence of mutual clarity is replaced by "spontaneous" assumptions and suppositions on the part of the individuals involved, on the basis of their previous experience. Each person is liable to think that something different is "clear." And sooner or later, misunderstandings and conflicts arise.

Communication concept

The sounding phase has already roused hopes or anxieties among those who took part in it, or who have heard about it. Quite probably, information about what you are doing will already have made its way down the grapevine. To a greater or lesser extent, the company has already started to move. So it is high time to inform the company about the project carefully, before the process of collecting the data required leads to a further intervention – and a more large-scale one this time.

Risks: It is not yet clear what the individual steps will involve, far less what will ultimately be achieved. So you hope to cause as little disturbance as possible, and keep everything on the back burner for the time being. You only want to provide full information once the project has been fully clarified, on the principle of "letting sleeping dogs lie." This reserve and restraint may also make things easier later on, if the project has to be quietly shelved again (cf. Chapter 8 in Part III, on "Handling Communication").

Gathering data

"No treatment without diagnosis" is one of our basic principles. To be able to make a diagnosis, you first need to have meaningful and reliable data. A separate chapter in the tool-box section of this book gives specific details on how to carry out this process of collecting data and reaching a diagnosis. Here, however, we would like to point out one particular hidden danger involved in gathering data, which is rarely taken into account in practice.

Risks: We mentioned earlier the importance of "unfreezing", the need to create an awareness of the problem and a willingness to accept change to begin with, at the outset of any process of change. Whether the situation in a company is "frozen" or has already "unfrozen" in many ways determines the quality of questionnaire results. If the situation is investigated at a time when those affect-ed have not yet "unfrozen", it is very likely that inaccurate data will be received

– because people who do not see the point of altering the status quo will be unable to provide a critical assessment of it. Equally, people who recognize the need for change, but see no way of implementing it and do not believe they can be successful, or who do not trust those who are propagating change, will also not make any effort to point out existing weaknesses when answering a questionnaire. They have come to terms with the situation as it is, have reduced their original expectations, and have set up a scenario for themselves that says, "Things could all be much, much worse than they actually are." In other words, there are true and "false" forms of job satisfaction – as D. Gebert already pointed out several years ago.

It is therefore completely insufficient to put unspecific questions about "satisfaction" and "dissatisfaction" in the traditional way. When collecting data – whether using questionnaire forms or oral interviews, with assistance from an outside specialist institute or on an in-house basis – questions need to be put that can provide sufficient clues to employees' feelings and attitudes, so that an assessment can be made of how much energy can be expected in implementing the changes, or how much resistance to them there will be, and where.

Diagnosis and force-field analysis

Even if the right questions have been asked, sufficiently conclusive answers have been received, and the whole flood of data has been condensed into a more or less manageable transcript of results, the material still needs to be carefully analyzed. This step consists of evaluating the existing situation, as indicated by the questionnaire, from the point of view of those affected by it and those with an interest in it:

▶ *Which aspects have special importance?*
▶ *What are the causes of the deficiencies identified?*
▶ *What can one conclude from this in terms of consequences and potential measures to be taken?*

Risks:
▪ Providing only very general information about the results, if any, within the company, and having the data interpreted in the back rooms exclusively by a small project team or by management.
▪ Giving preference to the point of view of a specific interest group, usually that of the more "powerful" people – following the principle "never bite the hand that feeds you."
▪ Falling back on the old "favorite solutions" and skillfully reading them into the data, perhaps even without noticing it.

Establishing a secure diagnosis, in particular, requires skillful and substantial dialogue in a situation that is free of dominance relationships, instead of flaunting the power of official positions in the hierarchy.

Developing a design and planning action

Once a reliable diagnosis is available, potential approaches to new solutions normally emerge almost automatically. Usually, lots of good ideas and specific suggestions are already provided in the questionnaire. During this phase, two things are important: thinking in terms of alternatives; and careful planning of possible implementations.

Risks:

- A single solution concept – a coherent and complete package of actions to be taken – is proposed and agreed on. No attempt has been made to consider what alternatives there are. The opportunity to achieve an optimal overall solution may have been lost.
- Concentrating entirely on thinking about the solution, but making hardly any effort to analyze the force-field involved: who will be in favor? How much commitment will they have? Who will be against? Who will try to keep out of it? What overall prognosis can be derived from contrasting these varying and partly contradictory forces and interests? Which steps are needed and how much time will have to be planned for in order to implement the intended solution in practice?

A specific appraisal of this type is an absolute precondition for developing not only outstanding development plans, but also practicable solutions.

Pilot projects and practical tests

The more turbulent the conditions, the more that fresh solutions need to be introduced in the form of open-ended experiments. In practice, too much time is almost always wasted in efforts to rescue old solutions and modify them to make them suitable for future challenges, instead of trying a new approach straight away. Particularly when computer-supported solutions are involved, the opportunity to question basic structures and processes is often missed, with the danger of allowing the computer to give fresh legitimacy to an unsatisfactory status.

If new solutions are still at the test phase, it is particularly important to provide careful, process-oriented guidance. There are always things that prove their worth straight away, while there are others that have to be adapted or altered. The solution has to be optimized in practice step by step – based on experience in everyday work and in dialogue with the managers, employees, and customers concerned. The term "learning organization" is genuinely appropriate here.

Risks: Times of change are times of transition; the old way of doing things no longer applies, but the new way has not yet established itself. If this transition period goes on for too long, it is easy for paralysis to set in. Important decisions are postponed, and speculation and wild rumors start to get the upper hand. Many people take cover and try to avoid taking a clear position, preferring instead to wait and see and keep all their options open if possible. People start behaving tactically.

The speed with which a decision needs to be taken, and the speed with which it should ultimately be implemented in practice, therefore have to be assessed from this point of view as well. The principle is: if in doubt, sooner is better than later.

Decision

Every decision in favor of a specific concept is always also a decision against other solutions. Abandoning potential alternatives in particular often leads to uncertainties and fears – and the temptation to delay the final decision again and again.

If the preconditions for the acceptance of radical changes by employees are in fact not present, a phase of propaganda work has to be conducted in order to create the required awareness of the problem. It would be quite wrong to water down the solution with shabby compromises and half-hearted measures – ultimately forfeiting the chances for genuine innovation.

A desperate search for all-embracing consensus, however, may also result from a lack of willingness to take risks. Sometimes it is not greater awareness that is needed, but action – taking the bull by the horns. Particularly nowadays, when less and less time is available, it is not always possible to convince the very last doubting Thomas of the necessity for radical changes. In addition, genuinely fundamental changes can only be explained and described up to a certain point. Someone who wants to learn how to swim has to get into the water at some point – and move about in it. In practical life, learning through theoretical knowledge and higher-level insight rarely takes place. Essentially, learning results from painful mistakes – and through the "faits accomplis" that life provides. In other words: those who are convinced that their "vision" is the right one sometimes need to take a courageous step. The "normative power of facts" – applied at the right time in the right place – certainly has its place in the toolbox of process-oriented management.

Supervising implementation

Most failures result from an assumption that taking the right decision is all that is needed, and that the project finishes there. But practical people know better. The old spirit does not give up the fight so easily. After all, it is not as easy to change mental attitudes as it is to change a shirt. But until the old patterns of thinking and attitudes have been replaced by new ones, they will always be trying to undermine the new organizational forms.

These tendencies to undermine or "reject" the process are in fact perfectly normal, and the only way to recognize them early enough and redirect them is to provide hands-on attention, encouragement, and support on the spot. If this does not happen, it is easy for a situation to arise that could be described by the participants as "Everything has been changed, but nothing has actually changed."

To ensure that the new conception is given life in practice, it may be necessary to carry out close-up monitoring of its implementation for an extended period. This implementation monitoring is an essential and independent phase of the process of change. It has to be professionally planned, and must not be seen as a natural process that can just be left to those who are involved.

Leadership in Transition

In Part I, "Scenario for the Future," we have already outlined the new image that the manager needs. However, developments moving in that direction are still progressing only very slowly. Managers are only human, after all, and it is always difficult for human beings to make fundamental changes. And that is exactly what this chapter is about – fundamental reorientation: a new understanding of the manager's role, and new qualifications.

And there is another aspect involved here that we should not overlook. So far as management is concerned, there is a positively paradoxical situation developing. On the one hand, management abilities of the sort that are urgently needed today and for the future are becoming an extremely critical bottleneck factor. At the same time, we are faced with a dangerous rise in the numbers of surplus employees, including those at executive levels. Unfortunately, in practice very few managers are capable of reorienting themselves and developing fast enough not to be left behind. Companies are therefore faced with an almost insurmountable "disposal problem" – unattractive though that term for it might seem.

Three serious obstacles

Pride in earlier experience

It is not everyone's favorite hobby to give up familiar ways of looking at things again and again, each time having to set off into uncharted territory. We are being asked to believe that yesterday's enemies are to become tomorrow's partners? And that the organization's past strengths, its product, and its market segment may soon begin to represent a threat to the company's very existence? However, a successful strategy for the future can only be developed if you are not trapped in the past, but capable of breaking out of accustomed patterns of perception, thought, and action. What seemed obvious yesterday has to be freshly justified if it is to continue to apply tomorrow.

Laziness, self-opinionatedness, and boasting about previous achievements – i. e., irrelevant and emotional factors – can prevent us from recognizing this and mean failing to implement the measures needed with the radical consistency required. This backward-looking attitude is often glossed over by pointing out the inestimable value of long years of experience. This attitude overlooks two things. First, although experience may make you wiser, it is just as likely to make you dumber. It can obscure your view of new ideas. Secondly, vast amounts of earlier experience are worth nothing whatsoever nowadays – because in the meantime conditions are now totally different, and sometimes even the opposite of what they used to be. Admittedly, much earlier experience is still valuable today. But it can only be valuable in a company if it is combined with a consistent attitude of receptiveness toward new opportunities.

Neatness and tidiness

"Even in their infancy,
most bureaucrats were already suffering
from the almost limitless size of their playpens."
Arnulf Herrmann

The term "bureaucratic mentality" has become more or less synonymous with the attitudes of people who only work within clearly demarcated boundaries – and only then when these boundaries are as secure as they could possibly be. The cliché of the "bureaucrat" may have arisen because regulations are particularly important in public administration. Having free scope for decision-making could actually be quite dangerous for a public official. Whenever an official acts on his own responsibility in a context that is not regulated, he runs the risk of being accused of exercising arbitrary power. So over the course of time, there was a natural tendency for regulations to develop concerning every possible event that might happen, so that there would be guidelines for action even in the most unlikely of cases. And in fact there are many administrative officials for whom what really matters is not solving a problem, but simply whether they have any responsibility concerning it – and if they do, that no possible claim could be made that they failed to observe regulations in dealing with it. Procedural correctness is more important than providing real assistance to the public in the individual case. This type of behavior is caused by the system. The "bureaucratic mentality" is a form of social maladjustment. It is not only seen in public bodies, it is also rife in thousands of businesses – wherever management bureaucrats have spent years ensuring that every single procedure is regulated down to the tiniest detail.

This mentality – originally developed with good intentions in order to prevent abuses of power and guarantee security and fair treatment for everyone involved – can become a serious obstacle in periods when conditions are unstable, because the whole environment is developing according to barely comprehensible patterns. It is not actually the regulation systems themselves that are the problem here, since regulations can in principle be suspended by deregulation measures. The problem is caused by all the people for whom t has in the meantime become second nature to work in regulated systems. Regulation has become a central part of their identity – and it is hard to change your identity just from one day to the next. It is a true saying that *"people are what they do"* – or to be more precise, *that "people become what they do if they do it long enough."*

The "entrepreneur type" that is invoked wherever you turn nowadays, and who is as hard to find as a needle in a haystack, has a different personality structure. For this type of person, the main aim is not to reach the safe haven of the point where his own responsibility ends, while ensuring his own lack of culpability in addition. The entrepreneur type sees that a problem exists and tries to solve it – if not one way, then another. His main interest is in the goal, not in the way it is reached. And it is no accident that this type of person is such a rare species. It is not only poor schooling and society in general that are to blame here; the world of business also needs to examine self-critically the way in which – from the start of the industrial era right down to our own time – most companies have been organized and managed. And to ensure that the last scales fall from your eyes, just think about the way things are arranged in the churches and in the army – institutions that have had a shaping influence on masses of people from time immemorial, and continue to do so today.

Good manners and conformity

> "*Don't burst a blood vessel*
> *if you've got no backbone.*"
> Stanislaw Jerzy Lec

Even those who are at the very top in management today started out, in their childhood, at the "bottom" and built up their careers according to the rules of the game that applied at the time. Good manners and conformity – plus a fair amount of opportunism, usually – were highly regarded virtues in the past. Working your way upward had its price. You might have started out with an upright backbone and firm principles, but after serving a sufficient number of years, your back gradually gets bent to a greater or lesser degree. However, stooping with a bent backbone means your overview is limited. Right up to the last minute before the final promotion, you have to go on being "well-behaved" to avoid threatening your career – as prominent examples have shown again and again, even recently.

Even in the very highest positions, there are conformist, "domesticated" salary earners, glorified pen-pushers, maneuvering in their well-behaved way through an established framework of thought and action. The streamlined "organization man" is a widespread phenomenon right up to top management level. The qualities that are needed today, by contrast, are entrepreneurial impudence, courage, unconventional thinking and behavior, courageous confrontation, a willingness to take personal risks. However, there is no way of getting round the laws of nature; you can tame wild ducks, but you can never make tame ducks wild.

An Update on managerial roles

Working *on* the system instead of *in* it

A manager attempting to create an organizational form that will be capable of reacting to turbulent market developments fast enough and flexibly enough is faced with the challenge of converting what used to be a hierarchically managed organization into a teamwork-oriented, self-regulating system. To achieve this, the first step is to stop doing all the management work oneself, to stop compensating for any weak points that arise oneself, and ultimately to stop accepting responsibility for everything oneself. And that means: working *in* the system. The manager's role is more like that of a "systems architect" and inspector, checking the system regularly, investigating the principles it runs on, and recognizing its susceptibility to errors, its strengths and weaknesses, its state of development and its potential. His most urgent task: analyzing errors and weaknesses occurring in the system and providing assistance by making improvements *to* the system.

Those who work *in* the system ultimately use their energy to maintain the existing system in its current state. When danger threatens and bottlenecks occur, the manager lends a hand himself. Doing things yourself actually always gives you a good feeling: you can achieve something that everyone else can see, and you can show what it is you are made of. But this type of short-term effort hides the failures in the system. It prevents them from being recognized early enough – and in the end it prevents them from being corrected.

Organizing learning

Those who work *on* the system basically follow the principle of the "learning organization." The people involved are constantly able to adapt themselves – adjusting their attitudes, behavior, operational measures and any structural and processing organization that is needed – to the changing demands of the appropriate environment.

This adaptation process does not take place automatically. It has to be stimulated again and again, communicated, encouraged, and organized. Creating appropriate frameworks for it and supporting the development of a corporate culture that encourages employees to take independent responsibility, show initiative, and control their own work – these are fundamental aspects of managers' tasks.

The following principles are important here:

- *Learning by doing*: people mainly learn things through practical action – and they learn things best when the process is jointly planned by a team and evaluated afterwards. The price: minor mistakes, occasional breakdowns. These are important opportunities to learn – an investment that ultimately always pays off. What is decisive is that the learning loop should always be integrated into the system. Without regular debriefing sessions, good results ultimately give rise to laziness – and bad results to recriminations.

- *Partnership-oriented learning model*: the traditional division of roles between the teacher or training supervisor, on the one hand, and the students on the other, may still be useful nowadays in many educational contexts. But self-regulation can only be learned in a partnership-oriented organizational model. To this extent, the manager is no longer someone who knows every-thing better, can do everything better, and who can therefore unilaterally claim the right to assess others. Instead, the system is subject to a shared learning process, in which the manager's roles and behavior can also be dis-cussed during debriefing.
- *Leaving responsibility for development with those concerned*: even medium-sized companies (large ones have always done this) are now increasingly investing in development programs for their employees. So-called "staff port-folios," "potential groups," and "goldfish ponds" are set up, and bosses are required to provide assessments of their employees and select potential suc-cessors. Bosses can supervise the development of junior staff in a sponsorship framework.

From the point of view of commitment to their staff on the part of management, it all sounds quite good to start with. But it can have problematic effects on employees. The "total care" provided may encourage spoiled behavior, which is anything but desirable in the turbulent times for which the preparation and training are being provided. Because people who have been selected for the "goldfish pond" without having made any significant personal contribution to the matter are hardly likely to think of asking, "What am I supposed to do next?" A sense of already having the field-marshal's baton in your bag from the start is not likely to encourage either modesty or a fighting spirit. And the term "gold-fish pond" is already suspect, anyway. Is it really a goldfish that is wanted: attrac-tive-looking, in need of care and attention, and liable to fall sick? Or would you prefer an employee whose curiosity, drive, and social competence mark him out?

Consultant and coach

Giving employees independence and responsibility can reinforce their sense of isolation and the stress of responsibility – particularly when they have not been accustomed to it beforehand. In a hierarchically structured organization, it is at least clear who has ultimate responsibility and who will therefore have to take the blame: the people "up top." But people who work on the principle of inde-pendent responsibility can no longer shift the blame onto others in that way. There is a whole world of difference between the two poles of "heteronomy through hierarchy" and "semi-autonomous self-regulation". To move an orga-nization in a responsible way from one pole to the other means that you have to plan for plenty of intermediate steps, each of which people can cope with. The trick is to do less and less yourself and transfer more and more scope for action to employees, on the one hand. On the other hand, you also have to provide the necessary support step by step in careful doses – but without permitting any reverse delegation. The one decisive principle is as difficult to put into practice as it is easy to state: *encouraging by challenging!*

In this context, the word "coach," originally a sports term, has long since become part of management jargon. It expresses some of the fundamental aspects of the leadership function that is involved, more clearly than the terms "advisor" or "consultant." Integrated, consistent performance orientation – and the motivation not to show off oneself, but instead make *others* strong and successful. Whether as "advisor" or "coach," the secret of success lies in knowing your partner and being able to make an accurate assessment of him – and adjusting the process to his individual learning curve. This means being a good observer and a sympathetic listener, as well as being a capable sparring partner when mistakes happen, personal conflicts arise, or difficult decisions need to be taken.

This switch in roles from "manager" to "coach" or "mentor" can only succeed, however, if the boss concerned:

- Has not got any hidden interests – i.e., is not trying to manipulate his employees psychologically and use them for his own purposes.
- Encourages critical thinking in a meaningful way – including criticism of his own role and personal leadership behavior.
- Is accepted by his employees as a capable and strong partner – someone they can learn from.
- Above all, has already succeeded in taking one difficult step: getting satisfaction not only from promoting himself and his own image, but also by encouraging growth in other people and their status.

As well as integrity and conviction, these things above all require considerable life experience and personal maturity.

The future: more teamwork

Flattening the hierarchy, "lean management" "bottom-to-top management," project organization, semi-autonomous groups, production units – all of these terms are just different ways of describing a fundamental development trend that is leading away step by step from an organizational model in which the roles of managers and those who are managed are clearly distinct, toward a model in which the basic component is the team. A team is a group in which management and leadership are carried out by different members, depending on the situation; in which the tasks of coordination and external representation can rotate between the individual members; and in which, in addition to having individual responsibility for specific tasks, there is common responsibility, shared by all, for the overall results.

Does this ultimately mean the end of hierarchical systems, the end of outstanding individual performances, and the end of distinctive management personalities? Our answer would be: no. Even organizations based on groups need various levels of control, and therefore a basic pattern of hierarchical order in the end. Even in groups, not everything can be done jointly, tasks and authorities have to be delegated to individuals, and individual performance can be rewarded. And even in groups, individuals differ from each other – there are some who have a strong influence, and others who have a greater tendency to conform. Even in groups, strong personalities will have more leadership activities than others, or will be able to carry out leadership tasks better.

Nevertheless, there will be "more teamwork" in the future in groups at all levels, for the following reasons:

1. In a team, an individual's strengths are activated, and his weaknesses are constantly being compensated for.
2. The direct and flexible interplay within a group means gaining the extra time needed in a fast-moving environment.
3. Teamwork is today virtually the fundamental precondition for innovation. Most tasks nowadays are just too complex for one person to be able to produce practicable and realistic solutions on his own.
4. A team is the ideal environment for individual learning (although it may not be the only really effective one). Groups are able to exert a much stronger educational effect, i.e. influence on individual attitudes and behavior, than the best-trained and most educationally talented hierarchical boss.
5. Cooperation among equals better matches the value systems of the top performers, particularly in the younger generation.
6. And last, but not least: a more or less well-functioning team carries out most of its own management, in addition to its operational tasks – meaning massive savings in management capacity and thus in overhead costs.

A qualified manager with experience in developing teams is capable of coordinating six to eight self-guiding teams of six to eight employees each. *De facto,* this corresponds to a management range of up to 50 people, well beyond what would be conceivable on the basis of directly managed individuals.

Group organization has tremendous advantages in terms of flexibility, innovative capacity, expertise development, and economic viability. The dramatic thing is that many executives and managers – particularly many who are at the top of their companies nowadays – have never experienced a genuine team from the inside in their entire lives. They are carrying out the tasks of management in the same way they learned them, the same way they have always been managed themselves: on the basis of clearly assigned individual responsibilities. Basically, they do not know what a genuine team is. The merest glimpse at the example set by most top executive committees in business throughout the country is enough to reveal this.

When business leaders – even those with the aura of being highly capable managers and charismatic leadership personalities – formulate their philosophies of management nowadays, it is often like listening to the Pope talking about pregnancy problems. Some of them genuinely believe they are making highly significant statements – and never realize that they do not know the first thing about it.

On the other hand, we should not idealize teams and teamwork here, and they must not be presented as automatic success stories – as if all you had to do was to set up a new group and leave it to itself for it to be able to direct and develop itself completely independently. Social science research has proved what is confirmed by practical business experience: *laissez-faire* is the best way of making mistakes in group work. In any company in which a team-oriented culture has not already been dominant for several years, group work first of all has to be learned by the employees, as well as by managers:

- approaching others instead of waiting for them to come to you
- sharing tasks on a partnership basis
- running meetings without hierarchical chairmanship
- listening to one another during discussions
- stating one's opinion in groups openly and directly
- dealing with other people's different views constructively
- settling conflicts of interest together – without an arbiter
- getting on with the job without needing to receive praise or blame from your boss
- coping with overlapping individual and group responsibilities
- depending on one's equals in important areas of professional life
- trusting colleagues and delegating power
- sharing responsibility for results to which others have also contributed.

Just as executives have to learn how to manage employees, a team has to learn how to manage itself. A little basic training is necessary to begin with. But in practice, competent guidance is needed as well – a mentor who can make the team aware of its scope for action, as well as its limitations; who can advise the team in difficult situations, without taking responsibility back on his own shoulders; who can provide support when it is genuinely needed, and refuse it when people are just trying to carry out reverse delegation; and who can also openly confront the team when performance is deteriorating, obvious problems are not being addressed, or agreed rules are not being observed. The principle of *encouraging and challenging* is equally applicable to the management of self-regulating groups.

Teams can become set in their ways mentally and forget to look beyond their own noses; they can get tangled up in internal quarrels and become unable to drag themselves out of the morass; or they may be living harmoniously as one big happy family but completely forgetting the surrounding environment, which they are actually closely linked to in their work. All of this *need* not happen, although it *can*. And even when things are running smoothly, teams – just like individual employees – have to be coordinated. Information transfer and communications have to be ensured. Incentives have to be designed in such a way that they are proportionate to individual and group responsibilities. Organizational changes have to be introduced and attended to more carefully. In brief, management is required – and highly qualified management at that.

Key factor: social competence

While it used to be mainly professionalism – based on a high degree of specialist skills and expertise – in dealing with the "hard factors" that characterized a qualified manager, in the future it is going to be the "soft factors" that more and more dominate the scene: influencing people and groups in constantly varying and often conflict-laden situations – and managing processes of development and change. An ability to recognize the patterns underlying turbulent developments, and to intervene and steer the processes using the motivations and energies that are present, is going to become a decisive competitive factor in the future.

The concept of "social competence" has in the meantime become an indispensable part of management jargon. But it describes a whole range of social skills, which in turn are rarely articulated with sufficient clarity and detail. In this section, therefore, we would like to give a quick breakdown of the essentials involved in it.

Taking basic human needs into account

The best-designed methods of enabling teams to achieve self-regulation will be useless if the people concerned have no enthusiasm for them, and therefore fail to implement them. And it is simply not true that everyone is desperate to take on more responsibility. Instead, there is actually a variety of different types of employee, and not all of these types are mutually compatible. In any company, employees with extremely different and sometimes contradictory expectations are thrown together.

For example, there is a particularly élite section of top performers, who have a constantly growing demand for self-management, self-motivation, and independent responsibility. This is the type of employee often described as the "departmental entrepreneur." He identifies himself to a great extent with the company, serves the company's requirements with commitment, and wants to make a career at all costs. More and more tasks tend to fall to this type of employee.

To keep this kind of employee happy, in addition to financial and career opportunities, it is primarily progressive organizational, control, and management tools that need to be provided. The trend is for management to be offered only in terms of agreeing targets, common resource planning, and consultation when needed – but without supervising guidance and without regulations.

In another group of employees, a growing split can be seen between professional and private life. They look for quality of life mainly during their leisure time, beyond the confines of what happens at work. Tasks at work are carried out in an unobtrusive way within an average normal range, but it is difficult and rare to get this type of employee to perform beyond the limits of this framework and take on any responsibility.

In yet another group, this distinction between private life and work is dissolving. They do not really need to work any more, since they have an assured income anyway; but they want to be active, develop themselves, and give their life meaning – sometimes simply in order to take refuge in some kind of occupation. But the work involved has to be attractive in itself and meaningful.

Others again regard work as a precious resource in itself. Having a share in it is regarded as being a privilege. This type of person is hard-working, conscientious, and adaptable – but does not like taking risks, and so is likely to be initially unresponsive to modern concepts of self-guidance.

In addition, there are people in special situations and those belonging to special social groups – e.g., older employees, former top performers who have been "shelved," people with disabilities, women with young children, women returning to work once their children have grown up, guest workers, etc. – all in all representing an incredibly broad spectrum of varying and sometimes contradictory expectations of work and the working environment. It is not possible to deal with this variety by simply lumping everybody together. A nuanced "cafeteria system" is needed if you want to do justice to the various requirements – diverse models for types of remuneration, working hours, forms of work and job, career development, participation in success and risks.

It is only in discussions with the individual employees themselves that one can find out what individual expectations and attitudes are, and what the implications of these are for the way in which the individual can be deployed at work. Our society today provides fewer and fewer sources of meaning in life. People are becoming more and more critical of the important traditional sources and suppliers of meaning in life – the church and the state, political parties, and interest groups. A yawning gap has opened up. If you value the type of employee who sees the company as being more than just a job to earn his living in, an employee who wants to develop himself through his professional activity, you have to offer him personal talks and an opportunity to address these questions of meaning.

Building trust

If you do not want to do everything yourself, you have to accept the need for co-operation and you have to delegate responsibility. But the basis for every form of cooperation and delegation is trust. In his book *Trust: a Mechanism for Reducing Social Complexity,* the sociologist Niklas Luhmann writes:

> "Without trust, only very basic forms of human cooperation are possible that can be dealt with on the spot, and even individual action is far too unstable for any planning to be possible beyond the safety of the immediate instant when

trust is lacking. Trust is indispensable to raise the potential for action in a social system beyond the level of these elementary forms.

Admittedly, you can also simplify the world to a great extent using distrust. But those who distrust others become more and more dependent on fewer and fewer people, since, as Luhmann describes it,

> *"Someone who distrusts others requires more information, while at the same time he is narrowing the range of information he is prepared to trust. He becomes more and more dependent on less and less information."*

When trust is lacking, one literally falls into a hopeless jungle of regulations, specifications, and control machinery. "Distrust organization" is the right term for this. "Trust is good, control is better" – this widespread attitude should be treated with the greatest suspicion. Those who act on that basis are from the outset incapable of building up working relationships based on trust. And sooner or later, this will be reflected in the company's economic viability – because there is nothing more efficient than collaboration based on openness and trust.

Teambuilding and team development

In view of the importance of teamwork for the way in which work is going to be organized in the coming years, it is clear that competence in dealing with groups is going to become an increasingly decisive criterion for management competence. It starts with one's own ability to integrate into a team. In addition, a good basic knowledge of the laws governing the processes occurring in and among groups is needed. A manager has to be able to judge when teamwork is indicated and when it is not – and if it is, in what form. He must be able not only to develop teams himself and lead them to success, but must also be able to make judgments and decisions at a *strategic level* concerning which people to select, which forms of training and management tools ought to be used, and what types of structure have to be set up in order to ensure that teamwork can be successfully established in projects or group structures in specific parts of a company.

Developing communications and feedback systems

This is a decisive part of the work the system requires: installing, maintaining, and cultivating internal and external communication networks; creating the necessary network links – and dissolving superfluous or outdated links and dependencies. Who needs what information when – and who has to get together with whom in what circumstances for working processes to run with the optimal efficiency and coordination? What forms of early warning, what periods of intermediate checking are needed in which places to ensure that development trends are recognized soon enough, so that incipient weaknesses can be corrected before the first big breakdown happens? The goal is: *a learning organization.*

The vital abilities required: wholistic, networked thinking and system-oriented action.

Capacity for conflict

Processes of change are processes of learning. Old habits and favorite ways of doing things have to be abandoned, thrown overboard, forgotten. And this cannot be achieved without conflict. Whenever something new is being created, there are hard collisions between interests, needs, opinions, and even firmly established ideologies. Single individuals, groups, and entire departments can get tangled up in open arguments, or in subtle forms of trench warfare. An ability to get to the bottom of things, and if necessary to show by means of tough but fair dialogue that earlier experiences and deep-rooted convictions have now actually become barriers to learning and obstructions to future development, and an ability to lead "hostile" parties in meaningful steps out of their blocking tactics toward cooperation – these are the key forms of competence for the future.

Tolerating contradictions

The world in general, and the working world in particular, have become complex and difficult to grasp. The clarity and unambiguousness of long ago have vanished. In complex, ultimately indefinite and temporary networks and fields of mutual influence, only those people will remain capable of action who can tolerate contradictions and live with ambiguities. This involves a very special form of resilience – accepting reality even when it is not completely comprehensible and plannable; tolerating uncertainty and being able to live with it, without trying to pretend to oneself and others that "everything is under control." Those who lack this ability will not only cause severe damage in their field of influence in the coming years, they will also begin to suffer in the end from a sense of their own "fate." And the more they suppress their problems, the more likely it is that they will fall sick sooner or later.

The problem of surplus staff and managers

Unemployment has already become one of the major problems of our time. What is new is that large numbers of managers are now also affected by it. There are various reason for this. First, when employees are dismissed in their thousands – and this is the case in many large companies nowadays – fewer managers are also needed. Secondly when levels of the hierarchy are reduced and group structures are introduced at the grass roots on the principle of "lean management," the demand for managers also drastically falls, even when the numbers of employees at the grass roots remain constant. Thirdly, in the new, networked organization, different management qualities are required from the ones that people used to be trained in. Many companies today are therefore facing the problem of having surplus managers.

The other side of the market economy

The market economy – even the so-called social market-economy – is essentially based on a free interplay between forces, on the dynamics of supply and demand. This includes, on the one hand, the freedom to recruit employees, and on the other hand the freedom to choose one's job – but it also involves the potential for contract termination, even without mutual agreement. It is simply a logical consequence of this mechanism that in times of full employment, employees have more bargaining power, while in times of low employment it is the employers who have the advantage.

Today, we have a long boom period behind us. Over all these years, rising income and career advances have become practically automatic. No one complained when lots of companies were going about wildly hiring new staff instead of sorting out their structures – the people who were hired did not complain, and neither did the unions. And during this period, lots of people switched jobs without batting an eyelid if they were able to earn more money somewhere else. And that was not the end of it – almost everybody regarded their success as being the exclusive and logical consequence of their own abilities and achievements. The notion that this might all be due merely to the affluent society, the continuance of which is not necessarily a law of nature, was simply ignored. People who distort reality to this extent have no choice when times change but to regard what they lose as being a terrible "injustice." Because something has been taken away that "belongs" to them – something which, in their view, was acquired by personal effort and which they have unilaterally declared to be their lifelong entitlement.

The fact that people who have been "loyal" to a company for decades can suddenly lose their jobs is part of the tragedy of the current situation. But it should be repeated: this is what the market economy means, and no one has any objections to it during the boom periods.

Feelings of guilt and maneuvering

The reductions in personnel that have become necessary almost everywhere nowadays are the logical consequence of the situation described above – the structural upheaval in the economy, exacerbated in many companies by years of culpable failure by management to do its most basic homework. It literally requires an existential crisis to force many companies to go over their books. And not everyone has understood yet that reducing the mountain of employees alone, without strategically underpinned structural changes, is not going to solve a company's survival problems. The most important thing that employers are hiding from today is: the sins of the past – and quite often their own inability to solve the company's current problems as well.

What does the problem of reducing employees look like from the point of view of the employer, from the management point of view? The first and most important point: quantitative growth is basically still regarded as the really normal form of company development. Consciously keeping a company at a specific size and ensuring that it remains healthy and successful at that level, or even intentionally reducing a company's size due to market changes in order to establish a new base for success after structural alterations – most managers find this type of thinking extremely difficult. The necessity for so-called "downsizing" or "capacity adjustment" – fine-sounding terms for job-cutting – is regarded as a blow of fate, as the effect of an unexpected but temporary economic fluctuation. The implicit principle for action is: cut costs desperately till you're past the trough – then you can start rebuilding again.

But if the changes are not approached in an active and constructive way, aiming for qualitative growth, and if the adjustment is treated from the start merely as an unavoidable, tragic decline, there are consequences involved. First, the situation will be ignored for as long as possible. Secondly, once you can no longer close your eyes to reality, you speculate about a miracle happening at the last minute – and delay taking the decisions that are needed for so long that a reasonable, humane and process-oriented process of change is no longer possible. And some people are so frightened of having to personally face the people the company is going to have to part with, that from the outset they prefer to leave things until undignified sacking is the only method left.

When action has to be taken at this stage, several forms of bad conscience are produced. First, because you yourself were responsible for helping to build up the surplus personnel that now have to be cut – and you yourself may have felt increased importance as a manager when you had growing numbers of people working for you. Secondly, because you played a major part in ignoring the problem and delaying action until the bulldozer and the chopper were the only tools left to deal with it. Thirdly, because you have at least some instinct for the existential problems that mass staff cuts create for families and individual lives.

These are massive psychological burdens – and they have to be put out of your mind if you are to remain capable of action.

And last, but not least, there is another factor as well: you have never done anything like this before. You basically have no idea of how to proceed in a situation like this. The lack of any clear plan, and a sense (once again deeply suppressed) of your own lack of ability and inadequacy, are what dominate the scene.

This mental state is no basis for offering qualified management in a crisis situation. Someone who is plagued by unconscious feelings of guilt and who has lost all creativity and professionalism is from the outset in no position to solve the demanding problems facing him in a practical and socially acceptable way.

Decline of middle management

Years ago, the trends guru John Naisbitt was already predicting an approaching drastic thinning out at middle management level. The tasks that used to be carried out at this level – collecting information and structuring it, channeling it, and passing it on – can be carried out faster, better, and at lower cost using modern information technology. Employees at the grass-roots level nowadays usually have both the qualifications to use these tools and an expectation of being able to do so, and of being able to control their own work in operational terms. The cuts in middle management seemed to come so suddenly and brutally because in the end, most people only addressed the problems when a) there was no longer any choice, and b) it was no longer so noticeable, since everyone else was doing the same.

But this necessary structural adjustment for management was a personal catastrophe for those affected by it. The end of one's world is always an individual matter. Those who have risen to the middle levels of the hierarchy not only have their "home" there, but also power, influence, and social prestige – and therefore their identity. Losing all of these is unbearable for many of them.

Executives are also needed at the middle levels in today's slimmed-down organizations. But the professional profile has changed: management tasks, now in the new position of being regarded as a service, involve providing employees with abilities and qualifications, attending during processes of change, and giving coaching to employees and groups. People who have become used to planning, controlling and administrating during their entire professional lives are not usually either able or willing to undergo such a radical change in their view of themselves.

The problem is often exacerbated by management attitudes that stand in the way of a "soft-landing" solution. People talk about the "paralyzed layer" that has to be "cut out to revitalize the company." On the principle "as soon as you've served your purpose they have no further interest in you," the high command can then rejoice in its illusory solidarity with the grass roots, in order to justify this surgical intervention to itself and the outside world. What is completely ignored in this process is who constructed the Moloch in the first place, and who lavished care and attention on it for decades. It is simply a matter of loyalty to stand by this common past – during which, of course, the company was built up and jobs were created – and now, when the environment has changed, to make fair arrangements for those who have to leave.

Many companies do take the latter approach, fortunately. But there are still too many that treat their surplus executives as the exclusive scapegoats. They are dropped by management like hot potatoes. It is a good way of avoiding responsibility – as well as saving money. Because "*We're not going to throw money after the people who are responsible for the dreadful state we're in anyway.*"

Taking the bull by the horns

Giving people bad news in such a way that the message is not watered down, but the person receiving the news is nevertheless not devastated by it, has always been one of the top skills in the art of management. There is always hot competition to give people good news. This leads to a flagrant, though understandable, form of incorrect behavior during restructuring processes that involve staff cuts. Although the course has basically been set and both the winners and the losers are known, information is not passed on and nothing is done. Result: everyone suspects the worst, no one knows anything specific. People start analyzing every detail of what goes on: who is getting invited to which meetings, who is being left out?

This avoidance behavior is disastrous for several reasons. In the first place, it is an expression of an abominable state of management culture to keep people in uncertainty about their fate for so long. Secondly, it gives those affected an excellent excuse for regarding themselves as victims and martyrs. Thirdly, at times like this pockets of dissatisfaction and frustration tend to build up all over the place, and they can spread throughout a company like an infectious disease. And if you haven't yet spoken to the people you actually want to keep, you are then risking losing your best people as well.

We can only recommend in the strongest terms here that people should be provided with information immediately and openly once the die has been cast – at a point when it is still possible to proceed carefully in relation to redundancies. This is *in the company's most vital interests.* Because all those who stay with the company are going to have their eagle eyes on the people who have to leave it. It is hard to motivate people in favor of a positive and shared future if they regard what is happening as ultimately unfair and have a sense that they, as the "winners," are inevitably contributing to the injustice being done to their former colleagues.

That is the psychological starting-point. What are the specific steps to be taken?

Three different situations

Situation 1:
Executives have been released, but they can be used internally – not working in the same duties and roles, but in more or less equivalent ones, sometimes even with fresh prospects for development.

This is the best case – but difficult conflicts can arise here as well. Because many executives have still not yet grasped what is going on in the world around them, far less what is about to happen. They think they still have a right to maintain their status and achievements, and have a claim not just to a specific grade but possibly even to a specific type of managerial work or even a specific position.

In these situations, if a normal discussion does not resolve things, then confrontation that is both open and tough is needed. At a time when everyone is affected by changes and many are affected by unemployment, it is not acceptable for a company, merely out of false consideration for individual executives, to delay the developments that need to be carried out in order to save the jobs of many.

Situation 2:
Simply in terms of numbers, there are too many people on board – some of them perfectly well qualified and reliable people. There is no way of using them internally.

There is really only one thing to do here: lay your cards on the table and discuss the situation with all those affected as soon as you have recognized it. There are always individuals for whom the opportunity to take early retirement from working life is actually not unwelcome, and others who have a good chance of finding a more suitable job somewhere else anyway. If you are not under acute time pressure, it quite often happens that the interests of the company and those of employees can be combined: a few functions that are not of vital strategic importance can be externalized through an outsourcing plan, and sometimes this can offer a group of employees an opportunity to set up business on their own – with some start-up help from the company. This opportunity for all or at least for a large proportion of those affected to find mutually agreed, tailor-made solutions, is only available when discussions with them are carried out early enough and openly enough. If you wait too long and suddenly find yourself under pressure, you are left with no choice but what unfortunately happens often enough in companies nowadays: sudden rough "disposal campaigns," which cause severe psychological burdens to those affected and which are followed by an irreparable loss of trust in the company. In some companies, the slogan seems to be: "People are our focus – and therefore our blind spot." The in-house title given to this type of project in one large corporation was "Operation Dead Wood." The very language used reveals the underlying thinking.

Situation 3:
There are too many executives, from the point of view of available abilities and qualifications. Requirements have risen drastically. There are only two possibilities: mass demotions – or redundancies. Often the only solution is redundancy.

This is one of the most unpleasant starting-points. First, because discussing inadequate abilities and qualifications practically always causes severe personal offense. Secondly, because there is almost always a bad conscience on the company's side. You are having to face the consequences of your own omissions in the past. Because requirements do not always rise in this way overnight. Basically, the executives concerned have been regarded as not being up to their jobs for a long time – but nobody wanted to tell them this, and no one took the initiative to move them to other, more suitable and more appropriate alternative posts soon enough. So in addition to the one piece of bad news, that they are losing their present job, they also have to face another – i.e., that they are not suitable for anything equivalent.

It is precisely in these particularly tricky cases that many bosses try to shirk their management responsibility. To begin with, they avoid the problem and beat about the bush – and then, when it is no longer possible to hide it, they go off on a trip and delegate the difficult talks involved to the personnel department (even though they spend the rest of the year complaining that this department is just a bunch of bureaucrats).

In our view, it is vital to clarify the situation openly and as early as possible, even in these difficult cases, initially in a one-to-one discussion between the person concerned and his direct boss. This kind of discussion is one of the most difficult tasks in management – but that is beside the point. The following steps are necessary, and have proved themselves in practice:

▶ *An outline of the requirements of the new post should be carefully discussed, and attention should be drawn to all the important and critical elements involved in it.*

▶ *Reasons should be given carefully and openly for why, or because of which requirements, the person concerned is not a suitable candidate. At this point the existing deficiencies should be clearly described, even if they have not been mentioned in the past – because in the present situation, only complete openness can help to reduce the damage.*

▶ *The remaining alternatives, e.g. demotion or redundancy, should be plainly stated. It should be made unambiguously clear that the preliminary decisions have been taken and that it is now only a question of establishing the specific way in which these are to be implemented.*

▶ *You must be prepared for the accusation that you have let things take their own course for too long, that you have not put your cards on the table and acted early enough and consistently enough. If your own conscience is not completely clear – and in practice no one having to carry out mass staff cuts can have a clear conscience – there is no use in wasting energy trying to justify yourself. Critical attitudes have to be permitted and endured. But this does not mean humbling yourself and putting on sackcloth and ashes. What matters is making it clear that the ways and means can be discussed, but that the basic decisions cannot be changed. Past mistakes, no matter whose they are, cannot be used to justify even bigger mistakes in the present.*

You can talk as plainly in this type of discussion as you want; many people are not willing to accept the realities straight away in critical situations. They react defensively at first: glossing things over, trying to behave appeasingly, offering explanations – sometimes even with strongly-worded accusations, or embarrassing assurances of their willingness to change. These initial reactions have to be accepted and borne with an appreciation of the situation for the person concerned – but without allowing the slightest doubt to arise about the finality of the decision.

Two things are decisive for the rest of what happens, and have to be made clear even during the first discussion. First, the *time by which the decision needs to be implemented*. Secondly, the *intervals for the further discussions* to be held in order to talk about specific ways and means together, and negotiate conditions. If this does not happen, there is a danger that nothing will be done – and that in the end it will only be possible to implement the redundancy through an unpleasant confrontation. Surprisingly large numbers of executives who have been given notice have a tendency to bury their heads in the sand. They hope to be able to "sit out" the conflict by doing nothing so that the problem will just peter out. Every week that their boss allows to pass without bringing the topic up again confirms them in this attitude.

Which people or bodies, in addition to the personnel department, should be included in further discussions depends not least on whether the person concerned has accepted the situation and started to adjust to specific steps during negotiations. A particularly important aspect is whether he succeeds in accepting some of the responsibility for the way in which things have developed into the present situation over a number of years – or whether he tries to present himself exclusively and one-sidedly as the helpless victim of a terrible injustice. In the latter case, it may be necessary in some circumstances to bring in other working partners or immediate superiors. Because as long as it is only the direct boss who discusses the problem of ability and qualification openly, some of those affected may take the view that it is only their own boss who has something against them and has decided to get rid of them.

In particularly difficult cases, it has proved useful to offer the person concerned an independent diagnosis of suitability for the job by a professional assessment consultant. On the basis of this type of examination – particularly by an external professional – no one can avoid facing up to his own strengths and weaknesses. In addition, this method of facing up to oneself can provide an excellent way of converting the crisis into an opportunity.

But an assessment alone may still not be sufficient. More extended psychological assistance may be needed to allow people to work through the subjective sense of a personal loss of status, the total questioning of their previous self-image, which they react to with the corresponding anxieties and blocking tactics. It should be remembered here that a person's self-image is not a purely inward psychological matter, but is closely linked to reactions experienced or expected from the environment. Basically, therefore, it is a matter of social status – of one's position in the network of family, friends, neighbors, colleagues and acquaintances. Only those who can work through this shock – i.e., relativize their "loss of social status" emotionally at least to some extent – can free themselves to face the genuinely important questions:

▶ *What are my inclinations and interests?*
▶ *What expertise and abilities do I have?*
▶ *What potential opportunities do these imply? And:*
▶ *What do I have to do to establish a new, meaningful job or activity?*

If the company is able to make some contribution toward professional assistance in this sometimes extended process of personal and professional reorientation, it indicates a constructive basic attitude on the part of management, and one that creates trust. And this in itself is already a small compensation for the omissions of the past.

In any case, the path from announcing the decision to its ultimate implementation for the person affected is a difficult process – and it has to be treated as such by the boss concerned. He has to take time for the discussions needed – and in these discussions, he has to involve himself in the difficult situation of the person affected. Only a step-by-step but continuous process of facing up to his new situation can help the person affected to get over the shock and take the action necessary to face the future. At the same time, however, the goal should always be kept clearly in sight – and the time by which the redundancy has to take place at the latest. This external pressure is also indispensable.

These recommendations may sound tough, or even "inhumane." In reality, however, the only thing that is really "inhumane" is what happens when the realities are not openly addressed. The problems are allowed to drag on; the tricky personnel problem is dealt with too late under extreme time pressure; and the parting takes place with open conflict.

We are making two assumptions here. First, that executives are not promoted against their will. They are basically well aware that they have taken on a demanding job with its associated risks – and they accept the appropriate rewards for this financially. Secondly, if executives really want to know what people think about them, whether they are matching up to requirements, they can always find out. In practice, it is extremely rare for a company to have sole responsibility for deficiencies in ability and qualifications in individual executives.

And finally, what is humane or inhumane can be measured only in terms of what happens to employees at the grass roots. It is astonishing in business how casually jobs can be cut in the manufacturing sector – and what pains are taken when it is management that is affected. Redundancies at the grass roots have long since become a large-scale business, and are dealt with using routine administrative methods. Even as low as middle management level, however, an employee who has been given notice is treated as an individual problem case. And at the very top, jobs and individuals are often never even questioned. In one well-known large company recently, a comprehensive program set up to analyze the cost structure, D.C.S. ("Determining Cost Structures"), was re-christened in company slang to mean "Directors' Chairs Safe."

Designing the process creatively

The real art of management starts when you are not just running routines and it is a creative search for new solutions that is needed. This by no means implies that every company has to reinvent the wheel. Best-practice analyses are useful for more than just conquering new markets. If you make a careful look around and check out other people's ideas and experiences without prejudice, you'll be surprised how many ways of doing things there are that you would not have thought of yourself. And once you have seen a wider range of possibilities and there are alternatives available, it is much easier to identify what the best plan is.

These are a few of the ideas that are now being successfully experimented with in practice:

- *Part-time work*
  This combines several advantages at once. Staff can be deployed according to the variations in work arising. Employees' needs can be taken into account more flexibly. And experience shows that people who work part-time are more productive on average per time unit than full-timers.
- *Job sharing*
  When two or more people share one job, it means that work is not only distributed more fairly, but in addition the improved productivity of each creates the same advantages as part-time work. In addition, it means that there are practically no more problems when someone is away. When people are off sick or on vacation, there is always someone else who can take their place who is familiar with the job. It should be emphasized that this method can also be applied to many management jobs. It is usually not anything objective that stands in the way of job sharing, but only mental barriers.
- *Starting a new business with a start-up grant or a corresponding cushion of orders*
  If you help as many smaller departments as possible on the way to entrepreneurial independence, it reduces the management burden, reduces central overhead costs, and increases the company's flexibility. With appropriate communications networking with the new, independent parts, a new type of network-based collaboration – a virtual organization – can be created.
- *Intermediate stop-off in a training company*
  Even if the time is not yet ripe to make the leap to starting an independent business, there are transitional steps that can be taken. A separate company can be founded with the task of training people to qualify them for new and different challenges. The resources needed do not all have to be supplied by the employer. Everyone who has an interest in preventing people from becoming dependent on welfare and ending up in the dark corners of our society can contribute: the employees themselves, their organizations, employment and social security offices, and all the other major public institutions with duties related to employment and the quality of society.

None of these methods represents a patent recipe that can be applied in every case. Only a combination of all available possibilities and working out situation-specific solutions can succeed. Various mixtures, and in particular transferring limited tasks or job packages to independent employees or groups, offer a potential that is still far from being exhausted.

However, two principles have to remain sacrosanct.

First, entrepreneurial responsibility for employees' own lives and planning for their future must remain with the individual employees themselves. When this sense of responsibility has been submerged and spoiled by years of affluence, it can and must be reinforced on the principle of *encouraging and challenging.* But when there is no willingness to take on personal responsibility, there is no basis on which advice and support can help people to help themselves and make a successful new start.

Secondly, no compromises can be made in the way in which work or the relevant business processes are organized. Without a clearly recognizable contribution to the net product, no intermediate stages, loops, or niches can be allowed simply in order to save jobs. The age of affluence when stokers were still employed on electric locomotives is over. This attitude may be branded as antisocial, but that is beside the point. The same critics would complain even louder, and justifiably so, if the company had to declare itself insolvent.

There is no doubt that new forms of working organization have to be found, and that new forms of agreement between employees, employers, and their representatives are needed. But better partnership is required for this than is generally seen in practice.

Hierarchy and Power: Enemies of Change?

Wherever fundamental changes are due to take place, vested interests are affected. Positions and privileges, delicate networks and spheres of influence are under threat. There are new opportunities as well, of course: eliminating obvious weak spots and friction, getting rid of what may be severe imbalances and injustices. But the cards are shuffled again, new winners and losers are identified, and influence is redistributed. One person's fresh hope is quite often another's worst fear.

So what, you might say – in the end, everyone's in the same boat. No matter how people's roles and interests happen to be distributed at the moment, they will all pull themselves together in the general interest, and reach a common consensus through constructive dialogue on how best to shape the future. Every-one just has to put their own interests openly on the table and be ready to re-cognize others' interests as being equally valid. In fair negotiations based on partnership, solutions can be found that will take everyone's interests into account appropriately.

This utopian vision of society is confronted with the actual reality: the fact that power struggles are the normal method of conducting debate, and power plays based on the principle of "everyone for himself." It is strategy and tactics, and sometimes almost athletic displays of power politics, that dominate the scene. Whether the conflict involves star wars or karate depends only on the weapons that happen to be available, as well as the positions involved in the hier-archy, ensuring power relationships that have a clear "top" and "bottom." It is just the same inside companies as in the worlds of politics, the church, the army, or soccer clubs.

If you want to change conditions, you first have to face two questions. First, "Why are things the way they are?" Theoretically, it would have been possible for things to change entirely by themselves. But it has not happened. And, "Why is it so hard to change the status quo?" After all, various efforts have already been made to change things. But without success.

The key topic is power. It is a question of who has an interest, and why, in things staying the way they are – what power the representatives of such inter-ests have, and how they are likely to use it.

The sociologist Heinrich Popitz, in his book *Processes of Power Formation*, describes in an unbiased, plausible way the mechanisms that give rise to power.

Machiavelli provided the recipes – and Popitz provides explanations of how and why these work. It may sound slightly theoretical from time to time when we refer to these explanations below. However, as Kurt Lewin wrote, "There is nothing more practical than a good theory." A great deal of what we observe in practical life could not be explained without well-based theories, and power is one of these fascinating phenomena. Its omnipresence in human life, its astonishing effectiveness, and in particular the multiplicity of forms it takes, are bound to rouse our curiosity. As David Hume once said, "Nothing appears more surprising to those who consider human affairs with a philosophic eye than the easiness with which the many are governed by the few."

But above all: only those who are familiar with the power game and the rules that operate in it have any chance of actually changing conditions, instead of running straight into a brick wall or charging against windmills like Don Quixote.

Problems of traditional hierarchical organization

The traditional model of organizational structure, with its strict hierarchical guarantees for power at every level, involves a number of severe problems that reduce its overall effectiveness:

- The cult of individual responsibility – an effect of the strict division of labor – leads to competition instead of collaboration, both at the individual level and at the level of groups and departments.
- Information, perspective, influence, and, in consequence, personal commitment increase toward the top and decrease toward the base – at a time when it is precisely "entrepreneurial thinking and action" that are urgently needed at the base.
- Thinking in terms of position and status instead of tasks and functions, prevents people from thinking and acting in dynamic sequences, i. e., in chains of processes.
- The route from "top" to "bottom" is too long, and too much information leaks away on the winding paths that run from bottom to top and from top to bottom.
- Having too many helmsmen both at headquarters and down the line who need to justify their existence every day and whose intervention keeps productive employees back from their work – the organization starts to become cumbersome.
- Due to insufficient networking and an imbalance in the distribution of power, individual weak spots in personnel can represent an intolerable danger for the whole organization, or large parts of it.

None of these items is a brand-new discovery by any means. It is well known how hierarchical structures first developed in their time – initially in the military, religious, and political fields – and what their legitimacy was based on. They based their legitimacy on the need to guarantee overall control, and in order to implement decisions effectively in a period in which giving and obeying orders was the accepted pattern of social interaction.

In the meantime, however, we have become aware of the disadvantages of the traditional form of organization in a completely transformed modern world. We are familiar not only with the advantages, but also with the conceptual basis of future-oriented organizations. But in practice, the corresponding changes are still taking place incredibly slowly. Why is this?

Every organizational change, no matter of what sort, also means changing the existing balance of power. Even modern, lean, decentralized structures cannot manage without power. Decisions are also taken in them, control is exercised, and people have to be influenced. It is the way in which this is done that is the question.

A contrast

The range of possible ways in which influence can be exerted is extremely wide. It extends from the ruthless and brutal exercise of violent force, to the legitimate authority of an official body, to fruitful persuasion – i.e., successful influence based on social competence.

In what ways do the methods of classic hierarchical power differ from those of social competence?

The classic hierarchy needs	Social competence needs
To use information and knowledge as a means to power, only sharing it selectively to allow tasks to be completed	Early, open, and comprehensive communications as the basis for a culture of management and entrepreneurship based on partnership
Management by decree	Self-regulation and individual responsibility
Conformity and subordination	Autonomy
Enforcement even of hidden goals and secret interests	Transparent goals, intentions, and interests
Obedience, "loyalty"	Independent thinking, critical questioning, open feedback
Clear and unambiguous order	Meaningful processes
Standardization	Variety of situation-oriented solutions

The classic hierarchy needs	Social competence needs
Division of labor, demarcation, and competition	Integration, collaboration, networking
Demonstrations of courage and strength as evidence of the ability to assert oneself	Admission of uncertainty and anxiety so that problems can be recognized at an early stage
Conflicts solved by arbitration	Conflicts solved by negotiation
Control based on basic mistrust	Trust not only as an expression of human respect, but as a method of achieving high efficiency

These are two completely different methods of exercising influence. We do not want to put things in crude black-and-white terms here, but you first have to be aware of the fundamental differences in order to realize that these are two quite contradictory "philosophies" or strategies. The fact that the two tend to get mixed up in practice does not make things any easier.

Why power structures are so hard to change

Those who are only familiar with the traditional methods of hierarchical power are likely to defend themselves tooth and nail against an organizational form in which the main thing required is social competence. First, because they do not believe they personally will be able to achieve the influence necessary in this type of organization; and secondly because they do not believe that this type of organization can actually work at all in practice.

The change that is on the agenda today involves more than just structural alterations; it requires a change of culture. This is a matter of values, inner attitudes and norms of real behavior – not least in the *style in which influence is exercised.* this is the one thing that is extraordinarily difficult to change in practice: *human behavior* – and most of all the behavior of people who are used to controlling others. And they are precisely the ones who would need to introduce these changes.

Another thing that can only be changed with difficulty is the real *distribution of power.* There is no dodging the fact that the new forms of organization will mean power being distributed more evenly in the company. But there is an old law: one of the ways in which those who have power will use it, is to make sure they never lose it. In other words, power has a tendency toward self-preservation.

Core elements creating power

- *Power is sexy*
Power has a virtually erotic type of attraction for those who have it – and those who want it. To maintain appearances, this attraction – just like erotic attraction – is systematically denied or suppressed. But this does not change the fact that the quest for power has a positively instinctual force in motivating human action.

- *My right → your right → our right*
People with power protect it by mutually confirming each another's "right" to have power and keep it. This cohesion is natural, because you have something to offer each other – the defense of shared privileges. This follows the basic pattern: *my* right (income, possessions, title, position) along with *your* power becomes *our* power – and thus a general, unquestionable right.

- *Enhancing power by showing it off*
People who have power enhance the impression it makes by using appropriate labels, status symbols, or insignia, such as titles, clothes, official cars, size and furnishing of their offices, exclusive access to special facilities, and other benefits that mark them out – and by showing off these insignia of power with a conspicuous and quite provocative naturalness.

- *Self-deprecation of the powerless and underprivileged*
This demonstrative naturalness in possessing power has precisely the desired effects on subordinates: they feel envy, they would like to belong to the same select circle, but they do not dare to basically question the existing balance of power.

   In addition, an almost law-like mechanism of self-deprecation operates. The unambiguous distribution of power makes people at the bottom feel free of all personal responsibility – the responsibility lies where the power is. You do your duty – and your superiors have the responsibility. This is the mechanism on which the Eichmann syndrome is based – an unholy alliance between those with power and their executive organs.

   And the acceptance of this power by subordinates, visibly evident in their submissive behavior, in turn confirms the powerful ones in their assurance that they have a "right" to their power.

- *Inability of the "destitute" to organize themselves*
Those who have nothing and want to acquire something need allies. But people only enter into alliances when they expect to benefit from them. In addition, they have to safeguard themselves against the risks involved in making bids for power. *Solidarity* becomes an indispensable condition.

   By contrast, it is difficult for the have-nots to form alliances with one another, because – in contrast to those with power – they can only fight to obtain something, while they have no common goods to defend. They do have certain aspects in common: they lack the same things, they are united in their condemnation of the existing distribution of power, they are all hoping for better times – but it is extremely uncertain how the power would be redistributed in detail if they were ever to acquire it. It is also unclear whether later, if they were really to gain power, they would still be able to trust their allies of today. All in all, there are more questions than answers – and they have nothing specific that they can offer each other.

The lack of the necessities of life which they share may provide a certain minimum willpower for changing existing conditions – but the unclear future and the incalculable risks normally prevent people from combining to achieve the solidarity that would be needed for common action. Consequently, those who have no power, in their inability to organize themselves, are more or less helpless in the face of an existing neatly structured power cartel.

● *Power gives everyone the safety of ordered conditions*
Once power has been clearly distributed – no matter how illegally it has been obtained or exercised – order has at least been established. People know what's what, and they can adapt to it. This order, which provides safety, would be endangered by anyone wanting to change these conditions.

● *Obedience is the citizen's primary duty …*
For many people, a "good upbringing" means bringing children up to be obedient, well-mannered, and conforming. These forms of behavior in turn stabilize existing arrangements and power structures in every field of life.

Disobedience, cheek, and resistance have always been regarded as socially undesirable "disturbances" and correspondingly as punishable. Critical thinking and open resistance are not actively encouraged today either in the home or at school. Consequently, the mental requirements and social competence needed for a healthy and natural way of influencing conditions in one's environment are lacking. The only choice left – apart from passivity, conformism, and "inner emigration" – is to erupt in aggressive and violent rebellion.

● *The strategy of partial power-sharing*
If somebody is absolutely dissatisfied with the existing distribution of power, and is becoming more and more of a threat to those who do have power, there is a particularly effective defense mechanism which the powerful ones have at their disposal: *the strategy of embrace*. The troublemaker is simply – and to a carefully restricted extent – allowed a share in the benefits. The price he has to pay: support and protection for the existing balance of power – from now on, in his own interests as well. In this way, he is at least temporarily immobilized, extricated from the solidarity of the have-nots, and turned into a support for the overall system.

Strategies for power changes

Change always also means conflict with "power cartels." The success of planned change is therefore in principle always endangered. Right up to the last moment before they are irreversibly implemented, strategies for change can be undermined when skillfully established, shrewdly stabilized power cartels that are constantly prepared to defend themselves think their interests are under threat. This is as true inside corporations as it is in the world of politics.

But it is not always those who have the say who automatically have all the answers. The goals of change are not necessarily compatible with the goals of those who have power. It is always possible that plans for change that are quite legitimate and valuable from an overall standpoint may encroach on a power cartel's territory, and make it bare its teeth. What is to be done?

If you want to weaken and change an existing power structure, it is not only good ideas that you need; you also have to build up a corresponding *counter-power* in order to achieve the breakthrough for your planned changes. The laws of how to create power remain the same – no matter what the purpose is that this power is to be used for.

These are the essential maxims for action for those who have decided to change the existing balance of power:

- Carefully establish for yourself whether you are really willing to take on the substantial risk initially – and be aware that you may have a long road ahead of you.
- Never let yourself be used for other people's unknown purposes, but always only do what you yourself consider correct and important.
- Neither condemn power in general nor its current possessors, but accumulate power yourself in a purposeful way and use it to change conditions.
- Question in principle and systematically all power privileges and status symbols; and in particular question the purpose of apparently "natural" privileges.
- Carry out open criticism of existing conditions and create resistance against notorious shortcomings.
- Propagate criticism, contradiction, and resistance as virtues – i.e., as competence – in order to put clogged up and ossified systems off their balance.
- Constantly be on the lookout for like-minded people and build up a core team of allies with whom you can recharge mentally and spiritually and plan all your intended steps together.
- Build up a wider network of allies step by step that can be carefully maintained and coordinated by the core team.
- Once your "power base" is stable enough: make preparations for solidarity and common action in implementing shared goals.

Experience in practice shows that the formal act of taking this last step is usually no longer necessary. Due to a whole variety of informal effects of the network, the attitudes, behavior, and spheres of influence in the environment change step by step, sometimes almost imperceptibly. Existing conditions then often move in the desired direction without anything more needing to be done, even before the carefully built up power potential needs to be deliberately exercised in a campaign of solidarity.

An age-old taboo demystified

You may have been getting a strange feeling in your stomach while reading this chapter. You may have found parts of it embarrassing, and started to wonder whether this book is propagating leftist ideologies or offering a user's guide to revolutionary or terrorist activities.

If so, it was because power is a *taboo*. It is not the done thing to talk about it – and when you do something forbidden, you are bound to feel odd about it. Power plays a central part in people's lives, but it is not a topic that can be officially discussed. Even people who formally possess immense power – top politicians or directors of large companies – regularly deny with complete conviction that they have any real power, or dramatically play it down, when they are asked about it. They are not even always aware that they are doing this, and it is often a quite instinctive reaction: one is simply a "mediator between various interest groups," "a public servant," or just "one of the company's many committed employees." It is the same as with sex: everyone knows that it exists and that it plays a vital role in human life, but it is just not socially acceptable to talk about it.

The strength of this taboo can be seen from the fact that power is never mentioned during managerial training. But power is in fact one of the most important tools for implementing decisions in management. In the context of a hierarchy, everyone is exposed to power every day – and everyone uses it every day as well. Directing and influencing large numbers of people is what you were hired for and what you are paid to do – but the topic of power "does not exist." Why not?

Basically, this is exactly where the fascinating journey into the anatomy of power starts. *Taboos are always – and sometimes even primarily – a method of preserving the existing balance of power.* As long as power continues to be a taboo, nobody will talk about it critically, and there will be no real danger of anyone questioning the existing balance of power or casting doubt on it and suggesting changes. The unwritten "prohibition" against talking about power in general, and about the balance of power existing here and now in a specific organization in particular, therefore also has a deeper significance.

In this book, we take the following point of view:

1. Power is in principle neither good nor bad. The only thing that makes a power "good" or "bad" is the purpose it is used for.
2. Power is a tool for implementing decisions inside organizations. It enables leaders to control large organizations without using power.

3. *Power should not be made into a taboo, but – in exactly the same way as all the other tools for management and exercising influence – it should be made transparent and should be regularly questioned with regard to its goals, its function, and the way in which it is being used.*
4. *Someone who wants to control processes of change in organizations and get things moving cannot afford to squeamishly avoid talking about power. He has to be aware of the laws on which the creation and maintenance of power are based. First, because sooner or later he is going to have to question the existing balance of power and perhaps change it. And secondly, because this cannot be done with good arguments and pious hopes alone. He has to have power himself in order to carry the changes through. And if he does not have power yet, he will have to build it up.*

So we can only warmly recommend to executives at all levels to study in detail the mechanisms by which power is acquired. It is a topic that is not only fascinating in itself, but also extremely useful in practical everyday life. To be a professional, you have to master the instruments you are playing; but deciding which melody to play is still up to you as well.

Charter for Managing Change

6

Primacy of transfer

When organizational changes are called for, there are plenty of intelligent people – top decision-makers and qualified specialists, as well as expensive advisers – who seem to think the job has been done once they have laid the necessary plans on the table. The greatest care and attention is given to the tasks of analysis and developing concepts, and usually most of the time involved is spent on these as well – so that the incubation period can take months, or sometimes even years. Finally, when the wisp of white smoke at last emerges from the holy of holies, there is a rush to put all these plans into practice – and then people wonder why something that has been so professionally produced, and which looked so logical on paper, does not work out in practice.

Actually, it is not really all that difficult to develop a good plan. Sometimes talking to the right people in peace and quiet is enough to clarify where you are headed. But planning and developing concepts is comfortable work. You can do it sitting at a desk, and nobody has to get their hands dirty. No wonder some people like to spend long periods keeping themselves busy with it.

No, it is not the planning involved that is the really critical part of the process of change. The one thing that is really difficult is implementing the plans. The trick lies not in drafting conceptual models and deciding on them, but in putting them into practice. It all depends on *transfer* – and this is the only way to measure success.

This absolute primacy of transfer implies what could be called a "charter for managing change": eight procedural principles that ultimately all serve one and the same goal, namely *ensuring that plans are transferred into practice.* When the critical bottleneck is termed "transfer," it logically means from the outset – even before a project starts – that the project's real goal is seen as being implementation, with careful attention being paid at each individual step to *creating the optimal conditions for putting the plans into practice.*

These are the eight principles at a glance (Figure 10):

- Target-based management
- No intervention without diagnosis

Figure 10. *Charter for managing change*

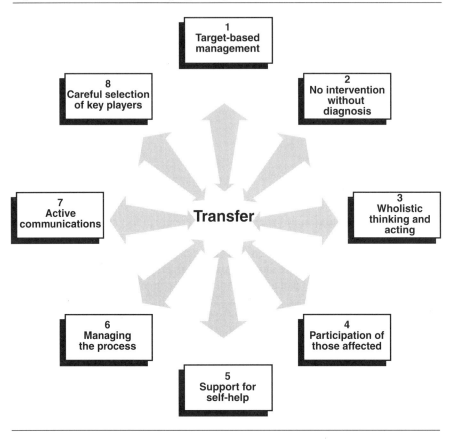

- Wholistic thinking and acting
- Involvement by those affected
- Support for self-help
- Managing the process
- Active communication
- Careful selection of key players

These principles represent an extremely effective conception of management. However, they are not just a list of miscellaneous options from which you can pick first one, then another, depending on the situation. The principles are mutually complementary, and to ensure success you have to pay attention to all of them imultaneously.

First principle:
target-based management

It may seem banal to point out something apparently so obvious first: *a project that is supposed to produce practical results has to be directed with the goal in mind.* It is one of the fatal misconceptions of our time to believe that management that is oriented toward people and participation – the view we support in this book – is not compatible with systematic planning, guidance, and control. A curse has been cast on everything that reeks of hierarchy and power by the defenders of a misconceived type of humanistic psychology – the "softies" and "psycho-freaks" produced by modern social science. To them, any kind of leadership is suspect on principle. But in reality, things are the other way round: without leadership, participation becomes a journey leading nowhere, and sooner or later you land up in the ditch.

The following points ought to be clear when work on the project starts:

1. **Initial situation**
   ▶ *Where do the problems lie?*
   ▶ *Why are changes needed?*
   ▶ *How is the need for action justified?*

2. **Goals**
   ▶ *What are the goals of the project?*
   ▶ *What concrete results is it intended to produce?*
   ▶ *What is going to be different afterward from the way things are now?*

3. **Criteria for success**
   ▶ *What criteria will be used to judge whether the goals have been reached?*
   ▶ *How will the project's success be judged qualitatively?*
   ▶ *How will its success be judged quantitatively?*

4. **Organization**
   ▶ *How will tasks be distributed – who will be doing what?*
   ▶ *Who is responsible for coordination and guidance?*
   ▶ *Who is responsible for taking decisions?*

5. **Planning**
   ▶ *What will be the phases of project? And what specific things will happen in each phase?*
   ▶ *What are the most important "milestones" – and what things need to have been achieved by the time each of these points is reached?*
   ▶ *What is the time schedule for the project? When should each of the individual phases have been completed, and when will the project as a whole be finished?*

6. **Monitoring**
   ▶ *How is the project's progress going to be monitored?*
   ▶ *When and how is each critical interim assessment to be made?*
   ▶ *Who is entitled to initiate corrective action when things go off course?*

Each of these six points is decisive for effective collaboration between all those involved in work on the project, for the economical use of available resources, for concrete results, and so ultimately for the process of *putting the project's goals into practice* later on. Creating the basis for target-based project management is therefore the first step that needs to be taken once the need for change has been recognized.

Second principle: no intervention without diagnosis

This is another apparent commonplace: at the beginning of any process of change, there has to be a *careful assessment of the situation.* Often this is the exact origin of disasters that follow later on. People think they know enough about the current situation, and they start developing plans – but without systematically analyzing the *actual situation* and without producing as concrete as possible a description of the *desired situation.*

In medicine, there is a principle that "treatment is only as good as the diagnosis it is based on." Nobody receiving medical care would question that. Transferring this principle to organization development, it could be formulated as "good analysis is half the battle in making a project successful." But even today, this is still not widely recognized.

The data needed to assess the current situation in a specific organizational unit can only be supplied by someone working in that unit. Quite often, the only people who know what can be sensibly changed in a unit are those who work there. At the beginning of every change project, therefore, a survey of the members of staff and management who are affected is almost always needed, so as to establish the following points:

▶ *What is running well?*
▶ *What is not running so well?*
▶ *What changes are indicated?*
▶ *How can they be carried out?*

If everyone involved has answered these questions, then usually all the material needed to develop successful solutions is already available.

It is usually advisable to conduct the diagnosis in four steps:

1. *Data acquisition*
   Survey
2. *Data condensation*
   Reducing the information to its essentials
3. *Data feedback*
   Informing all those involved about the results
4. *Data analysis*
   Analyzing links, defining weaknesses, pointing at possible solutions

Admittedly, even good analysis is not enough. In some companies, there is actually too much analysis – and not enough action. And there are situations in which analyzing the existing situation produces absolutely nothing. For example, when it is a question of building a new factory in open countryside; or if the organization in an existing enterprise needs to be totally over-hauled to make way for new activities; or when a business is on the point of totally collapsing and has to be "turned round." But these are special situations. In most cases, it is advisable to start by examining in detail the situation you want to change. It is only once you are familiar with the insides of your alarm clock and its mechanisms that you will be able to repair it when it breaks down.

Third principle:
wholistic thinking and acting

One of the most frequently seen reasons why projects for change fail is that there are technocrats at work, who have taken into account all of the techno-logical, structural, and economic aspects of a problem during the planning stage – and who have just as rigorously ignored all the human and interpersonal aspects involved.

These sins of omission begin even at the stage of *analyzing the existing situation*: the technological and economic structures and processes are examined in detail – but the working atmosphere, staff motivation, management style, de-cision-making processes, and cooperation within and between the individual organizational units are not issues at all.

This one-sided way of looking at things continues at the level of *work organi-zation*: the project is systematically planned and tightly organized – but nobody is interested in whether staff understand and accept the goals of the project or not, whether individual committees have the right people on them, and whether the employees who have been appointed are capable of carrying out the speci-fied tasks within the allotted time.

And at the stage of *drafting the future organizational structure,* the same pat-tern is repeated again. For example, a draft is drawn up with an organization plan as thin as a beanpole, with as few hierarchical levels as possible and a wide spread of management responsibility – and nobody bothers to check whether this structure is consistent with the dominant management culture, or whether the abilities and experience of existing managers will enable them to take on such a wide spread of responsibility.

Wholistic thinking and acting in organizations means not just looking at the "hardware," but also at the "software." The phenomenon of the "organization" basically has to be seen from three points of view:

- *Structures*
  Structural organization, process organization, management systems.

- *Behavior*
  Motivation and identification, communication and cooperation.
- *Culture*
  Written and unwritten laws and game rules, principles of reward and punishment.

Wholistic thinking and action also means paying careful attention to significant *networks*. In the effective structures of a complex organization, it is not just the structure and internal constitution of the individual organizational units that are important. Between human individuals, groups, and organizational units, dynamic *interactions* also take place in practice. There are always weak points where it is not possible to trace the causes back to any specific organizational unit. The reason is that they are purely the results of a *dysfunction* in the *interplay* between units.

For example, if a company stipulates that every five-figure or six-figure invoice has to be individually checked (and in some public administration bodies, you can find swathes of ten or twenty signatures on the invoices in their files), you can be more or less certain that not one single invoice will in fact be carefully checked. Because everyone will assume that the invoice circulated to him has either already been checked several times, or that it is going to be checked later by any number of other people. And ultimately, no one can be accused of negligence. Each of those involved is basically acting quite rationally. If they all had the bright idea one day that each individual invoice ought to be carefully checked according to rule, the whole company would soon break down altogether, because everybody would end up just checking invoices. The solution to this problem is of course not to reprimand individual employees to pay more attention to their work; it is to change the regulations.

If, when you are assessing the *initial situation,* designing *project work,* and drafting *new concepts,* you keep in mind the fact that the organization is multidimensional, and at the same time pay attention to the important networks involved, then you will be in no danger of overlooking vitally influential factors. You will be able to recognize and solve problems long before the project – which may be an expensive one – starts to run aground.

Fourth principle:
involvement of those affected

There are three good reasons for getting the employees who are affected by processes of change actively involved in the project work and advance decision-making:

1. *Better decisions – more practical solutions*
   Only those who are immediately concerned will be aware of all the details involved, and which aspects need to be given special attention if the new organizational form is actually going to work in practice.

2. *Creating motivation*
   Those who have been actively involved in producing solutions are then personally committed to making them work in practice.
3. *Identification with the company*
   Those who are actively included in project work and advance decision-making will feel they are being taken seriously as partners, and will personally identify with the company.

But the decisive aspect is that, from the very start – even before the existing situation is analyzed – staff should become actively involved. Only if you know the initial situation and understand the background to it will you be able to stand by the consequences with conviction.

There are two particularly widespread prejudices that need to be dispelled here.

Prejudice no. 1: "*Getting employees involved costs a lot of time – more than is usually available in practice.*" Yes, getting staff involved does take time – longer than a solo management effort would take. But the time spent repays itself several times over, both during and after implementation. In addition, if there really is extreme time pressure, it is easy to make quick progress when staff are motivated. In nine out of ten cases, however, any extreme time pressure is management's own fault from the very start. They have been letting problems stand for years on end, and have been slow to take decisions even in connection with the project – and everybody knows it.

Prejudice no. 2: "*If everyone is going to be given a say, we'll end up just talking and not getting any work done.*" Wrong: employees do not actually want to have a say on every single question. They only want to have a say on questions that directly affect them in their everyday work – and due to their knowledge and experience they do also have useful things to say about this. One of management's important tasks is to organize work on the project in such a way that everyone is involved at the point – and only at the point – where they are both able and willing to contribute something personally.

Effective participation is not just a question of management style; it is essentially a question of organization. The tasks involved in change projects are usually so complex that they require expert teamwork. Putting together teams and developing them are therefore absolutely central aspects of organizing participatory problem-solving processes. In its turn, this means that a *basic knowledge of group dynamics* is an indispensable equipment for executives with a leading role in innovation projects.

Fifth principle:
support for self-help

In the end, the work involved in processes of change is based – in spite of the leadership it requires – on the *decentralized self-organization* of the staff members and groups involved. Project work basically takes place in a framework and an atmosphere free of hierarchical constraints. At the same time, the work is innovative, and therefore demanding – involving *arrangement tasks* and *conceptual tasks* going beyond the daily routine, and often even beyond the existing training and experience of the individuals concerned. For most of those taking part in the project work, this usually makes it interesting and motivating, as they learn new approaches to questions and play a part in shaping new solutions. However: often, people find that they have got out of their depth. They have reached the limits of their competence – and sometimes gone beyond.

- In the course of their professional education and further training, not everyone has yet learnt the methodology of the processes involved in problem-solving and decision-making. For some, working on organizational structures and processes is completely new territory, and people who are meeting colleagues with quite different jobs from different areas for the first time sometimes have to absorb so many new things at once that they are not in a position to contribute anything themselves.
- Not everyone knows how to take part in discussions and cooperate effectively in a team that has no hierarchical leader. The only way some people have of dealing with conflicts is to avoid them. There are people who have never been told before that they have a bad habit of interrupting; other people do not have the confidence to express an opinion different from that of their superior in the hierarchy when he or she is in the room; and there are highly paid managers who think nothing of canceling long-planned meetings whose date has been jointly agreed on, simply because they have thought of something better to do.
- It happens in almost every large-scale project that a staff member is not released by his immediate superior for important project deadlines, even though everything has been arranged previously; or that, to carry out its tasks, a team finds that it needs funding that has not been budgeted for. Also, it is often necessary to adjust plans or postpone deadlines for external reasons.

In short: during every process of change, and in every project, no matter how well-organized, there are always situations in which the team's work is delayed or obstructed – and the members of the team, due to a lack of the necessary expertise or ability, are not in a position to solve the problem by themselves.

From the very start, management therefore has to be prepared to offer active support when and where it is needed. Depending on the situation, the following types of support can be required:

- *Feedback*: when there are difficulties within a group, it is sometimes enough if you just hold a mirror up to the team – i.e., tell them directly what a critical observer notices – and the group itself will do what is needed, on its own initiative.
- *Training*: supplying the theoretical foundations (e.g., organizational theory) and methodological know-how (e.g., problem-solving techniques) o behavioral training (e.g., communication and cooperation within the team).

- *Moderation*: external support in work conferences and workshop meetings: structuring working processes, moderating discussions, visualization.
- *Advice*: personal coaching by a manager, support from in-house experts, or guidance from external advisors – either due to particularly demanding specialist problems, or in acute conflict or crisis situations.
- *Decisions*: making resources available: manpower, finance, rooms, materials, deadlines.

No matter which particular type of support is needed or indicated, the goal must always be to allow the staff member or team concerned to become *independently active again as soon as possible*. Support has to be aimed exclusively at the immediate need, and it has to be delivered in doses that are as small as possible. Everything that goes beyond this becomes a temptation to carry out reverse delegation, and leads to a loss of independence. There are even situations in which the only really effective support that can be given consists in giving *no support*. In any case, the principle is: *If you want to provide effective support for self-help measures, you always have to have one foot on the retreat.* The fact that some managers or advisers find this difficult is beside the point. The feeling that they are needed is often too sweet a temptation for people to resist.

Sixth principle: managing the process

Whenever there are complex work processes involved in putting a product together, flexible fine-tuning is needed. In the chemical industry, for example, work processes have to be constantly supervised and regulated to ensure that production is continuous. Sensors are installed at all the critical points, regularly measuring the local pressure, temperature, and mixture ratios. The values are sent to the central controlling facilities by established feedback mechanisms, and the slightest deviation from set values leads to sensitive corrections in the energy or material input. And when there are serious deviations, production is run down or even stopped so that serious breakdowns can be prevented.

It is exactly the same with work processes in which human beings are involved: what matters is *adjusting the speed,* ensuring *constant maintenance procedures,* and carefully *finishing each important stage of the work before the next is started.* In the sphere of human work, process management is actually much more important than in the field of purely mechanical work processes. The complexity of human beings far exceeds that of any machine. And when a large number of people are working together in alternating roles and groupings – which is what happens when change processes are being initiated – it is simply not possible to predict where and when a malfunction or loss of power is going to take place. The only thing you can do is keep your finger constantly on the pulse of events – and intervene to provide guidance when the situation requires it.

There are two factors that make events in humans and in interpersonal relations both interesting and difficult to predict:

First, although human beings are still more intelligent than computers, the speed at which they can absorb and process new information is comparatively limited. In other words, projects for change are not just *work processes,* they are always also *learning processes.* Each individual and each team has its own specific learning curve, and this can always only be extrapolated from each current situation. Taking manageable forward steps during a process of change always involves making demands of the people involved, but not excessive ones; making sure they are not left behind because the pace is being forced; giving them an opportunity to "digest" the individual steps of the work and appreciate the inner logic of the way the project is going.

Secondly, when you are working with people, you are not just dealing with objective – and hence ultimately logical – matters, but always with emotions as well. What affects people inwardly – their needs and interests, their hopes and fears, what makes them happy and what annoys them – influences their behavior much more than visible, external factors. So if you are working with people and want to win them over to shared goals, you have to take their *inner state,* their *feelings,* and their *mood* into account. And a magic wand is not necessary for this – people themselves provide signals indicating their emotional state. But you have to pay attention to these signals and take them seriously – and you have to be prepared to stop and wait when tensions suddenly arise, or a noticeable loss of enthusiasm starts to spread.

Managing the process presupposes three things:

- *Regular process analysis:*
  - ▶ "Management by wandering around": talk to the people at the front about their work- and listen to what they're saying!
  - ▶ Carry out regular progress reviews together and hold debriefings.
- **Working on resistance and conflict situations:**
  - ▶ Accept any resistance that arises – discuss it and find out what caused it and what the background to it is.
  - ▶ Agree on common procedures that are acceptable all round.
  - ▶ Never suppress conflicts, but lay them on the table – get the parties who are involved round a table to discuss and clarify the background to their differing opinions and diverging interests.
  - ▶ Negotiate the solutions to conflicts on a basis of partnership.
- **Circular planning:**
  - ▶ Flexibility in detailed operational planning.
  - ▶ Guidance that takes the facts of each situation into account.
    (But: consistently maintain the phase plans and established deadlines!)

There are four aspects that always have to be carefully borne in mind:

- **Energy**
  Who has the "ownership"? Who are the most important allies and promoters?

- **Power**
  How can the "key hierarchies" and the informal "opinion leaders" be motivated?
- **Force field**
  What are the factors and influences facilitating the project, and what are the ones obstructing it?
- **Networking**
  What is the environment that the project is situated in?
  Who has to be actively included or informed?

Not all resistance can be overcome, and not every conflict can be solved. Someone whose job and livelihood are seriously threatened will have no motivation to take a committed and creative part in reorganization work. People whose bosses have repeatedly lied to them about planned changes in the past will not suddenly start trusting management again just because of a few declarations of intent or encouraging words, and will not be prepared to do their utmost to achieve a common goal. In relatively normal circumstances, however, conflicts hardly ever arise in practice that cannot be resolved through open and constructive discussions based on partnership.

Seventh principle: active communication

Most people are neither dumb nor rebellious. It is comparatively easy to manage them, and they are even surprisingly willing to cooperate with unpopular measures – provided they have understood the purpose and accepted that it is useful or perhaps even necessary. This means: management has to be convincing – and the basis for this is lively communication.

Since communication is such an important topic, we have devoted a whole chapter to it ("Handling Communication"). But a few remarks can be made here initially.

- *Information is not communication.*
  If you want to win people over to your plans, you have to talk to them – face to face. You have to respond to their needs and concerns, their hopes and fears – in an open dialogue. And you have to be willing to agree with them over ways to proceed that they are going to be able to follow.
- *This cannot be achieved only through individual contacts and team discussions in a top-down direction through the management cascade.*
  Meetings and events have to be organized with large numbers of executives and employees – to ensure that everyone gets the same message, and can put questions straight away and experience "live" dialogue with management. Without occasional dialogue meetings at regular intervals involving larger groups, it is almost impossible to guide large-scale projects efficiently nowadays.

- *Even if it is only information that has to be conveyed, interactive methods must be used whenever possible.*
  Information markets or presentations, followed by discussions in small groups and an opportunity for questions and comments in a plenary session.
- *In large-scale, comprehensive projects, a distinct communication design has to be developed.*
  It has to be clear before you start who is to be actively included in the process of information flow at what intervals and in what form – and who is responsible for the corresponding activities.
- *General interest in the project has to be consistently maintained.*
  This involves providing reports about interesting activities during the course of work on the project. The project has to be kept in the news, and employees have to be kept interested in it. A lively, up-to-date project news-sheet can be an extremely useful medium for this.
- *"Management by wandering around"*
  Regular direct contact with the people at the front, with the grass roots. Talking to people. Answering questions – but also putting questions. This is indispensable – both to get a sense of the "temperature" and to provide the persuasion needed.
- *And last, but not least: it all has to be enjoyable!*
  "Active" means being vivacious, spontaneous, cheeky, uncomplicated. Plus having a good sense of humor. There is no place here for showing off, using flashy jargon, bureaucratic fussiness, or deadly seriousness. Otherwise dullness and boredom start to set in.

Eighth principle: careful selection of key players

If you want to change anything in an organization, there is a law you have to be aware of: *processes operate through people.* This is particularly true of processes of development and change. In every great revolutionary movement or reform movement there is one person, or a small group of people, without whom history would have been different. In a sports club, a village community, or a business, it is always a minority that gets things moving forward. The majority can be won over to an idea by pioneering thinkers and forerunners. But it never initiates changes itself.

If you are making plans for change, there are three questions you need to ask yourself at the outset:

1. *Who are the most important potential "allies" you need to get on your side?*
2. *Who are the "opinion leaders" who have to be won over to the idea if the majority is going to come on board too?*
3. *Who has got what it takes to direct the process of change – or the important stages in the work it involves?*

In practice, unfortunately, these three vital questions are too often never even asked. Employees are nominated as project managers purely because they are not too overloaded at the moment with other work, or because "they ought to be given a project to manage for once," as a "reward" for services rendered, or to encourage their personal development. And when the staffing of a project coordination team is discussed, the question is, "Who are all the people that need to be represented here or taken into account to avoid things getting out of hand?" The single really decisive factor – whether a person is suitable – is totally forgotten. The project is allowed to run aground.

There is more awareness today than there used to be that, in normal organizations, you have to make sure that "the right person is in the right place" when people are appointed to posts – although terrible mistakes are still made. But it is still not widely known that a professional personnel policy is just as important in project work – even though the effects of unsuitable staffing in project teams are felt much more quickly, since the people involved are outside the established hierarchy and outside their specialist routines. Also, they do not have very much time to get used to each other. Professional leadership is especially important here.

When staff are selected for *leading and coordinating functions in the context of change processes,* the following criteria have top priority:

1. *An open, honest, and straightforward way of dealing with people*
   An ability to create trust is probably the most important requirement for successful project work.
2. *Proven ability to work with others in a team*
   Project work basically takes place in teams – and it is only when the teams are working properly that it produces useful results.
3. *An ability to listen and put oneself in someone else's emotional position*
   Only someone who is able to take notice of others and promptly recognize resistance is going to be able to guide processes correctly.
4. *Having the courage to make decisions – and the resoluteness to push things forward*
   Decisions constantly need to be taken during a process of change – and sometimes unpleasant ones. Someone who is unable to act promptly will miss opportunities that will never return. Problems will escalate into crises.
5. *A high level of acceptance among employees and management*
   It is hard to believe how easy it can be to get things done – if they are just suggested by someone people like to listen to; and how anything at all can turn into a problem when the wrong person proposes it.

Any other qualifications can be acquired by training courses, if necessary. The personality and behavioral requirements, however, have to be assessed in advance. They cannot be acquired in the short term, if at all, by training.

Of course, you cannot put the requirements too high for every single position that needs to be filled. In the final analysis, in every organization you have to live and work with the people who are already there. But no compromises should be made on the decisive coordinating bodies and management functions. A lot can be changed while a project is running if it proves necessary: the distribution of the tasks, the timetable if necessary, even the goals that are being aimed for. But mistakes in the staffing of key positions are almost impossible to retrieve.

The question of leadership is today a fundamentally different one from what it was five or ten years ago. At that time, it was still possible now and again to allow an incompetent manager or project leader to create trouble. But today, the price that is paid for good or bad management is paid quickly and paid without mercy – and as often as not, large numbers of people and jobs are affected by the consequences. So it is not just a question of effectiveness, but ultimately also a moral question, to make sure that the right people are in the key positions.

Experience shows that there are people who are suitable, due to their skills and personality, for pushing forward processes of change – and that there are others who are unsuitable from the start. In practice, putting the right person or the wrong person in the key position is often what makes the difference between the success and failure of a project. There is no faster, more efficient way of getting changes moving and implementing them successfully than picking the right people and putting them in the key positions. With a few really capable people all working toward the same goal, cooperating with each other and pulling together, you can move mountains. But it depends on the people in the first place. Ultimately, it is the people who manage the processes.

Figure 11. The ten most important "dos" and "don'ts"

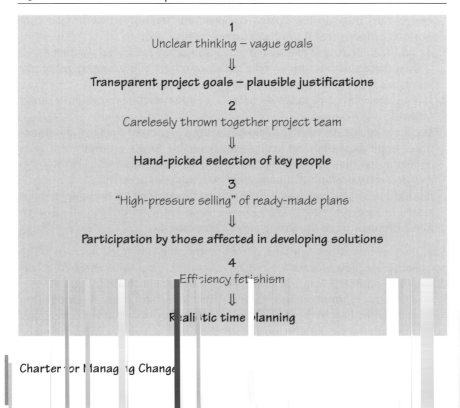

1
Unclear thinking – vague goals
⇓
Transparent project goals – plausible justifications

2
Carelessly thrown together project team
⇓
Hand-picked selection of key people

3
"High-pressure selling" of ready-made plans
⇓
Participation by those affected in developing solutions

4
Efficiency fetishism
⇓
Realistic time planning

5

Cold start

⇓

Careful preparation and "kick-off" phase

6

Pet ideas as a "hidden agenda"

⇓

Pet ideas initially laid openly on the table

7

Acting on a rigid timetable

⇓

Sensitive and flexible management of the process

8

Forcibly breaking down resistance

⇓

Constructive handling of resistance

9

Avoiding conflict

⇓

Exposing and working through conflict

10

Cabal politics and secret diplomacy

⇓

Freedom of information – active communication

Part III
A look into the
Tool Box

Tools and Procedures
of Corporate Development

1

Many roads lead to Rome: an overview

Basically, there is an almost bewildering variety of methods, tools, and procedures available to drive forward a corporation's development. To clarify things, we have used the following categories to arrange them in an overview (Figure 12):

- *target subject of the intervention*
  - ▶ The individual
  - ▶ The group
  - ▶ The whole corporation, or vital parts of it
  - ▶ The corporation's relevant environments
- *Mode of intervention*
  - ▶ Primarily using soft factors
    (information and abilities, attitudes and behavior)
  - ▶ Primarily using hard factors
    (structures and processes, systems and regulations)

We use the word "primarily" here deliberately, as there are tools and procedures that are difficult to classify as being clearly one or the other, since the approach involved uses both hard and soft factors.

You can really just use a self-service approach to select whatever seems particularly appropriate for managing change processes in your company. Some of the items are ordinary management tools that can be virtually taken for granted, and these need no more than a mention here. Others seem to us to require some explanation, particularly as you may be applying them on your own if they are suitable. We will describe these briefly here, and further details are given about many of them in later chapters.

The individual as the target of interventions

Strategies and concepts can only work to the extent that they are accepted and implemented by the people who are going to be affected by them. Whether this

Figure 12. Tools, methods, and procedures incorporate development

Soft factors Attitudes and behavoir	**Hard factors** Structures, processes, rules of the game

Individual

- Acquising management Know-how
- Analysis of functions/tasks
- Bonus and profit-sharing
- Training in social skills. e.g.
  - Conducting a discussion
  - Chairing a meeting
  - Cooperation
  - Decision-making
  - Conflict-resolution
- Agreeing and checking targets
- Employee appraisal and selection procedures (e.g. assessment center)
- Incentive systems
- Personnel development plans
- Personal coaching
- Sensitivity training, group dynamics
- Job descriptions
- Work organisation
  - Job enlargement
  - Job enrichment
  - Job rotation
- Individual career and life planning and counselling
- Salaries, working hours, and social benefits
- «If this was my company...»: departmental analysis by employees
- Socially acceptable models for demotion and leave

Groups

- Team supervision
- Sociogram
- Team structures. e.g. semi-autonomus groups
- Project organization
- Team development
- Peer group for self-help
- Quality circle
- Team coaching
- Confrontation meeting
- Profit-center organization
- Established management tools, e.g. target agreements

Company or departements

- Corporate identity
- Organizational/ departmental diagnosis
- Lean management
- Corporate culture
- Organizational/ departmental development
- Total quality management
- Employee hearings and workshops
- Reorganization of structure and processing
- Process-oriented mission development
- Regular employee surveys
- Established mission statement
- «Sensor» team
- Forming communicating, and controlling strategy

Company and environment

- Customer surveys
- Marketing concept
- Customer council
- Public relation work
- Standardized comparison with competition

happens depends very much on the framework in the employees' working environment. The environment can make it easier to act, it can provide active support – or it can make things difficult or almost impossible. The more that individual employees differ in their expectations, values, and qualifications and the less it is possible to lump them all together, the more worthwhile it is to pay attention to specific individuals, get to know their personal assumptions and expectations and do justice to these with tailor-made measures.

Further training in leadership and management

Our behavior is substantially determined by the mental patterns that we hold. For example, we have a very specific image of what it is that makes a meeting a good or bad one – no matter where the image happens to come from. It is this "model" that guides us when we have to conduct a meeting. It also guides us when we are participating in a conference, making us feel satisfied or dissatisfied with the venue.

We have similar conceptual patterns for "leadership," "communication," "cooperation," "conflict," and many more. Any steps that will serve to make us conscious of these mental images, test their usefulness for today's requirements, and contribute to developing them and bringing them up to date, are helpful. These include examining the theory behind modern concepts of leadership and management, as well as undergoing training in the skills that can be derived from these theories – such as how to conduct an interview with an employee, how to chair group discussions, which models of decision-making or of dealing with conflict are appropriate in which situations. Training courses can provide valuable dry-run exercises that provide assurance, improve mental fitness, and ultimately help to change behavior.

Sensitivity training

Social competence, i.e. an ability to deal successfully with other people – particularly in tense situations – is being demanded more and more. If you hope to achieve it, you have to have good sensitivity for other people's feelings. This in turn presupposes that you are *in good touch with yourself* – i.e., you are aware of your own feelings and know what effects they have on others. Many people can do this quite spontaneously, with excellent results. However, a good level of expertise in a subject is not always combined with the required social competence. Courses in "sensitivity training" can help people to explore the way in which they act in a group situation, discover blind spots in their perception, and test new forms of behavior. Various methods are on offer for achieving this, and the tried and tested ones include: group-dynamic behavioral training, transactional analysis, theme-centered interaction, and the systemic approach derived from family therapy. The goal is always social learning through experiencing oneself in a group.

Decisive criteria for using or recommending this type of training are that participation must be voluntary; there must be professionalism and competent leadership; and there must be an environment in which people can open up toward unaccustomed ideas and experiences without being afraid of getting hurt, and can experiment with new forms of behavior.

Coaching

Often the problem does not lie in the fact that executives lack the required theoretical equipment, methodological expertise, or goodwill. Instead, it is a matter of identifying – during the hectic rush of everyday operations – a specific way of implementing concretely and consistently in management practice something that one actually knows and in principle wants to do. People do not leave themselves enough time to do this; in other words, they have different priorities.

If you have a consultant at your side, it means you are committed to regular, critical checking of your behavior and methods of operating in the working environment – and therefore ultimately committed to a confrontation with yourself. The topics involved can be brought up either by the manager himself or by the coach. Your own role as an executive, your methods of operating when dealing with employees, colleagues, and customers, your treatment of emotional involvements, strategic considerations regarding company or departmental development, questions of personal career planning and life planning, can all be dealt with. The goal is not only to team up to carry out reflection and analysis, but above all to develop scenarios for action and alternatives for decision-making.

However, this type of "private consultancy relationship" does not relieve the manager of the need to get direct feedback from employees, colleagues, and customers. A coach must never become the main professional contact and advisor – an *éminence grise* secretly pulling all the strings behind the scenes.

Structural and organizational regulations

The effectiveness of employees depends not only on their qualifications and abilities and the way in which they are managed and motivated, but also on how clearly and attractively their work is structured. Does each person know exactly what is expected of him? Does he know which criteria are being used to assess him when, how, and by whom? Are people's fields of responsibility and resources clearly assigned and regulated? Do people know what they have to do to get on and what happens if performance drops off? Are these regulations up to date and attractive?

Against the background of this type of question, *duties and jobs* can be analyzed. Is the employee only being regarded as a means of implementation in this context, or as someone capable of acting independently and responsibly? Is he essentially regarded as being merely a tool available to the company, or have the duties and jobs been designed in such a way that employees can develop themselves to the full in relation to their needs and their own lives?

It has long since been proved that meaningful job enlargement, job enrichment, and job rotation are extremely good ways of killing two birds with one stone – giving impetus to company development while at the same time ensuring personnel development.

Instead of having *areas of responsibility* and *incentive and promotion systems* that are simply prescribed by management, the people affected can *participate in developing them* – this is another way of enhancing the attractiveness of working conditions.

It is still by no means taken for granted that work can be guided by reaching *target agreements* instead of by giving instructions. It is even rarer to see appropriate *controlling systems* being used to allow individuals or groups to control the quality and success of their own work in such a way that they can take countermeasures quickly enough and independently when things go off course.

At a time when the demands being made of individuals are changing faster and faster, when working conditions are getting tougher, and when organizational structures are at the same time constantly having to adapt to changing requirements, it is easy for an unpleasant atmosphere to develop – there is pressure to work harder, things seem to be uncertain and unpredictable. People become increasingly afraid that they will suddenly no longer be able to meet with these unpredictable demands. Consequently, it is not only *formal and motivating patterns for promotion* that have to be created, but also *formal and attractive paths for demotion,* which one can adapt to and trust. But the reality in many places today is still totally different: the people lower down, who are bursting with ideas and energy, are not allowed to act – and the people further up, who are in a position to act, are no longer capable. It is not future achievements that are rewarded and lead to promotion, but past ones – and sooner or later, everyone reaches a point at which he is simply getting in the way. This is not a new insight by any means. Everyone basically knows that things cannot really work like this. But only a few companies have started to give detailed thought to socially acceptable ways for both promotion *and* demotion.

A very simple question

White-collar workers have a tendency to accept problems in their working environment as a kind of inevitable fate, simply because in the end it is not their own money that is involved. Getting them to ask themselves the question: "If this was my company, what would I change?" can break down established blocks on perception and thinking, and release creative ideas. The target for this kind of exercise can be the individual employee, a group, a department, or a division.

This exercise can be approached in various ways: a *general written questionnaire* on this main theme has the advantage that everyone can be invited to join in and feel their advice is being asked for. On the other hand, if everyone is asked, it can also lead to nobody really feeling he is being genuinely asked. It has therefore also been found helpful to *pick out individuals or areas according to their strategic importance,* and ask them for a contribution in a more purposeful way. A special variation is to form an *interdisciplinary analysis team* to develop suggestions.

The questions asked can be left completely open. But a ready-made tool can also be used – e.g., a checklist for company analysis (see Part III, Chapter 14, "Criteria for Successful Management")

Aiming at the group level

Not everybody may be aware of this yet, but: *a group is more than the sum of its individual members.* A whole range of social psychological studies have demonstrated that groups have special dynamism and power – particularly in dealing with conflicts and solving problems. Given the right conditions, groups develop a *high degree of self-control and self-organization.* How are these advantages best used?

Daring to use more groups

Many organizations are completely over-regulated. Thick manuals and a flood of internal instructions and rules are the evidence of this. Everything is regulated down to the finest detail. The perfection of the regulations bears no relation to their significance. Except of course in situations in which observing quality and safety standards precisely is a matter of life and death – e.g., in air traffic control or in the medical field. Over-regulation creates zones of low responsibility. Everyone can hide behind the likely deficiencies and omissions of the other people who come either before or after him in the chain of individual jobs. Ultimately, he is even glad that these deficiencies exist, since they relieve him of any need to provide his own contribution on time.

Alternatives to this include:

- Transferring to group work any task areas and problems that are best dealt with by shared interdisciplinary thinking and action.
- Clearly describing to these groups their purpose and tasks, giving them the strategic information they require, and negotiating with them the appropriate framework, rules, and resources – but also leaving it up to them how things are regulated in detail and how tasks and roles are distributed in specific ways – e.g. which member of the group is to have which tasks and duties.
- Some tasks can be assigned to this type of ' semi-autonomous group ' on a permanent basis, while others can be treated as projects with a clear time limit.

However, this type of group also needs to have a say in personnel development, qualifications, and performance-related payments.

The meaning of "system maintenance"

This type of group organization can only become genuinely effective and unfold its full potential if sufficient investment is made in the development, maintenance, and servicing of both the organization and the human relationships within it. A group cannot be turned into a functioning team simply by providing organizational rules. Conflicts can develop between the members of the team. Groups can also lose their energy, rigidify, and degenerate to become an end in themselves. Some companies have a plethora of obsolete project groups or study groups rolling gently forward without clear goals, without leadership, and without any special commitment from their members. The social contact provided by the team and the status that is sometimes associated with being a team member are often sufficient motivation – and if there is no boss there to dissolve the team, it can survive for months or even years without having any real function or specific task to fulfill.

If you want to prevent this type of degeneration, you have to ensure stocktaking at regular intervals: there must be critical questioning and repeated justification of goals, tasks, of the composition of the group, role allocation, and the rules of the group culture, as well as provision of resources and abilities. If any of these has ceased to be justifiable, the group will have to be dissolved.

Team-based organization of structures and processes, and dynamic systems of self-organization, therefore do not reduce costs in terms of time and energy, but simply shift them from one place to another. Instead of the costs created by fussing over details and inventing all sorts of regulations, there are the costs involved in maintenance. What you gain is: flexibility and time – through smaller, faster-reacting entrepreneurial units.

Whether it is a matter of a hierarchically structured department or division, an interdisciplinary project group, or a semi-autonomous group – subjecting yourself to a "system check" once a year is the least that any organizational unit can do. This type of *team inspection* can take up to several days. It can be carried out within the unit concerned, or it can be directed by an external chairperson.

What is decisive is:

- Every *dimension* that is relevant for efficiency and motivation has to be examined, and in particular:
  - *Performance from the point of view of external or internal customers*
  - *Quality of methods and procedures*
  - *Role allocation and interplay with one another*
  - *Working atmosphere and job satisfaction*
  - *Strategic perspectives*

- *Sufficient* time must be available to ensure that any problems that are identified are not simply touched on superficially, but worked through calmly with a view to solving them.
- An *atmosphere* has to be created in which it is possible to express and accept criticism constructively.

Various models for system maintenance

However, annual spring-cleaning is not always sufficient. Depending on the situation, it may be necessary for a team to undergo a shake-up in the form of *team supervision* or *team coaching* at short intervals. There are two advantages to this. First, inadequacies and faults do not have to be left for a long period without being attended to until the next servicing takes place, but can be dealt with without delay. Secondly, it is possible for more complex problems to be dealt with in small, manageable steps over an extended period. In addition, if the intervals are shorter, the "law of recognition" begins to operate: certain types of bad habit simply do not arise in the first place, because people know that they will be brought up at the next meeting anyway. The group's self-help system is made more effective.

A special, but tried and tested, method of checking the internal interplay in groups consists of having the group observed by someone trained in psychology during a routine discussion, and who can provide specific feedback information afterward (process feedback). Video recordings can help make a particularly strong impact with this type of feedback.

But a group can also get an insight into its inner life and clear up disturbances by explicitly discussing the structure of its emotional relationships. A "sociogram" can be used to analyze what types of relationship the members have with each other and the ways in which this system of relationships affects the group's performance and the way people work together in it. To do this, relationships between individual members of the group are assessed using specific questions (e.g., "who is or is not close to whom?") and then shown in a diagram in the form of a social "map," so that each member of the group can clearly recognize his place within it. However, having a working basis for trust in the group as a whole is essential in this type of exercise, so that the inevitable "rejections" that emerge can be coped with. In addition, enough time has to be invested to allow members to discuss the results together. Otherwise, the tool will not only cause considerable damage, but all the learning opportunities it can provide will have been lost – on the principle "saw a lot, learned nothing."

If it is the interaction between two groups that is being discussed, mutual working relationships can be clarified and renegotiated using what is known as a *confrontation* or *conflict resolution meeting*. In view of the increasing practical importance of this procedure, we have described it in detail in a separate chapter on "Conflict Management".

Quality circles

Setting up a quality circle means:

> *Giving employees an opportunity to join together in groups and think systematically about improvements that could be made in their own workplace and in the immediate working environment.*

Other possible terms for this kind of group might be *learning group* or *workshop circle*. People working in a quality circle are officially permitted to do what they would be doing unofficially anyway: think about everything that makes their job difficult and seems absurd – and what would make their job easier. The energy that is normally wasted in useless complaints can be converted into shaping solutions constructively. This approach, which was initially only used in production sectors, has for some time now also been applied in the service sector.

However, the success of quality circles depends on the following factors:

- *Motivation*: "*every desire must come from the people …* " – i.e., employees have to have a real need to deal with these questions. Obviously, the desire to do so has to be exclusively voluntary.
- *Infrastructure*: suitable meeting room, equipped with aids to visualization.
- *Facilitating*: competent chairing and methodological support for the group.
- *Coordination and guidance*: a committed individual or a small steering group can serve as the "hub" ensuring that ideas and suggested solutions are thoroughly checked and followed up.
- *Support from the hierarchy*: genuine willingness – particularly in middle management – to benefit from the circle.
- *Corporate culture*: a culture inside the company that is characterized by participation and comprehensive quality thinking.
- *Collaboration with the works committee*: if necessary there must be an appropriate agreement between management and the works committee.

In practice, there may be threats to this basically sound approach due to the following factors:

- *Employees are not properly prepared for this type of involvement.* Only the organizational framework is created, and employees are then expected to suddenly generate virtually miraculous energies. But they have not been sensitized and prepared in the right way. There is a lack of awareness of the problem needing to be addressed, and not enough trust that management is serious about the whole exercise.
- *Middle management is not actively included.* On the one hand, there is the danger that suggested improvements by employees will be generally regarded as an attack on managers and their duties. New ideas are dismissed in advance – because people think they ought to have come up with them themselves. On the other hand, there are always weak bosses who will feel their own executive authority is being undermined if solutions to vital problems are solved by employees without their involvement, or even against their will.

- *Quality circles are prescribed companywide for everyone simultaneously* – instead of starting with small cells where there really is energy available, and allowing this movement to spread step by step like a prairie fire.
- *Employees feel exploited.* People who show commitment must feel that this is going to be rewarded in the shorter or longer term. The rewards can of course be made in different kinds of "currency." Money is not necessarily the decisive factor. Recognition is often enough, provided it is from the "right" people. What is certainly indispensable is the experience that things do actually change, that one can really "get things moving."
- *An appropriate public awareness is not created.* Lively reporting of what goes on has always proved to be an outstanding way of encouraging people and strengthening their resolve. On the one hand, it is a matter of providing the groups with a forum in which they can present their results, as well as presenting themselves – through reports in the company's general newspaper, in their own publication, in the form of original poster campaigns, or in the framework of an information market. On the other hand, this type of publication can also be provoking and challenging to parts of the company where these processes have so far been resisted.
- *Depending exclusively on "training facilitators."* Competent facilitating is important – and in areas in which people are not used to discussing things with one another, it is even indispensable. But it is only one of several absolutely necessary conditions. And attention must also be given to ensure that those who become chairpersons do not fall victim to the temptation to use this simply as a way of attracting attention to themselves, reducing the employees – who are in fact the main players – to the role of extras.

Keeping the whole company in view

Organizational change

Optimizations and modifications are not always sufficient to ensure market survival. In many cases, only a more radical "change of model" helps. There are two criteria that can be used as touchstones for ideas and as guidelines for action:

- *Organizing from the outside inward*
  This means orienting the organization consistently according to the principle of the *process chain,* which basically consists of three elements:
  - Recognizing the customer's demands and the market situation.
  - Converting the diagnosed demand into solutions for the customer through appropriate products or services, without loss of information or time.
  - Putting the tailor-made product on the market successfully.
- *Committing oneself purely and exclusively to productive added value*
  The second touchstone criterion is the question of the productive added value. Each function, every point, every person and every action that needs to

participate in the process chain has to be assessed according to the productive added value that it can contribute. Everything that does not stand up to this test must be removed from the chain.

"Unproductive" intermediate elements would cause the least damage if they simply did nothing. If that was all, they would merely be a cost factor. Understandably, however, they try to justify their own existence by actively doing things. In order to attract notice, they market their activities. Their action – precisely because it has no direct productive added value – only leads to other people becoming involved and getting distracted from their real tasks. Areas like this therefore not only cost the money needed to support them, but their own activity also creates further unproductive activity. This causes losses of both time and information – as well as creating annoyances.

Over time, every organization starts to develop useless fat, which can often only be reduced by systematic "slimming" campaigns. The fat often consists of headquarters staff whose only duties are to shuffle numbers backward and forward, producing more and more reports, wasting other departments' time with requests for all sorts of data and reports, and tinkering about with theoretical models – without ever contributing to the solving of actual problems in a responsible way.

Employee opinion survey

A tried and tested method of challenging the whole organization at regular intervals is to carry out an employee opinion survey every two or three years on all the topics that affect work and the working environment.

The advantages are obvious:

1. Management can get an insight into the overall state of the company as its employees experience it. Norman Wiener's phrase, "I don't know what I've said until I've heard the answer to it" can be extended to the whole range of management action here. We do not know what we have done until we see employees' reactions to it.
2. The regular repetition of the survey provides insights into the extent to which the company, and specific areas or aspects of it, have developed or changed over time.
3. Including the whole company in the questionnaire allows the individual areas to recognize their own relative value and see in which ways they are better or worse than the average for the company, or for other departments they can compare themselves with. These comparisons allow targeted development steps.

Organizational diagnosis is particularly important as a tool for company development, and we have therefore devoted a separate chapter to it.

Corporate mission

A mission statement that is not just a piece of glossy paper but contains accepted and effective guidelines for strategic planning and company management is another part of the sound framework needed for company development. Methods of developing and using a mission statement are described elsewhere.

Binding management tools

A common and binding agreement on the management tools to be used provides both executives and employees with an important framework for guidance. The same procedures and tools apply to everyone in relation to controlling performance, human resource management, informing and communicating with people in the division and the rest of the company, reaching decisions, planning, budgeting, and controlling – both as in theory and in everyday management practice.

On the one hand, this common basis makes useful cooperation within management easier, while on the other it encourages the establishment of a shared company culture.

The importance of outside views

Archimedes is supposed to have said, *"Give me a firm spot on which to stand outside this world, and I will move it."*

All types of living systems aim to achieve a state of internal rest using as little energy as possible. But creative unrest is the precondition for change. If internal energies and points of view are not sufficient to lead the company out of a potentially fatal state of rest and complacency and make it restless and searching, the only alternative is often to provide it with a view of itself or an image of itself as seen from the outside.

- *How do customers regard the company?*
- *How are service departments in particular experienced and assessed by their internal customers?*
- *How is the company doing in comparison with its relevant competitors?*

The information needed can be supplied by one-off ad hoc actions, or by standardized, regular customer surveys and comparisons with competitors, or by a permanent customer advisory council.

Another way of rousing internal energies consists of exploiting publicity work. Every company presents itself to the public in a variety of ways – through commercials, sales promotions, the way it deals with complaints, general press and publicity work, and sponsorship and lobbying activities. These investments in influencing customers and other relevant environments can also be used for a secondary purpose without much additional effort: you need to communicate internally as well about what you are doing on the outside. A media report, or a successful response to a commercial, etc., can strengthen employees' sense that it is good to be part of it all, and that it is rewarding to be working for this particular company. Whenever this outside view – in whatever way – might threaten to impair motivation and identification, appropriate countermeasures need to be taken.

Managers usually give a great deal of thought to what means they can use to achieve great things – and give too little thought to exploiting to the full things that are already available.

Beyond individual tools

"*One swallow does not make a summer*" – and a single tool, used in isolation, is not capable on its own of providing the decisive momentum needed for company development. If it is company development that you want, the following fundamental aspects need to be taken into account.

The wholistic view

In complex problem situations, it is often only a combination of different, but well-coordinated measures that will help. Only a detailed diagnosis can identify where it is that we can intervene simultaneously with usefully coordinated steps – e.g., in strategy, structure, processes, behavior, attitudes, qualifications, working conditions, resource allocation, and regulating areas of responsibility.

Example: An association whose main task is to represent the interests of its members in public wants to prepare itself for the future. The resources available for the association's work are constantly diminishing, while at the same time the standards expected of its activities are rising. It decides to carry out an intensive analysis of the efficiency of work at branch offices. Responsibilities are clarified, duplicate work is identified and eliminated, working processes are restructured using up-to-date technology, and employees receive intensive training on how to deal with one another and with the association's members and are groomed in better cooperation.

Despite all this, two years after completing the reorganization project, the association goes into crisis, and its continued existence is threatened. Important members threaten to resign because their interests are not being represented in proportion to their significance. It is not a new threat, but it now looks as if it is actually going to be carried out. In reality, the reorganization project had ignored the *overall political situation in the association*. Although there was an awareness of the growing threat to its survival, there had been a reluctance to grasp the nettle and face the fact that there were covert informal interest groups with mutually obstructive expectations within the association. On the contrary:

it had been hoped that communicating with one another better might stabilize the foundations for shared values and interests. There was a failure to disclose these diverging interests and allow open confrontation between the various expectations and demands – even at the risk of finding out at an early stage that common representation of interests might actually be impossible in the present form.

If the *strategic dimension* is not taken into account and examined, there is a great danger that, even when the project results are in themselves quite good, they may ultimately prove to have been obsolete.

The mind behind the tools

It is not the perfection of the tools that determines whether or not they are successful, but the purposes they are used for. It is the style and spirit of the project that will be seen as its real message. Those who are affected are bound to notice whether it is literal execution of tasks and formal correctness that are being emphasized, or common goals and needs. Pure social engineering alone is not capable of releasing lasting momentum. There are companies with all sorts of elaborate forms of communications tools and procedures – information markets, in-house newsletters and customer newsletters, the latest communications techniques ranging from employee surveys to "open-door" policies. In spite of all this, the working atmosphere and employees' motivation and identification with the company are anything but good. The tools do not work, because employees actually have the feeling that they are being used as "tools." Higher management is not really interested in their opinions. It is simply going through the motions in order to make itself look good to the company's directors and the public.

Observing the energy in the system

Every social system has only limited resources and energies. It is important on the one hand not to demand *too little* of the system – otherwise we will not achieve either the necessary awareness of the problem or the sense of setting out on a fresh adventure that is going to be needed. On the other hand, there is no point in demanding *too much* of the system either. If management declares too many things (or even everything) "important" all at once, employees will start to regard nothing as being particularly important any more.

The tools used have to fit the company's culture

Just like the human body, a company has its own immune defense system." Anything that is not compatible with the dominant culture risks being rejected.

Large numbers of campaigns that were actually quite useful in themselves become a complete mess, with masses of energy being wasted, because the company's "body" has not been prepared for them and adjusted to them properly. For example, if employees' opinions have never been consulted in the past, it is pointless to carry out an employee survey without carrying out the appropriate confidence-building measures to prepare them for it. Attitudes of objection and distorting results are almost bound to be the reaction.

"How" is more decisive than "what"

It has often been observed that it is not the finished product, but the processes involved in creating it – for example, the common development of a mission statement, visions for the company, management principles, and management systems – that produce real impetus for development. Provided, however, that the process can be designed as an intensive form of dialogue. People from very different areas and different levels of the hierarchy get talking with each other during this period, and get to know and appreciate one another and their special situations and viewpoints. This releases genuine synergies without anyone really needing to talk about it. The same phenomenon can be seen when a "corporate identity" or "corporate culture" is developed and formulated with substantial participation by one's own employees (instead of by outside experts, no matter how good they are). The wealth of ideas and sense of commitment that emerge, which have previously been slumbering within the company, are often astonishing.

Usually, it is not the tool that provides the decisive momentum, but the *process of developing it*. Employees sense that management is taking them seriously enough to offer them active participation in developments. It is participation by those who are affected that makes the developments themselves become the decisive process.

Organizational Diagnosis

2

Every human organization is a complex and sensitive organism. If you tinker about with it without taking account of its internal connections, you risk doing more damage than good. The first thing needed for managing change effectively is a clear basis for decision-making. With a good diagnosis, you are already half-way there.

There are of course situations in which it is visions, goals, and strategies that are needed, and not diagnosis. There are situations in which not much analysis is needed, because the diagnosis has been perfectly clear for some time – to anybody with their eyes and ears open. In addition, taking a diagnostic attitude is one of the decisive preconditions for successful individual action – curiosity about what the situation really is; skepticism in the face of prejudices; an ability to put questions and listen carefully to the answers; always trying to put oneself in other people's position; sensitivity to undertones; an ability to learn from one's own actions and their effects. Successful management is based to a considerable extent on this type of action-oriented diagnosis.

But organizational diagnosis also involves *planned and systematic procedures for acquiring information about the organization's internal conditions.* Diagnosis must be a deliberate action or special phase during the course of a project. There are always situations in which it is necessary to throw light on the organization in a systematic way in order to make the preconditions for change transparent.

In this chapter, we concentrate on the methodology of systematic organizational diagnosis.

The bird's-eye view and the worm's-eye view

There are three psychological barriers that in practice often stand in the way of careful organizational diagnosis. These barriers are all either directly or indirectly connected with hierarchical thinking, which is still deeply rooted even in our modern performance-oriented organizations.

The first barrier is the fact that practically every decision-maker, as a privileged member of the organization, already has a more or less fixed opinion about which things are generally running well, which things are not working, and what needs to be changed. These opinions have almost never been completely wrong. But experience shows that they are never completely right, either. Each executive has a special perspective on the organization – and because of his position in the hierarchy and specific duties, he almost never has all the relevant facts. When you are a successful manager, possibly at a high level of responsibility, a great deal of modesty and experience in life is needed to accept that your own point of view might at best represent a useful working hypothesis – one that needs to be carefully checked out before any decisions with potentially serious consequences can be taken on the basis of it.

The second barrier consists of the assumption that bosses at the lower and middle levels know best what the strengths and weaknesses of the actual situation are, and consequently what needs to be done to lick the organization into shape. This assumption is not a completely false one, either. Each manager can contribute something useful to an assessment of the situation. But each manager only has a limited part of the important information needed. Everyone has a blind spot. And some of them can therefore find it difficult to recognize weaknesses – quite apart from actually mentioning them – because this would automatically lead to the question of why they themselves had not long since remedied such deficiencies in the course of their normal managerial work.

The third barrier consists of a reluctance to ask the opinions of people who only know the organization from the "worm's-eye" point of view, people who have their noses deeply buried in the operational details, who have no experience in managerial duties, who may not have had any further education, and who have never given a single thought to the overall strategic and structural context of the organization. But precisely this is the decisive point: it is those who do the actual work on the very front line in the company and with the customer who should be asked what is running well from their point of view, where there is unnecessary friction, and what ought to be changed. They have the everyday experience and detailed expertise and familiarity with all sorts of practical information that needs to be taken into account if the process of change is going to be successful.

Full survey or representative cross-section?

Of course, there are always specific questions in practice to which only a restricted group of people are going to be able to contribute. But if you want to get a picture of the overall state of an organizational unit, the employees at the grass roots are always the most important sources of information.

In smaller organizational units, there is really only one answer to the question of how many employees should be included in a survey: *all of them*. But if the staff consists of hundreds or thousands of people, the volume of the work involved becomes a problem. In terms of the justifiable cost–benefit ratio, the question becomes one of how to make an appropriate selection. Choosing suitable questioning methods can allow the costs involved to be limited even when there are large target groups. For example, you can ask a limited selection of employees and managers individually, a larger number in groups, and the whole staff in the form of a written questionnaire campaign.

If there is any doubt, the decision should always be in favor of including everyone in the survey, not only from the point of view of achieving a sufficiently broad database, but also with a view to asking every employee if possible and thus stimulating broad interest in the common project.

Contents of the survey

A comprehensive check-up of this type needs to cover strengths and deficiencies in all the important dimensions of the organization:

- **The structures:**
  - *Structural organization*
  - *Processing organization*
  - *Working space and external working conditions*
  - *Management systems and management tools*
- **Behavior:**
  - *Motivation and identification*
  - *Working atmosphere*
  - *Management style*
  - *Information flow*
  - *Decision-making*
  - *Teamwork*
  - *Collaboration between teams, functional responsibilities, and departments*
- **Management culture and corporate culture:**
  - *Written and unwritten laws and rules of the game*
  - *Degree of regulation and formalisation*
  - *Usual forms of communication and cooperation*
  - *Principles of rewards and penalties*
  - *Mission statement and management principles (as written – and as practiced)*

It is decisive that not only *weaknesses* should be searched for, but also that explicit and careful questioning regarding *strengths* should be carried out. The first and most important reason for this is that things should not be changed that do not absolutely have to be – on the contrary, existing strengths need to be recognized, taken advantage of, and expanded on if need be. Secondly, employees will be much more willing to mention existing weaknesses in specific terms if they have also been able to describe the positive sides of the actual situation.

Most people generally tend to get annoyed only about the things that disturb them – and to take for granted (and possibly not even notice) everything that is satisfactory. If equal weight is given to asking about strengths and deficiencies, it has a salutary side effect: the people who are asked will make a balanced assessment of their working situation and will not fall into a one-sidedly critical attitude to their professional environment.

Even in well-managed companies, in particular, there is often a marked "grumbling culture" among employees. People have got used to being able to voice their critical opinions freely all over the place – in the process completely forgetting how much there is that they can actually be very happy about. Some people even need to be sent to outside seminars so that they can hear from their colleagues about the kind of conditions that exist in other companies.

How should questions be put?

In principle, there is a very wide range of methods available for acquiring data. Five methods of questioning that have proved particularly important in practice can be sketched out here briefly: *individual interviews, group interviews, hearings, diagnosis workshops, written questions (standardized questionnaire).*

- **Individual interviews**

  Personal individual talk
  Semi-structured (topics are specified, open dialogue takes place within the framework of the individual topics)
  Time required: ninety minutes to two hours

  Advantages:
  - Personal and individual talks
  - High degree of openness
  - High degree of interaction (quality of communication)
  - Depth of analysis
    (allows very precise understanding of operational context)

  Disadvantages:
  - Time-consuming
    (with large target groups usually appropriate in combination with other methods)

- **Group interview**

  Groups of 5 – 7 people
  Semi-structured discussion (as in individual interviews)
  Time required: 3 – 4 hours

  Advantages:
  - Larger target groups can be covered
  - Important points become very clearly recogni ble
  - Very lively
  - Group activity encourages team culture

Disadvantages:
- Not as much individual openness
- Group dynamics may interfere with discussion
  (not everyone receives equal attention)
- Two questioners may be needed
  (if internal employees with no experience in chairing teams are used as the questioners)

● **Hearing**

Short questions to a large number of people, each of whom is only available for a limited time (alternating composition of the question group)

Time required: half a day (but only part-time presence of the individuals being questioned is needed)

Advantages:
- Fast overview of the overall situation and key topics
- Many people can indicate initial trends in the shortest possible time with the least effort
- Can also be organized even at short notice without any problems
  (interview partners can be brought in flexibly, depending on individual availability)

Disadvantages:
- Limited depth of analysis (problems cannot be discussed in detail)
- Openness regarding awkward topics is limited
- Depending on the specific management culture and personnel involved: risk of becoming a "fairground" event

● **Diagnosis workshop**

Groups of 20 – 25 people
Workshop event with facilitator
(Collecting and condensing the information using a question-card technique, probing deeper on individual topics using work in smaller groups or plenary discussions)

Time required: one day

Advantages:
- Great variety of results, wide range of aspects presented
- At the same time: priorities are clarified
- Flexible deepening of the analysis is possible

Disadvantages:
- Relatively large amount of organizational preparation necessary
- Large amount of time required for individual participants

- **Written questions**

  Standardized questionnaire
  Answers using scales ("multiple choice" procedure)
  Computer-aided evaluation (anonymous)
  Time required (individual completion of questionnaire):
  30 minutes to one hour

  Advantages:
  - No problems in managing large target groups
  - Recognizable priorities resulting from quantitative distributions
  - General acceptance of the results ("objective" image)

  Disadvantages:
  - The results (numbers and percentages) are usually difficult to interpret (they provide hints as to the major problems, but do not provide any background information to help understand the context)
  - Satisfactory response rates are the exception
    (wage-earning employees often find it difficult to use pencil and paper anyway)
  - Anonymous (impersonal) and written ("bureaucratic") way of addressing employees

Written questionnaires are basically appropriate for establishing statistical distributions. It is usually advisable only to use them in connection with other more interactive methods that are more analytically productive.

Standardized written questionnaires seem to us to be particularly useful when they are regularly repeated (e. g., every two years). This allows not just the current values to be identified ("snapshot"), but also any changes in the values since the previous questionnaire (developmental trends).

Thanks to computerized analysis, even in large companies it is now possible without special effort or extra costs to provide each manager at any level both with the average values for the company and also those for his organizational unit directly – not just for his own personal information, but to serve as the basis for discussing the current position and having a problem-solving session with his team. However, experience shows that top management needs to explicitly request this intensive processing by managers and check that it is being carried out. Otherwise all their good resolutions will be swamped by the hectic activity of everyday business.

However, the most sensitive and nuanced tool for questioning is always a personal discussion with an individual. Usually at least a representative selection of employees can be questioned in individual talks. If it is not possible to talk to all employees individually, it is advisable to supplement individual talks with group interviews or diagnosis workshops. The greater effort and costs that these involve in comparison with written questionnaires always pay off in the end. After data have been gathered in individual discussion with those affected, there is usually not much more analysis that needs to be done – the most important links are clear, and good ideas and suggestions for specific measures are usually already available. It may be possible to implement several items without any more ado. There is no substitute for the quality of these results.

External institute or do-it-yourself?

The question of whether an external institute should be used, or whether the survey should be carried out by one's own employees, does not usually arise in practice. Management assumes from the outset that neutrality, objectivity, and professionalism can only be ensured by using an outside body. However, we take a different view. Neutrality and objectivity cannot always be ensured even by an external institute – and if you are unlucky they may send you students or part-timers whose only previous experience is in doing non-stop standardized interviews with housewives about washing powder.

In addition, neutrality and objectivity are by no means the only criteria for the method that is chosen. It is equally important to produce results that are based on *genuine understanding of the working context in the company.* It may also be important that the *expertise* developed during the survey should remain within the company, instead of departing again along with the external consultants. Finally, whether the survey is going to achieve nothing more than data collection, or is going to make a major contribution to *the development of internal company communications,* is also important.

With regard to professionalism, there is no doubt that this can also be ensured by selecting and training the employees to be used and by giving the project the appropriate supervision. We do not mean to argue here that external consultants should never be used, but that they should be used if possible to "help people to help themselves," to train your own employees on the job, so that expertise is transferred *into* the company (see Figure 13).

Helping to carry out an internal survey is a motivating challenge for employees, and a genuine form of job enrichment. "I have got to know the company properly for the first time," is a comment that is often heard. The employees selected have to be released from their normal work to some extent for a time during the survey, but experience shows that they are also able to carry out practically the full quota of their normal activities during this period. The interest provided by the additional task mobilizes undreamed-of extra energies.

However, what is decisive is that those conducting the survey should be carefully trained for the tasks involved. People who have never conducted an interview before need to be introduced to the methods, so that they can carry out skilled discussions aimed at diagnosing the company's condition (see Figures 14, 15, and 16: "Basic diagnostic attitude," "Methodological tips for holding discussions," "An interview guide"). The training involved requires limited expense and effort, and usually two or three days' training are sufficient.

Figure 13. Using your own employees as opinion pollsters

Advantages:

■ First-hand information is kept in-house

■ Greater practical relevance of the analysis

■ Flexible organization (questioners already in-house)

■ Builds expertise within the company

■ "Job enrichment" for the employees involved

■ Valuable training for the employees involved

■ Experience shows that questioning by colleagues in one's own company is highly appreciated

■ The survey makes an important contribution to the development of a lively communications culture within the company

Requirements:

▶ Extremely careful selection of questioners (social abilities!)

▶ Training of questioners for their tasks (2–3 training days)

▶ Formation of self-guiding teams with fixed target groups to survey

▶ Project-style organization

▶ Support for teams during analysis (facilitating/visualization)

Figure 14. Basic diagnostic attitudes

What is the interviewer supposed to do?
Ask, listen, ask again – ask, listen, ask again –

What for?
To grasp and understand the individual point of view, subjective opinion and personal perceptions of the person he is talking to.

Why "ask again?"
First: because not every answer is immediately comprehensible.
Secondly: because it is not a matter of collecting facts, but of understanding the background and context.

What requires special attention?
The way in which the person being asked perceives his job situation: his feelings, basic mood, "emotional state".

What is the interviewer not supposed to do?
Contradict, correct, discuss – or attempt, as someone who is supposedly
or actually "better informed," to explain how things "really are".

What qualities mark out a good interviewer?
Curiosity, interest in people, empathy with other people
(who have different experiences, interests, and opinions) – i.e., among other
things, a certain amount of modesty!

What is the interviewer's function?
To convey the "message" of the person being asked – not to convey his own
opinion.
To be an honest mediator between the person questioned and the project
management.
To be a committed reporter – not a referee!

What is the function of the person questioned?
To be a competent provider of information about what is happening in his
working environment – and about his responses to it.

Figure 15. Methodological tips for holding discussions

- *Open dialogue within the framework of individual topics*
  What is involved is a "semi-structured" interview – i.e., the topic areas
  are pre-set, and all have to be addressed. However, free discussion can
  take place on the individual topics.

- *Making things specific with practical examples*
  – "Can you give me a practical example of that?"
  – "Are you thinking of a specific case?"
  – "What was the occasion that gave you that impression?"
  – "When were you last in that situation?"

- *Asking about solutions as well as about problems*
  – "Why is that happening – and how could it be changed?"
  – "Who could or would have to do what to remedy this?"
  – "What would you do if it was your company?"

- *Getting back to the subject*
  When the person being questioned gets carried away into too much
  detail, interrupt and lead him back to the subject with an appropriate
  suggestion:
  – "I'd like to take up the following point again ... "
  – "You were saying just now ... "
  – "Going back to the question ... "
  – "What I didn't understand properly a moment ago was ... "

- *Keeping an eye on the time*
  More or less keep to the time set for the individual phases of the discussion - i.e., lead on to the next question soon enough (unless both participants have enough time and are not under pressure). In case of doubt, only mention one topic briefly (asking about the most important point in it spontaneously), but never leave out any topics.

- *Statements about people are important – and almost always tricky*
  The working situation is shaped in a major way by the people in the working environment. Above all, problems are often experienced only in relation to people, and related back to people. Statements about individuals are therefore always important and must be recorded. But the person being questioned must not be intensively "grilled" concerning people he is critical of. The dangers: an embarrassing situation; bad conscience; impairing the openness of the discussion.

- *Watch for the "body language"*
  The inner attitudes of the person being questioned towards specific questions and his feelings in relation to his job situation are sometimes not expressed through the spoken word, but by facial expression, gestures, or silence – i.e., by what is not said.

- *Keeping notes using keywords*
  The most important statements made during the discussion should be noted using keywords – but it is not necessary to write down everything that is said. The interviewer is mainly in direct eye contact with the person being questioned, and should only look at the page now and then. Tape recorders are strictly forbidden. Only very experienced interviewees (prominent public figures) manage to maintain naturalness during an electronic recording.

- *Put down a word-for-word record of particularly apt sayings*
  Particularly apt formulations or characteristic statements should be noted word for word, and visually marked out for later evaluation. Quotations are a very vivid way of documenting the emotional background, and make a decisive contribution to the liveliness, plausibility, and persuasiveness of the results.

- *Unrewarding interviews or parts of them are part of the job*
  Some interviews are more rewarding than others. And there are some questions that bring out a lot from one person, but very little from another. "Blank" areas in interview records are perfectly normal. You don't need to record results at any cost.

- *Quick summary after every discussion*
  After each discussion, take a quarter of an hour on your own in peace and quiet to arrange your notes, go over the talk in your mind, and make short extra notes about personal impressions or the course of the interview, the atmosphere, and the person questioned (openness, mood, behavior).

An interview guide

By far the most important working tool for an employee survey is a guide for discussions. The care taken in developing this is an investment that is well worthwhile. It is not a matter of putting the same questions in every single interview. The questions also have to be put in such a way that those being questioned understand them and can respond to them appropriately. In addition, the interview guide has to be designed in such a way that the questioner can relate his discussion notes to the individual questions immediately. This makes work easier later on when the data are being analyzed.

In practice, questionnaires are almost always far too long. Too many clever pen-pushers have spent too much time at their desks racking their brains about all the interesting things that might be found out now that they are going to be in touch with the people anyway. The result is that the interview becomes a stupefyingly tedious and nerve-racking business of ticking off individual questions. The upshot is an impressive mountain of data – and not enough understanding of the background.

Figure 16. An interview guide

A Sample guide that has been used for various employee-run surveys in large companies -always supplemented by a few interesting, company-specific questions. In the working documents for the questioners, the interview records, the questions are spread over about eight pages (letter-size, including a cover sheet for personal data), with enough space after each question for handwritten notes (keywords and quotations).

1. **Opening the discussion** (5–10 min.)
   - Personal introduction of the interviewer
   - Information:
     - Aims, procedure and time plan for the employee-run survey
     - Number and selection of people questioned
     - Most important topics for the discussion (overview of what is coming)
     - Procedure during analysis (confidentiality in particular)
     - Notes taking (keyword notes)
   - Give an opportunity for questions ...

2. **Current job** (5–10 min.)
   First of all, your job. I see here that you work as ... I've got a vague idea of what that involves, but only in a general way. Could you just briefly tell me what a normal working day involves for you – what exactly you do from the morning to the evening?

3. **Motivation** (5 min.)

What are the good things about your profession? What is it that you like about your work?

What is it about your job that you enjoy? What is it that gives you satisfaction or makes you proud of what you have done?

4. **Down side** (5 min.)

Every profession also has its down side. What are the unpleasant circumstances or problems that are usually encountered in what you do?

5. **Positive aspects of what happens in the company** (5–10 min.)

When you think about the way things run in everyday work – which things are running well in your view? Which things do you think have been well organized? Which things should stay the way they are in the future? What are the things that have proved their worth as you see it?

6. **Critical aspects of what happens in the company** (15–20 min.)

   – *Which things in your everyday work are not running so well as they could or should?*

   – *Are there things that make you worry about the future – e.g., about the efficiency of the work, the safety, the working atmosphere or your own enjoyment of your work?*

   – *As you see it, what might happen if nothing is done?*

   – *As you see it, what are the causes?*

   – *How could these problems be solved? Who would have to do what?*

7. **Management and cooperation** (5 min.)

   – *How do you regard the atmosphere, management and collaboration in your own working environment, particularly in your team? How well or badly do people get on with one another in it?*

   – *Do people have contact with each other outside the company? Of what sort?*

   – *Do people have a say in the way that work is designed and organized, or do they just receive orders? Are they asked for their opinion? Can they make suggestions – and are these taken seriously?*

   – *What qualities do you particularly appreciate in your boss? Which ones are you not so keen on?*

8. **Contact with people higher up** (5 min.)

   – *Do you occasionally have contact with bosses higher up in the company?*

   – *Which of these do you regard as pleasant, and which as less pleasant? Why?*

9. **Cooperation with other departments** (5 min.)
   - Which other departments and divisions are you occasionally in contact with in everyday work?
   - As you see it, which aspects of collaboration with them work well? Which work less well? What ought to be improved?

10. **Information and communication** (5–10 min.)
    - As an employee of a not particularly small company, you usually want to receive some information about what happens when, or what doesn't, what goes on in the company as a whole and about things that are coming up in the near future. How do you normally find out about important news?
    - Who talks to you on what occasions about this sort of thing?
    - What written information do you receive? How useful do you find it?
    - Are there questions you would like to have an answer to, but have not got one yet?

11. **Personnel policy** (5 min.)
    - How do you regard the company's personnel policy overall?
    - What sort of professional and personal encouragement and support do you expect in this company?
    - Do you feel that you receive adequate support and advice with regard to your professional development? If not, who ought to be doing what?
    - What is your overall experience so far of your contacts with people from the Personnel Department?

12. **Company management** (5 min.)
    - How do you regard the management of the company as a whole and the policies of the Board of Directors?
    - As you see it, are there questions that the Board of Directors ought to be concerning itself with intensively?
    - If the Managing Director himself were to ask you to give him a suggestion about something – what would you say to him, in one sentence?

13. **Company's image** (5 min.)
    - What sort of image does the company have for the public, as you see it?
    - As you see it, what is it that makes the company attractive as an employer, and what makes it less attractive?
    - What is your personal response to the company's commercials and ads that appear in the media?

It is not a matter of getting as many questions as possible answered in the shortest possible time, but rather of conducting a *skilled dialogue* within the framework of the individual questions. This requires an appropriate script, which is provided by the interview guide. In addition, you should not allow people who are fanatical about figures and or perfectionist about methodology to lead you into putting too many precise, so-called "closed" questions. Someone who is only allowed to say "yes" or "no" is not going to have the feeling he is taking part in a genuine discussion. By contrast, open questions activate the flow of thoughts and discussion – and this is the only way of getting beyond the bare facts to an understanding of the vital background and contextual information (see the example interview guide given in Figure 16).

What to do with the data?

The first thing that has to be coped with after a survey is the confusing variety of the data. Dozens or even hundreds of discussions lasting one or two hours produce a mass of information. The material has to be condensed. In-house employees usually need some support with this: facilitating, visualization, data preparation and presentation of the essential findings.

Condensing the data requires particular care. What matters is identifying what is really important and summing it up. Typical statements cited verbatim can make a fundamental contribution to illustrating and understanding trend results that are formulated in more general terms. On the other hand, no statement may be included in the report that could be traced back to an individual source. In addition nothing should appear in an official report that might compromise an individual in the company.

Appropriate routes for information about the results then need to be found. Decision-makers have to give particularly intensive attention to the results, because they are the ones who are going to have to set the course for subsequent action. At the same time, however, it is very important that all employees should be informed about the results openly. This is the only way of ensuring wide acceptance for the measures that need to be taken on the basis of the survey.

In a large company, it is also useful to explain separately to the management personnel in the larger organizational units the specific results that relate to their areas of responsibility. This should at least be provided as an option – for those who regard critical results as being a valuable extra contribution to management information, and not just as an unsuitable way of denigrating people.

Organizational diagnosis as a management tool

In the ultimate analysis, a comprehensive organizational diagnosis is not possible without consulting the members of the organization who are affected. In many companies, however, employee surveys are taboo. Management is afraid of waking "sleeping dogs," or encouraging "exaggerated expectations." What this means is that they do not want to put themselves in the position of being forced to act. Or: management does not believe that a survey of employees will be any "use." It believes that everything that can be done has already long since been done by the existing management. The fact that employees are in truth the only genuine "experts" concerning what is going on right at the grass roots is not yet a very widespread insight.

What happens much more frequently, however, is that earlier survey campaigns have killed off the idea forever. The results were not reported openly, or no practical consequences worth mentioning were seen – or both. The result is that employees are simply no longer prepared to cooperate with "snooping" questionnaires.

This is very unfortunate, because particularly in large companies, employee surveys are an extremely valuable tool – not only for creating a basis for decision-making, but above all to mobilize *energy for change* within the company. There are always too many members of staff whose main goal consists of maintaining the status quo. Questionnaire results are extremely elegant "arguments" for change that speak for themselves. They provide a natural justification for decisions that would otherwise have to be pushed through with a great deal of effort and against massive resistance.

However, a survey is always a distinctive, culture-forming type of intervention. The communications theorist Marshall McLuhan originated the famous saying, "The medium is the message." As with every other medium, the outward form of an employee survey also contains a "hidden message." In the case of a written survey carried out by an external market research or opinion research institute, this message is: "We wish to obtain statistical data," or "We carry out our communications in writing." In the case of detailed individual discussions, the message is: "We are interested in your personal opinion," or "You are important as an individual." Group discussions give the signal: "Teamwork is what is needed with us." If the questions involve not just the proper functioning of structures and processes, but also management style and the working atmosphere, the message is: "We are not just concerned about efficiency, but also about good working relationships between people." And if in-house employees conduct the discussions, it means: "We are looking for dialogue with each other inside the company."

This is not a general judgment opposing written forms of survey in the company. Questionnaire surveys can certainly be the appropriate method for certain purposes. The choice of method ultimately depends on what you are aiming for. And two questions always arise at this point. First: "What do we want to know?" Secondly: "What do we want to achieve?"

No matter what the answers to these two questions and the consequent choice of method are – two conditions have to be met first before a detailed diagnostic exercise is entered into: you have to be willing to provide open information about the results; and you have to be prepared to implement the results by taking concrete steps.

Management
by Agreed Targets

3

"For those who know not where to sail, no wind is the right one."
Seneca

Leadership and management by agreeing targets with people is anything but a new discovery, either in business or in any other field. The idea was brought to Europe from America several decades ago – originally termed MBO ("management by objectives"). In the meantime, target agreements have become an established component of management tools in most larger companies.

Why are we including the topic in this book?

First, because in practice this tool is surprisingly often used in a fashion that completely misses its original point. In many cases it is no exaggeration to say that it is just being used as an excuse.

Secondly, because independent employees and organizational units can be managed and developed in a skilled way only by using formalized target agreements and checks. If you are not familiar with this tool, you should not even start trying to move your organization towards lean and decentralized structures.

Meaning and purpose of targets

One of the most widespread and also damaging evils in the working world – and in human life in general – is a loss of meaning and lack of perspective for the future. Those who cannot see the point of their work are incapable of finding it motivating. And those who can no longer find any meaning or perspective for the future in their lives in general fall victim to depression and sooner or later try to escape from their lives in one way or another.

Having a goal in front of your eyes is the best possible remedy for tiredness, discouragement, and inner emptiness. If you can see the larger context in which your work has its place, if you are aware of the chain of processes into which your own tasks are incorporated, it enables you to mobilize your energies. And if you can see your own contribution – no matter how small it may be in relationship to the whole – as being important, valuable, or even indispensable, then you are able to see past the end of your own nose and make a contribution to the success of the whole. No matter what your own situation, you will be thinking and acting in an entrepreneurial way.

Setting a goal for oneself or for others means defining the result that is being aimed for – to begin with only a result, not the means of achieving it. The goal provides orientation, but does not create restrictions. On the contrary: it is precisely the goal that opens up new potential fields of action. It forces you to think about the orientation of your own actions and look for solutions and methods allowing you to use your energies in a directed and therefore economical way. It also spurs you on – by offering the potential for independent action and the opportunity to achieve testable personal success. Particularly in the field of management, that is particularly hard – being able to look back on a job well done and say, "I did it!"

If you want to ensure that "entrepreneurship" is more than just a fashionable but empty term, there is no way of avoiding managing yourself and your employees via targets. People who have always been managed using detailed catalogues of operational tasks have never learned how to think and act independently. They have not learned how to accept genuine responsibility. And unfortunately, this is also true of masses of the people in today's corporate hierarchies, right up to middle management and above: at higher or lower levels of expertise and intelligence, all they do is execute allotted tasks. And often enough these are tasks that could be completely dispensed with anyway to the immense benefit of the whole system.

Achieving orientation towards goals is one of the basic preconditions for self-organization and self-direction in lean organizations.

Things that should not be confused with "targets"

Job descriptions
These define areas of tasks and assign responsibilities – as far as possible not in the form of interminable catalogues of individual activities, but by marking out a framework of responsibility. So it should not read, "He does … " but "He ensures that … " A job description indicates the framework within which the employee's goals can move. The goals give specific content, constantly updated, to the expectations of the employee that are described in general terms in the job description.

Tasks
Setting up a task means assigning the task of doing something specific. In this case, depending on the situation, many things can be (but need not be) handled in more or less the same way as with setting a target: orientation toward the result; defined scope for action; defined parameters for success. The main difference lies in the fact that a target usually concerns higher-level aspects, without defining the path along which it has to be reached. By contrast, tasks can be extremely simple and therefore so narrowly defined that not the slightest room is left for indepen-

dent thinking and action, for creative and conceptual work. Even someone who works like a robot can do a decent job – provided it is defined properly.

Activities
These concern only real actions, carrying things out, operational activity. This does not exclude meaningful higher-level targets and tasks. These can, or should, provide the framework within which the activity is carried out. But this orientation is often lacking. One logical consequence of this is indifference – withdrawal into oneself and alienation. Another possible consequence is operational rush, which is simply a desperate attempt to achieve distraction from the inner emptiness involved – on the principle, "We lost sight of the goal, so we redoubled our efforts."

Planning
While the target establishes the direction and the task defines the path, plans serve to prepare intended activities in detail.

Although planning is important in fulfilling complex tasks, in today's age of high-speed change, it needs to be understood and dealt with in a new way. Plans tend to mean that you are no longer fully prepared for contingencies. They give you a deceptive sense of security. Phrases like the following illustrate this dilemma: "Planning means replacing accident by error." "The precision of the data is completely out of proportion to their relevance." "The more precisely you plan, the harder accidents hit you."

Resolutions and intentions
As the proverb says, "The road to Hell is paved with good intentions." In contrast to a genuine target, intentions or good resolutions are not ultimately binding. They provide the indispensable raw material, in the form of imaginary test runs, out of which resolute action can emerge when the time is ripe and the situation is favorable. But intentions can also be used to provide a comfortable cushion on which it is easier to sleep. Intentions are the most sophisticated form of self-deception – the ideal way of maintaining a sense of one's own firm will, without ever actually having to do anything or change anything.

What sort of management targets can be set?

The targets can be broadly divided into four categories:

1) Work targets in the framework of normal descriptions of duties affecting current business.
2) Work targets that go beyond the normal framework and may eventually involve special commissions or projects.
3) Developmental targets or targets for change relating to employees, groups, duties, or organizational units (affecting for example organization, interplay, behavior, qualifications, etc.).

4) Developmental targets relating to oneself (affecting, for example, management behavior, communications, qualifications, etc.).

It is not a matter of picking the whole of the business apart into its smallest details and providing it with specific targets. In business life, many things are often already extremely well regulated and running well, and do not need any special targeting and planning in order to make sense. Targets are appropriate wherever there is a discrepancy between desired conditions and actual conditions, and when the way to achieve the desired condition is not immediately obvious (when the way is obvious, it is not targets that are needed, and instead specific measures have to be planned and carried out).

Examples of quantitative targets:

- *"Increase returns by X percent with costs remaining constant."*
- *"Cut X number of jobs in central administration."*
- *"Reduce inventory by X percent."*
- *"Acquire so-and-so many new customers in target group X for service Y."*
- *"Reduce the average processing time (or development time) from X to Y hours (or days, months, years)."*

Examples of qualitative targets:

- *"Resolve the conflict between department X and department Y."*
- *"Get employees to understand, accept, and support the goals of the restructuring plan."*
- *"Introduce semi-autonomous production groups and get them functioning."*
- *"Develop new appliance type X to the point where it is ready for production."*
- *"Introduce target agreements in the whole section and implement them appropriately at every level planned in the draft scheme."*

The art of management does not consist of doing everything right, but of tackling the right things properly. It is not the number of targets that shows quality and leads to success, but having the right priorities.

Dictating targets and agreeing targets

"That's all we need, everybody setting their own targets – setting targets is management's job!" People who talk like that show that their basic thinking is not oriented toward people and processes. They are suffering from a deepseated sense of insecurity. They do not feel that they are in a position to arrange targets on a basis of dialogue. And you can be pretty sure they have a poor view of human nature at the back of their minds.

Agreeing targets has nothing to do with grass-roots democracy. It simply means that targets and priorities have to be carefully thought out, discussed and agreed on before they are set. It is only agreeing targets through dialogue that can ensure:

⇨ *that the targets have really been understood and accepted;*
⇨ *that the priorities have been set properly, without incorporating conflicting targets;*
⇨ *that targets are not formulated without attention to the necessary funds and resources.*

Giving individuals a say in setting their own targets is therefore not a matter of handing out personal treats; it is justified by the nature of the process involved.

The fact that scope for action does not mean total freedom, and that some higher-level goals only leave a limited amount of freedom of action with regard to the individual targets derived from them, is another matter. What is decisive is that the targets should be tested and assessed in their overall context by getting together with those concerned – i.e., in a process of dialogue – instead of just being thrown out off the top of one's head.

No matter where the stimulus for a target comes from – whether it is one's own idea, part of a framework plan coming from further up in the company, or the result of an open discussion aimed at assessing the current position: anything that is not internalized by people to become part of their own sense of duty has little chance of ever being implemented. It is the same as with smokers: you can give them attention; you can talk to them till you are blue in the face; as their doctor, you can threaten them with imminent death; you can confront them with color TV pictures of the lungs of chain-smokers who died young; you can turn your back on them and reject them – but it is only when they decide for themselves, when they take entrepreneurial responsibility for their own health, that they will actually stop smoking.

Individual targets and team targets

Tasks and working structures are constantly becoming more complex. In modern lean organizations, teamwork with a high degree of self-control is becoming more and more important. Management tools have to take these developments into account. If teams have a common task and are supposed to be organizing themselves independently in order to reach it, the targets have to be agreed with the team – instead of bilaterally with its individual members.

It may be useful or even necessary to set individual targets in addition. If this is the case, the process of agreeing targets for the individual takes place together with the whole team, i.e. with all of the colleagues involved, and not with the boss at the next level up.

Figure 17. A hitparade of failure for agreeing targets

These are the most frequent deficiencies that are seen in practice in the process of reaching agreed targets:

1 **It is not targets that are agreed, but activities.**
   Target agreements have been confused with operational planning.

2 **Targets are not agreed, but given as instructions.**
   No dialogue takes place.

3 **There are only quantitative goals: turnover, headcount, reject rate.**
   Everything affecting the "soft factors" is ignored as irrelevant.

4 **Target agreements only take place from the bottom up.**
   Consolidated input from the grass roots – no willpower and entrepreneurship on the part of management.

5 **No clear company goals to use as a starting-point.**
   Each department is just looking after itself – instead of paying attention to its function for the whole company.

6 **The agreed targets are not compared horizontally.**
   No one knows what anyone else is doing – priorities and resources have not been coordinated.

7 **No monitoring and checking is carried out to see whether the target has been met.**
   Hindsight will be used to find reasons why the target could not be met.

8 **The target agreement is not linked to employees' standing.**
   There are neither rewards nor penalties – the whole thing is completely unimportant.

The main principles

Targets can guide behavior toward success all the more effectively the more consistently the following principles are observed:

Targets have to be set high, but must be realistic and achievable.

Targets can fail to serve their purpose for two reasons. Either because they do not represent a challenge, therefore ultimately have no effect. Or because they are felt to be unrealistic and incapable of being achieved from the very start. In the first case, opportunities for success and development are missed, and in the second frustration and resignation are created. In both cases, valuable energy is wasted. Not providing enough of a challenge is just as dangerous when targets are set as creating too much of a challenge. When there is no momentum or stimulus, nothing will move. Pressure caused by expectations that are too high, or even a belief that a target cannot be met anyway, leads to loss of motivation and barriers to action.

The art of agreeing targets therefore lies in setting each hurdle exactly as high as can be jumped – according to the employee's capabilities, available funds and resources, and any support that may be needed.

Clear description of the state that is to be reached

"*Where do I want to go?*" or "*What do I want to achieve?*" are the decisive questions, and not "*What has to be done?*" Targets are states that have to be reached in the future, anticipated results of activities, and not descriptions of activities. It is clarity and putting things in concrete terms that is needed. Many lead-runners drop out of the race too soon, knowing the direction in general, because they think they have already reached the goal – or they run past it because they don't recognize it.

Achievement of the target must be measurable or checkable

If it is not possible to check whether the target has been reached, whether it is a quantitative or a qualitative one, then the target is pointless. At what point in time is what state to be achieved in concrete terms? What are the measurement criteria or index values that need to be reached? On the basis of what criteria is the outcome to be assessed? If you set the goal "developing customer orientation," for example, it is advisable a) to specify what "customer orientation" means specifically, and b) to establish in advance what criteria and what procedure are going to be used to assess it at a specific time.

Defining scope for action and boundaries

Being an entrepreneur does not mean having complete freedom; it does not mean being able to do or not do whatever you want at any time. Instead, a good entrepreneur has a very precise awareness of what he can and may do and where his boundaries lie – when and where he can act, when and where he has to show consideration for whom, has to take other people's interests into account, has to win other people's support. The "in-house entrepreneur" also has to have a precise awareness of his field of action in order to proceed in a target-oriented way:

⇨ *Scope for action*
⇨ *Responsibilities*
⇨ *Available funds and resources*
⇨ *Limits, conditions, restrictions*
⇨ *External information and communication*
⇨ *Rules regarding consultation with the boss.*

It is while these topics are being negotiated that it becomes clear whether the boss is serious about managing by target agreements – or whether he is setting the most demanding possible targets but withholding the means and decision-making powers that the employee would need to meet them.

Planning time and milestones

If you have ever built a house, you know how important the planning of the stages and deadlines are. If you only have the overall time in your head, you are going to be on a fool's errand. Above all, you are going to think you have plenty of time still for far too long, and then get into a rush of activity at the end – and you will finish up botching things.

- *When is the overall result to be available?*
- *At what times are partial results to be expected?*

These questions have to be answered during the process of agreeing the goals.

One target must be compatible with the others

Agreed targets may not only have no effect, they may even be damaging – namely, when contradictory targets are being aimed for and conflict between them is inevitable. The individual's targets must be balanced with those of his colleagues sufficiently to ensure that no conflicts over priorities can arise. But that is the easy part. The most dangerous conflicts are the ones that the individual himself creates, because he has simply turned everyone's wish list – his own or his boss's – into a catalogue of targets, without examining it. And when two different targets turn out to be incompatible when seen in the light of day, then sooner or later energies are going to be bottled up. He will be like Buridan's ass, which starved to death in front of two equal-sized haystacks because it could not decide whether to go to one or the other – and there was no one there to take one of them away.

Ensuring networking, clarifying interdependences

Nobody, no team, and no department, is an island unto itself. Not all plans can be realized without other people, functions, or departments being affected in one way or another.

- *Who needs to be informed, who may need to be asked for assistance or support?*
- *Who might have targets that would clash with mine?*
- *Where could there be valuable synergies if things could be coordinated in time?*

Questions like these – looking both to the left and the right – have to be carefully clarified before starting.

Estimating costs

Equipment, personnel capacity, budget and forms of support cannot be estimated only once they are needed. Of course, you cannot calculate the anticipated costs down to the last cent at the time when the target is agreed, when the method of achieving it has not yet been established. But you can make a rough estimate. This is sufficient to expose the biggest mistakes that may be buried somewhere in a catalogue of targets. Many people think a good entrepreneur is a man who is always making generous investments. In fact, the successful entrepreneur is the one who knows precisely when and where he should invest how much – but also when and where he needs to consolidate.

Making sure targets are checked and audited

If you want to direct your actions toward a target, while at the same time being prepared for unexpected events and developments, you have to proceed in a process-oriented manner. You need an early warning system that will allow you to recognize the danger of deviations from the target course early enough for corrective measures to be taken. Three things are important for this.

1) *Defining the criteria based on which it can be judged whether or not you are still in the target corridor.*
2) *Planning of "checkpoints" at various times for intermediate assessments and identifying the current position.*
3) *Binding agreement that the employee must contact his boss on his own initiative as soon as he notices potential deviations from the target course that he does not think he can correct on his own.*

It may also happen that one is obliged to correct not the procedure, but the target. But target corrections are out of the employee's scope for action in principle. Quite apart from eventualities of that sort, a half-time progress assessment process should be definitely included in the plan and implemented.

Assessing priorities according to importance and urgency

There are two quite different reasons why a target can have priority. Either because it is important – i.e., it is of fundamental significance. Or because it is urgent – i.e., postponement of it is not possible. After an initial brainstorming session, the "wish list" is almost always a) a mixture of the two and b) far too long. Important and urgent targets therefore have to be distinguished to begin with, and then arranged in a sequence of priorities. Then it can be decided how many targets and which ones in each category can be realistically tackled.

Less is more

When too many targets are set simultaneously, it is almost inevitable that not all of them will be met – perhaps even none of them. Setting up a whole forest of targets provides people with an excellent opportunity for fragmentation, jumping from one thing to another and completely exhausting themselves in a dramatic effort to do their best. Setting priorities is what is needed – and the right priorities too, if possible.

The process of agreeing targets

Verbal agreements by superiors with employees that take place "in passing" in an isolated, accidental, and completely unconnected way have nothing to do with competent target agreement. Target agreements are a tool of management. If this is supposed to benefit the company in any way, then – like any other tool of management – it has to be used in a coordinated way and requires a certain amount of formalization.

The process of agreeing targets starts at the very top of the company. It is company management that sets the overall framework: the strategic direction for the company in the coming year, the most important targets and priorities, and the corresponding rough allocation of resources. There may already be emphases given here that are quite specific, and which can substantially influence the targets of the individual departments or divisions – for example:

- *Which customer target groups are we going to focus on in particular?*
- *What are the areas in which new products should be developed as quickly as possible?*
- *What needs to be changed with regard to organization or cost structure?*
- *What index values need to be improved, and by how much?*
- *What resources are available – and how are they to be used?*
- *Which principles have top priority this year?*

It is obvious that commitments of this type cannot be made all on your own and just off the top of your head, and that ideas, opinions, and suggestions from executives and employees – if necessary right down to the grass roots – need to be gathered and taken into account in advance.

But the first and foremost binding target is set at the very top. It is the product of the preceding discussions within the company, but its important emphases express the will of top management.

Practical experience shows that the initial momentum for decisive developments sometimes comes from the grass roots, sometimes from the middle levels, and sometimes from the top. Company management need not, and cannot, give birth to every single good and important idea itself. But its task is to ensure that the right ideas are generally accepted, by setting the appropriate targets and allocating the resources in the right way.

Once the targets have been formulated at company level, what matters is breaking them down into the corresponding divisions and departments at the next level down:

- *What does this mean for us?*
- *What contributions do we need to make to ensure that the company's targets can be met?*
- *What specific goals are implied for us?*

On the same pattern, the process can then be continued downward level by level. This means that each employee with whom targets are agreed first has to know his superior's targets in order to set his own priorities appropriately.

It does not mean that all individual targets have to be exclusively and directly derived from the targets at the next level up. There are department-specific targets that also need to be set even when there are no guidelines from above. What is crucial is that the company's strategic direction should be understood by all its employees and supported by an appropriate alignment of departmental activities.

As mentioned earlier, the process of agreeing targets is not finished once the targets have been set: target planning has to be checked at regular intervals – at least once, half-way through, together with the boss responsible. Having to see the boss again guarantees that the targets are kept in mind and continue to be binding. Otherwise it is easy for the year to run on the principle "strong start, weak finish."

Keeping written records

Formalities and the churning out of paper should be kept within narrow limits. Two things are sufficient:

1. A front-page overview with two parts:
   a) The overall strategic emphases and targets for the company that provide one's own work during the period concerned with its framework, direction, and meaning.
   b) A list of all agreed targets in keyword form.
2. One page per target, with keywords recording specific agreements and most important conclusions from discussions (see Figure 18, "A master chart for target agreements").

This minimum documentation is necessary to ensure that you know afterward what has been specifically discussed and agreed. "Later on" here means at the time of the intermediate assessments, and certainly at the time of the final assessment, which is then not only closely linked to assessments of employees' achievements, but also forms the basis for the next round of target agreements.

"All theory, my friend, is gray"

In practice, this saying seems to apply to the way most people regard target agreements. Hardly any other tool of management has been familiar for so long, is regarded by everyone as "natural" – and is so inconsistently applied (see Figure 17, "a hitparade of failure..."). There must be good reasons for this, particularly since managers – in their own view, at least – are people who think and act in particularly rational and reasonable ways.

Figure 18. A master chart for target agreements

1. **Target**

2. **Reasons justifying action**
   Starting point, current status

3. **Addressee**
   Or person concerned

4. **Relevant overall framework**
   Part of which larger-scale chain of processes

5. **Measurement units**
   Criteria for assessing whether the target has been reached

6. **Time-frame**
   Including milestones

7. **Basic approaches to action**
   Strategies, special procedures

8. **Costs**
   Funds/resources

9. **Framework**
   Standard values, networks, communications

10. **Priority**

There are two possible explanations.

First: It is not always pleasant to require clear thinking of oneself and others and to get to the bottom of things together with them. You have to argue things out face to face. You can't always just ooze charm. You sometimes also have to tell employees what you think they are capable of and what they are not. Or tell your boss what resources and powers you are going to need to get people to take a specific target to heart.

Secondly: It is very risky to take up a clear position. It means being brutally dragged out of the cozy niche where you had made yourself so comfortable. You become exposed. You become measurable, checkable, controllable. You become accountable. How are you going to keep your options open to think differently later? You have lost your human right to freedom.

One might think that it would primarily be the employees who do not like to show their bosses all the cards they have in their hand, who would rather not be checked up on. And they do indeed exist. But when alibi exercises are being carried out in a company on a more or less universal basis, it can be safely assumed that it is the top management level that is taking the lead with inadequate target agreements. Because that is where genuine leadership is being demanded. When you are on the executive committee, you can't pretend you are just a member of the supervisory board. It is not a management tool that you can simply administer from above. You yourself are personally challenged. And the worst part of it is: you yourself can be checked. Because employees need to know their boss's basic goals before their own can be discussed and set out. If you are used to setting targets for other people and defining their freedom of action, you don't like to have to take yourself in hand. This is why it is quite often the Olympians at the very top who get the worst forms of mental diarrhea when they are exposed to competently executed target agreement procedures.

Reducing agreed targets to the absurd

In many companies, the top performers have the hurdles regularly set higher for them every year, in a more or less mindlessly automatic process – particularly when the agreed targets have been met, or even when they only look as if they are going to be met. You don't want to make the effort of defining new targets, resources, and incentives with every single individual in fair negotiations. You act on the simple maxim: where there's a lot, there's usually more to come.

Those who are faced with this are acting perfectly rationally if they decide to incorporate the mechanism into their calculations in the future. They have to protect themselves against being punished for setting demanding targets and producing competent performances; against having unachievable goals or unsustainable targets forced on them; against letting themselves and their whole department be squeezed dry like a lemon. They will do anything to set lower goals in the future and incorporate sufficient reserves – or they will ensure that the targets will be seriously missed for once. In other words, this is the best way of converting executives who are able to think and act in an entrepreneurial way into cunning subordinates busy with tactical maneuvers.

At some (usually perfectly predictable) point during the second half of the year, tremendously hectic activity, not to say panic, breaks out in many companies. There is a sudden risk of not meeting the targets, there are obvious discrepancies from the planned figures. Instead of the situation being investigated together with everyone concerned, a sudden intervention comes from above like a clap of thunder. People in management think they can show their strength by decreeing from above that all previously agreed targets and all the agreements connected with them are suspended. A state of emergency is proclaimed. Current budgets are curbed across the board, freezes are ordered here, there, and everywhere, the riskiest cost limits are dictated. Independence and scope for action within the company have had their day.

In company management it is the same as with traffic. In spite of all the care and attention you give to driving, it can happen that you suddenly find yourself forced to hit the brakes hard. However, the frequency with which you have to do this depends a lot on your personal style of driving. Some people have had an ABS system installed for years and never used it. Other people need it every time they have to stop.

If you let the behavior needed in emergency situations become habitual, the tools at your disposal are going to start wearing out. When it is a matter of survival, people are creatures of habit with long-term memories. Employees who have been through this type of grand braking maneuver twice in a row are already expecting it to happen a third time. And they are usually right. The result: they are extremely reserved in their commitment to target agreements because they are assuming from the start that the agreements will be suspended even before the planning stage is finished. The proclamations of a state of emergency will soon lose their ability to scare people. After a time, people begin to take them perfectly calmly, because they know that the whirlwind comes round

Figure 19. Checklist of essential items for agreeing targets

These are the points you need to attend to if target agreements are not going to degenerate into mere alibi exercises:

1 Agree on targets – not measures to be taken

2 Agree on targets – don't dictate them

3 Higher-level goals are the starting-point for a dialogue about targets.

4 Targets for current business – targets for development and change

5 Balance between quantitative and qualitative targets

6 Challenging, but realistic and achievable targets

7 Reaching the target can be assessed by defined criteria

8 Horizontal coordination of individual targets

9 Agreed targets must be recorded in writing

10 Target agreements are achieved in a coordinated process from the top down.

11 Checking the course to the target – deviations from the course are recognized soon enough, and course corrections are made

12 Reaching the target is a vital element in assessing employees' capabilities and qualifications

once a year. The consequence is that energy and inventiveness are not used to produce extra performance, but to undermine the system.

Is agreeing targets out of date?

Have targets and target agreements become obsolete at a time when the environment has become unstable and unpredictable; when it is chaos management that is being propagated; when Lao Tzu's saying "the way is the goal" has entered management thinking; when the "learning organization" becomes the model for company management oriented toward the future? Does it make sense any more to set targets when everything is changing so fast? Are target statements not already ripe for the trash can before they have even been put down on paper? Do commitments like that not make people insensitive to unexpected changes in the framework? Do they not encourage the myth that economic and political events can be planned? Do they not give people a false sense of security in the end?

The answer is: yes – if targets are not set against the mental background of a turbulent environment, and if the targets are not approached in a process-oriented way, and you behave instead as if reaching them was like moving along a railroad track in a tunnel. If you have ever sailed on the high seas, you will know what process-oriented thinking means: checking your current position again and again; taking account of the changing winds and currents and the resulting drift; being driven through storms; getting stuck in a calm; having to repair a torn sail, a broken boom, or a leak in the ship's side now and then. And last, but not least: keeping the crew happy. The course has to be constantly redefined – but the target remains the same. Even hundreds of years ago, it was the targets that took the great explorers, equipped with nothing more than a compass, a sextant and their astonishing navigational talents, to the ends of the earth and back again in their wooden ships.

Facilitating processes 4

Whenever and wherever it is change management that is needed, there is a need for facilitating. There are several reasons for this. First, an ability to act as a facilitator is increasingly becoming part of the normal equipment of any executive who wants to mobilize his staff and develop his team. Secondly, innovative work in workshops, project teams, and groups is constantly increasing – and this often requires process management of one sort or another. Thirdly, the need for large meetings for staff and executives is increasing – and nine out of ten times, these are sure to require process managers.

Of course, you can hire external, professional process consultants now and then. But it is better if your own employees can develop process facilitation skills alongside their normal jobs. Then the expertise can remain in-house, and staff can be used more flexibly. In addition, taking on tasks as a process facilitator is practically always regarded as a form of job enrichment.

However, running meetings needs to be learned and practiced. There is more involved than just asking people to make comments one after another. Looking expectantly round the table when a question has been asked and saying "Yes?" when someone's hand is raised – even the most untalented manager can do that. And he almost always does do it then as well – whether the situation requires it or not. The result: all the life goes out of the discussion. Some people may have advanced quite far up in the hierarchy without ever having given a thought to what "facilitating" actually means, and without ever asking themselves if there is anything about their personal style in conducting meetings that might need to be improved.

This chapter provides a quick summary of the essentials of Facilitating, providing a basis for training facilitators, or for your own "on-the-job" self-training:

– *The facilitator's role*
– *The essentials – or what it is that matters most*
– *The facilitator's specific tasks*
– *Tips for using a facilitator*

The facilitator's role

Someone who takes on the job as group facilitator first needs to be clear about his duties and his role.

- *What is the role of a facilitator?*
    - Active service provider for the overall group
    - Consultant on useful and efficient working methods
    - Consultant and support provider for communication
    - Consultant and support provider for cooperation
    - Team coach
- *What is* not *the role of a facilitator?*
    - Team spokesman
    - Expert adviser
    - Head teacher
    - Referee capable of awarding penalties
    - Detached onlooker
    - Outside observer

The essentials: what really matters

1 *Creating an atmosphere of openness and trust*
   This is the most important thing: an atmosphere of openness and trust, and an easy, relaxed way of dealing with one another. This is the only way to achieve productive work, and the only way that learning can take place. It starts with openness and honesty, as well as a sense of humor, on the part of the facilitator. He is important as a role model.

2 *Communication: controlling dialogue*
   Having a good understanding between the members is alpha and omega of teams. The facilitator needs to ensure that people listen well, ask questions well, and explain things well – instead of talking at or past each other.

3 *Team development: helping people to help themselves*
   Not doing everything yourself, but ensuring that the team members become active themselves and stay active: that they become more sensitive to the quality of communications in the team; and that they learn how to "trouble-shoot" and repair their own ways of interacting.

4 *Seeing the overall team as a "client"*
   Always keep an eye on the ability of the overall team to function properly. The principle is: every team member is an important partner! Be available and responsive to all of them. Don't give anyone preferential treatment, never denigrate anyone, don't try to shake anyone off or exclude them.

5 Not putting yourself under too much pressure

The facilitator does not always have to have everything "under control." He is not a magician. He does not have to understand everything straight away. It is not his "fault" if things come to a stop at some time, or people get annoyed. The one and only thing that is decisive is that he should make a sincere effort to support the team in analyzing and working through any difficulties that arise.

The facilitator's specific tasks

What opportunities does the facilitator have to exercise influence?
What are the tools he has at his disposal?
What can or must he do specifically?

● *Clarifying the background and context*

You can only be a good facilitator if you understand exactly what people are talking about, what is being said by whom, and what the background and context of the questions and problems are that are being discussed by the team. What this means is that the facilitator needs to have a clear understanding about things himself. But he also has to ensure for the team's sake that when there are complex problems involved – and they are almost always complex – hasty conclusions are not drawn and rash "solutions" are not produced, but rather that the background to a situation is carefully analyzed.

Put specific questions yourself ...
For example:

- *"I don't think I understand this yet. What exactly is it all about?"*
- *"I don't understand that. What's the connection?"*
- *"What was it that made you take that opinion?"*
- *"How did this situation develop?"*
- *"What do you think the reasons for this conflict are?"*
- *"Why do you think your colleague was so annoyed?"*
- *"What sort of sense did you make of that story?"*
- *"What do you think the deeper-lying causes of this problem are?"*

Or you can stimulate the team to clarify matters ...
For example:

- *"Have you any idea why your colleague X takes that opinion?"*
- *"Is everyone already clear about how this situation developed?"*
- *"Are the reasons for this conflict already clear? If not, ask again!"*
- *"Let's not apply any treatment before we've got a clear diagnosis!"*
- *"Don't give advice before you've understood the problem!"*

- *Ensuring good understanding*

Ensure that the team members listen to each other properly and understand one another – instead of talking past each other (the specialist jargon for this is "controlled dialogue").

For example:

- *"Did you understand what your colleague just said?"*
- *"Are you sure that your colleagues have grasped what you mean?"*
- *"Let him finish what he's saying, so that he can get his point across."*
- *"Could someone who was listening just state what he thinks it means so far – then Mr. X will be able to see what still needs to be explained and what doesn't."*

- *Ensure that people stay specific*

Make sure that abstract matters, points that are too general or are just not comprehensible are made understandable in specific and concrete ways (examples, further information, analogies).

For example:

- *"Could you put that in concrete terms?"*
- *"Could you give us a practical example?"*
- *"That's too abstract for me, I don't understand it."*
- *"When were you last in that kind of situation – and what exactly was it like?*
- *"What do you mean, 'we ought to'? Who ought to do what?"*
- *"Could you describe step by step what exactly happened?"*

- *Ensure visualization*

Complex connections between things should be illustrated visually (e.g. using drawings on a flip chart).

For example:

- *"Let me try to sketch that in a diagram – maybe I can make it clearer."*
- *"Could you just make a sketch of who reports what to whom, otherwise it'll take us ages to get a picture of the situation."*

- *Sequence of speakers*

It should be carefully considered if and when the facilitator should assign a sequence of who speaks in turn, and when he should not.

In a small team (up to about seven people), the participants in a discussion can usually speak spontaneously. In larger groups (from about 10 people upward), however, it may be necessary for the facilitator to assign a sequence. And with big groups (from about 20 people upward), there is usually no other choice.

If a lot of people in a very large group all want to speak at the same time, it can be difficult for the facilitator to keep track. The first trick is then to make a note of the names, so that no one will be missed out. But if new participants continue to raise their hands before all of the people in the queue have yet spoken, then you have to draw attention to the waiting list:

– *"It's Mr. X first, then Mr. Y, then Mr. Z."*

And it's no disgrace – and in fact it will avoid frustration – for the facilitator to state that he or she has lost track:

– *"I'm not sure any more who all wanted to speak, or even what the order was. Could those wishing to speak please raise their hands again?"*

When in doubt, being open about it can be a great relief!

But even in a large group, the facilitator can let a spontaneous discussion run freely for a certain time if he has the impression that there is something important happening. Sometimes a good idea or a fundamental insight can only arise because at the right moment the facilitator has *not* intervened. However, it is important that he should be able to justify this. Otherwise the participants will notice a "leadership vacuum" that will cause uncertainty.

● *Mobilizing silent participants*

People don't all have to speak for exactly the same amount of time – and certainly not everyone has to speak on each topic. But overall, the facilitator has to ensure more or less balanced amounts of participation by mobilizing those who have been silent.

For example:

– *"You haven't said anything for a long time."*
– *"I'd be interested in hearing your view about this."*
– *"Is there something you've been quietly thinking?"*
– *"You've been listening to all this for a long time now. What's your impression?"*
– *"When someone has been quiet for a long time, it doesn't mean he has nothing to say. What about you?"*

● *Putting the brakes on the talkative ones*

If individual participants are taking up too much time, they need to be held back.

For example:

– *"I'd also be interested to hear other people's opinions."*
– *"If you go into that much detail there will be no time for anyone else to speak."*
– *"Let other people get a word in."*
– *"Now that Mr. X has given his opinion in detail – what do other people think?"*
– *"There seems to be a duel going on between Mr. X and Mr. Y. What do other people think about the issue?"*

And another good tip here: if you want to stop someone who is talking too much, just stop looking at him! Eye contact with you, as the helmsman or helms-

Figure 20. Overview of the facilitator's tasks

- *Clarify background and context*
- *Ensure good communication (controlled dialogue)*
- *Make sure people stay specific*
- *Ensure visualization*
- *Establish the sequence of speakers*
- *Mobilize silent participants*
- *Put the brakes on the talkative ones*
- *Get back to the subject*
- *Establish what is essential*
- *Sum up interim conclusions*
- *Clarify differences of opinion and interest*
- *Work out conflicts*
- *Review communication process with the team*
- *Give the team feedback*
- *Give individual team members feedback*
- *Talk about feelings and perceptions*
- *Show your own feelings*
- *Time management*
- *Record results*
- *Ensure clear agreements*
- *Joint process review and "post-mortem"*

woman, signals "importance," "attention value," and "interest," and lack of eye contact by contrast mean "disinterest." You will find that this works four out of every five times!

- **Getting back to the subject**

If the team gets carried away and one topic starts leading to another, until you suddenly find you are talking about something completely different, then you have to lead it back to the subject in hand.

For example:

- *"I think we are getting off the subject. The question was … "*
- *"Is what we are discussing here important to the subject?"*
- *"Does anyone know what it was we actually wanted to talk about?"*
- *"The question at issue is still … "*
- *"Can somebody tell us what it is we're actually talking about just now?"*
- *"Mr. X originally wanted to discuss the following: … "*

Here too, there are exceptions. The apparent "sidetrack" may actually be an as yet unrecognized main thread. If you notice that there is an important subject involved that has previously been pushed aside, you can make it explicit. If you are not sure about your diagnosis of it, you can check it out briefly – together with the participants.

● *Working out what is essential*

When the discussion begins to lose direction and starts going back and forth, it may be that the participants have lost the thread. People who are "in the thick of a discussion" can easily lose the overall view. The facilitator has to keep an overall view, however, and if necessary restore the "focus" on the topic.

For example:

- *"The discussion is basically revolving around the following central question: …"*
- *"The topic that everyone is skirting round here is: …"*
- *"The following connection seems to me to be decisive: …"*
- *"Sometimes you can't see the wood for the trees. But the essential point is: …"*
- *"To sum up the previous discussion, it is basically a matter of the following question: …"*
- *"Now that we have seen and understood how the problem developed, what we have to do is see how to solve it."*
- *"We've been discussing the sensible thing to do now for long enough. The question now is, who is going to do it?"*

Or when several topics get mixed up:

- *"I think we ought to distinguish between two questions – firstly …, and secondly …"*
- *"At the moment we're discussing several questions all at once: in the first place …, in the second place …, and thirdly …. Let's take one at a time, otherwise we're going to get things confused."*
- *"It seems to me there are two different things involved here that have got muddled up – namely: …"*
- *"You're talking at cross purposes. Mr. X is talking about the question …, while Mr. Y and Mr. Z are talking about the question … Which of the questions do we want to discuss first?"*

- *Summing up interim conclusions*

The discussion can start to go round in circles if the participants are not clear enough about everything that has already been explained and spoken about.
For example:

- *"I'd like to just sum up what we've worked out so far ..."*
- *"We can note the following results so far: ..."*
- *"There are a few things we've already established, namely: firstly ..., secondly ..."*
- *"What has the discussion shown so far?"*
- *"To make sure we're not going round in circles: what information can we already assume as a basis?"*

- *Clarifying differences of opinion and interest*

The participants' need to show harmony with one another can sometimes lead to them not noticing contradictory positions, or minimizing them. If the discussion continues as if nothing had happened, it will run aground later on all the harder.
For example:

- *"Does everybody here really have the same opinion about this?"*
- *"Could you just tell me what you think Mr. X's opinion actually is?"*
- *"You're being very silent but you're shaking your head and giving us black looks – what are you thinking?"*
- *"Just to make sure we're not just being polite here: what you are saying is actually the complete opposite of what your colleague Y just said a minute ago."*
- *"Can anyone say which of us he thinks supports Mr. Z's views?"*
- *"Before you go on, let's just check how many people share your opinion."*

- *Working out conflicts*

Not every difference of opinion has to be discussed in detail, and not every conflict of interest has to be resolved. But if having a constructive discussion might be endangered, then you need to talk about it.
For example:

- *"There's a difference of opinion here that we need to talk about."*
- *"Before we go on, we all need to understand the background to these two contradictory standpoints better."*
- *"We don't all have to have the same opinions the whole time. But we should at least have a good understanding about which of us here holds which opinions – otherwise there may be bad feelings in the rest of the discussion and you can be sure nothing good will come out of it."*
- *"Let's just make quite sure these two standpoints are really as irreconcilable as they seem at the moment – and what exactly the disagreement consists of."*

- *"I suggest that the people who have only been listening so far should say what they think the contradiction here consists of."*
- *"I'm not sure whether we can solve this conflict just now, or even need to – but I'd like to get a better grasp of the background to it at least."*

- ● *Reviewing communication processes with the team*

If the quality of communications within the team is seriously in need of improvement, it is useful to take a break and talk about it.
  For example:

- *"I think we should leave this topic for a minute and turn our attention to the way in which we are discussing things here."*
- *"What do you feel about the discussion that's going on here?"*
- *"If an outsider had been listening to this discussion for the last half hour, what sort of impression do you think he would have got?"*
- *"Why is it that we're not getting any further here?"*
- *"I'd like to ask for some critical comments about what is going on here at the moment."*

- ● *Giving the team feedback*

Another way of making the team sensitive to the quality of communications is for the facilitator to provide direct feedback about it.
  For example:

- *"Has anybody else noticed that no one has been interrupted today when they were speaking?"*
- *"Since we had that discussion about the team's power structure, the atmosphere in the room has relaxed incredibly."*
- *"These good results were only possible because everyone felt able to speak freely."*
- *"What strikes me is that no one is listening to anybody else."*
- *"It's not one discussion that's going on here, but two or three at the same time. There are constant side discussions going on."*
- *"I'd be curious to know what you feel about this – my impression is that people aren't talking openly here and we're all beating about the bush."*
- *"No one who has spoken in the last fifteen minutes has been allowed to finish what he was saying. People keep interrupting."*
- *"Some people here are keeping a low profile and not saying anything at all. Does anyone feel the cap fits?"*

- ● *Giving individual team members feedback*

Situations come up again and again in which it is useful to mention the behavior of an individual team member.

For example:

- *"I think it has been very helpful for this discussion that you keep asking to check whether you have understood the other person properly."*
- *"You're sometimes a difficult person to have a discussion with – but what I like about you is that you are so open. You don't beat about the bush, but say what you're thinking and what you feel about things. People at least always know where they are with you."*
- *"If you as the boss start thumping the table as soon as someone states a slightly different opinion, you needn't be surprised if no one says anything any more."*
- *"It strikes me that you basically only speak when I ask you things directly. Why do you think that is?"*
- *"The contributions you make here are always very intelligent but non-committal general remarks. But I'd be interested to know what your personal opinion really is. Are you for or against?"*
- *"You never say anything and keep staring at the ceiling, or out of the window, or at your watch. You're giving us the impression that the subject and the people here are terribly boring for you."*

● *Talking about feelings and perceptions*

People are primarily guided by emotions in their behavior. But discussions mostly take place at a purely rational level – i.e., too intellectually. The facilitator always has to make sure that the emotions going on at the subliminal level are made transparent.

For example:

- *"How did you feel when you found out your department was going to be split in two?"*
- *"You are all reporting facts here. But what do you feel about the way these things are developing? What sort of reactions does the new situation trigger in you?"*
- *"How do you think your boss felt when you told him you would be leaving the department?"*
- *"Describe how you feel when you recall what happened then."*
- *"How did you feel inside on that occasion?"*
- *"How would you react if somebody treated you like that?"*
- *"You are describing it all in such a dry and matter-of-fact way, as if you weren't directly involved at all. Did you have any feelings about it?"*

● *Showing your own feelings*

The facilitator has to be approachable. He can and should also show his own feelings.

For example:

- *"It's great being facilitator here. You all understand each other so well, I've got nothing to do!"*

- *"After the interesting results from the last meeting I've been looking forward to today's."*
- *"I'm glad to be able to act as facilitator again for a team where everything isn't so stiff and formal."*
- *"It worries me that people keep fooling around here."*
- *"I feel completely powerless as facilitator here when everything gets into a muddle and nobody listens to anyone else."*
- *"I'm serving as the facilitator here, but I would feel better if I was not the only one here who was worrying about time management."*
- *"It annoys me when I get here at exactly the time agreed and then have to sit around twiddling my thumbs with just one or two people because half the team isn't here yet."*

● *Time management*

Keep an eye on the time and always start leading on from one working step to the next in plenty of time.

For example:

- *"We should be winding this point up now or the time will be over and we won't have got where we wanted to."*
- *"Is there anything important left to say about this topic? If not, let's move on so that we don't lose any time."*
- *"If we start talking about this new question just now, we won't be able to finish discussing today's actual subject properly. I would suggest leaving the question to another time."*
- *"We should be finishing up on this, otherwise the whole plan will get muddled up."*
- *"There are two choices here. Either you can go on talking about this new question that has come up – and then the main topic that was planned will not be dealt with. Or else you can concentrate the discussion on the original subject and postpone the new question to another time. Which of them is more important to you?"*

● *Recording results*

The facilitator has to ensure that the results are briefly summed up and noted down at the end of the discussion (or at the end of the conference work). Otherwise people will forget what was discussed or worked out when.

For example:

- *"Can I ask you just to list the most important conclusions of the discussion – then I can note down some keywords for each point on the flip chart."*
- *"Can someone try to sum up the conclusions?"*
- *"What are the most important items we've learned or worked out today?"*
- *"I would suggest that you should briefly sum up the conclusions of your discussion and note them down – otherwise you might have to start over from the very beginning again next time."*

- *Ensure clear agreements*

To keep things progressing, it is critically important to make sure that tasks are assigned and clear agreements are made.

For example:

- *"What specifically needs to be done now – who is going to do it by when?"*
- *"Who is going to deal with topic X, and who is going to deal with topic Y? What are their tasks precisely?"*
- *"Who is preparing the minutes? By when?"*
- *"Who is going to be informing whom about this discussion, and in what form?"*
- *"When and where is the next meeting taking place?"*
- *"How will the individual team members need to prepare for it?"*

- *Joint process review and "post-mortem"*

There should be no meeting without an analysis and evaluation! A common critical review – with an assessment of emotions and "post-mortem" – considerably enhances the learning effect for everyone involved, and helps the team to manage itself better in the future.

The facilitator can mention the main questions briefly, or write them up on the flip chart for everyone to see. Not everyone has to say something about every question – but everyone should at least make a short remark.

Useful main questions:

- *What do I think about the results of our discussions? How satisfied or dissatisfied am I with the conclusions?*
- *What do I think about the efficiency of our work? Has good use been made of our time?*
- *What do we need to pay more attention to in the future?*
- *How did I feel about the atmosphere?*
- *How were communications between people? What was good – and what was not so good?*
- *What was the facilitating like? What was helpful? What would you like to be different?*
- *What is my mood like at the end of the conference? What kind of feelings does it leave me with as I go home?*

Practical tips for using a facilitator

- *When should someone special be used as process facilitator?*

- Almost always if the workshop group is larger than seven or eight people.
- If the workshop participants do not have much experience in conducting discussions and organizing meetings or in the techniques of problem-solving, decision-making, visualization, and team development.

- If all the participants – including the head – wish or have to be free from facilitating tasks in order to devote themselves entirely to the discussion (this is almost always the case with team development or strategy workshops).
- If the composition of the group as a whole is tricky in personnel terms, or if the participants do not know one another.
- If the subject is so explosive that controversy or perhaps even conflict can be expected in the discussion.

● *When should an outsider be used as process facilitator?*

- When facilitator skills are needed, but no one in-house who has the right qualifications or abilities is available.

● *When should two or more people be used as facilitators?*

- In meetings with very large groups, particularly when they involve phases with subgroup work that needs to be supported by a facilitator.

● *When is a facilitator not needed?*

- If the formal head (superior or project leader) can and is willing to act as facilitator himself.
- When the people in the team are so familiar with one another and experienced in workshop meetings that no special facilitating is really needed at all.
- If methods of directing a meeting and chairing discussions are to be learned by all the team members and the facilitator job is meant to rotate round the team members as part of their "on-the-job" training.

● *What is the difference between the roles of boss, employee, and facilitator during a team workshop?*

The boss
- is and remains the boss even during the workshop;
- leads the team and, together with his employees, is responsible for the content of the workshop, for achieving its goals, and for its results.

The employee …
- makes an active contribution and shares responsibility for the content of the workshop, for achieving its goals, and for its results.

The facilitator …
- advises the team on how to proceed and on methods of working;
- conducts various phases of the discussion, or (depending on what has been agreed), all of it;
- manages the process and procedures, or at least ensures that the team works in a specific way;
- takes care of the quality of communications and participation;
- intervenes when the rules are not being observed;
- pays attention to subliminal disturbances, tensions, and conflicts – and when appropriate articulates them in a constructive but clear form.

Figure 21. Visualization

- **What is the purpose of visualization?**
  - *Interim results*
    Working through challenging problems within a team is a highly complex business. To make the working process as target-oriented and effcient as possible, it is absolutely necessary for interim results to be recorded and put in a visible form for all the participants. It is only when everyone has the same overview of the same data in front of them that the next working step can be planned and carried out in a coordinated way.
  - *Drawings and graphics*
    Images and pictures can often make it much easier for people to understand complex questions more quickly and clearly than verbal explanations. Visualization is an important tool for overcoming complexity!
  - *Keeping minutes of decisions*
    Documented final results in the form of the minutes of the meeting are the basis and necessary precondition for planning and checking on further steps in the process.

- **What does visualization involve?**
  - *Sticking to the essentials*
    Only the most important points or aspects should be recorded.
  - *Conciseness*
    Note the keywords in telegram form – not long-winded prose!
  - *Legibility for everybody*
    Large, clear writing that can be read by everybody in the room.
  - *Form suitable for everyone to use*

Able to be structured and restructured: can be taken apart and rearranged, can have parts removed or added ...

- **Flip chart**
  - Indispensable as a "notepad" in the plenum or small group: minutes of the discussion in keyword form, checklists, minutes of results

- **Portable free-standing pinboards**
  - This is the best medium for common work on complex topics
    Indispensable for collecting and structuring data using cards
  - Ideal for large-area graphic displays
    Organization charts, networks, matrices, complex diagrams, etc.
  - Allow extensive visual display to be transported
    Graphics and text can be flexibly moved out of the way and brought back again when needed.

Plenum and group work

The ideal size for working groups is about five to seven people. A group of that size is big enough to ensure the necessary variety of ideas, opinions, and abilities, while at the same time being small enough to allow direct and lively communication between the whole group.

As soon as the group starts to get any larger than that, ways of working have to be developed that will ensure that everyone can take part in the working pro-

	Plenum	Small groups
Function:	Integrating the whole group	Mobilizing individuals
Advantages:	■ Everyone is present ■ Everyone can see everyone else ■ Everyone hears the same thing	■ Lively discussion ■ Active participation ■ Personal contact
Disadvantages:	■ Limited dialogue ■ Limited participation ■ Quasi-"public" results ■ No overview possible	■ Only intermediate steps are possible ■ Immediate pressure for
Suitable for:	■ Creating transparency ■ Creating a sense of community ■ Exchanging information ■ Clarifications, reaching agreement ■ Gathering opinions ■ Creating "loyalty" and committment to common actions and projects	■ Developing ideas (brainstorming) ■ Developing concepts ■ Systematic analysis ■ In-depth discussion and debate ■ Specific details ■ Detailed planning

cess actively enough. Plenary sessions become more cumbersome and have a paralyzing effect after a time. The human resources that are present cannot be used to their best any more. Work in subgroups becomes an important tool.

The dynamics and efficiency of the working process basically depend on maintaining useful interaction between group work and plenary sessions.

● *When should groups be kept as small as possible?*

- – When the participants still have to get to know one another.
- – When particularly personal problems are involved.
- – When what matters is every individual being able to contribute ideas.

● *When are larger groups preferable?*

- – When the number of groups necessary would otherwise be too large. More than three presentations of group results one after another at the plenum have a tiring effect.
- – When it is more a matter of gathering ideas, rather than in-depth discussion.

● *When should all the groups be given the same task?*

- – In principle, whenever something new has to be developed: ideas, approaches to solving problems, strategies, plans of action.
- – When it is important to get as many alternatives and variants as possible, so that they can be compared.

● *When can different tasks be assigned?*

- – When all the basic questions have already been cleared up, and it is "routine" work that is being distributed, so that progress can be as fast as possible.
- – When specific, detailed plans are needed on various previously elaborated individual topics.

● *When should the composition of small groups be changed?*

- – As often as possible – at least for each new topic (getting a good mix of people is important for developing relationships evenly throughout the overall group).

● *When should the composition of small groups be left unchanged?*

- – When several working steps on the same topic take place one after another.

● *What is not suitable for group work?*

- – Editing texts that are longer than one sentence (this should be reserved in principle for individual work).

Personal Feedback

5

Collective maladjustment

It is a sad, but true statement: our civilization is sick. We no longer live a natural life. We behave toward each another in an alarmingly artificial way. Stiff, ritualized activities dominate the scene. Openness and honesty seem to have been lost. We have simply forgotten an ability we still had as children – to tell each other spontaneously what we think and feel. We can think of a thousand reasons why it would be hurtful, or even dangerous, to be open in direct contact with people. And we even still believe this.

It is the present crisis that is forcing us to reevaluate things. The social sciences teach us that openness and trust in interpersonal relationships are associated with effectiveness; that without openness, fruitful teamwork is not possible; and that all the new, "lean" concepts of organization simply cannot be made to work alongside the behavioral norms of the past.

And before you know it, age-old human virtues such as spontaneity, being emotional, being able to cope with conflict – which used to be systematically condemned in the field of management – suddenly become strategic factors for success. In many companies today, therefore, we are facing for reasons of sheer survival a need to learn and practice from scratch something that is actually quite natural and normal: how to be open with one another – in the way that is necessary for, and not an obstacle to, fruitful coexistence and cooperation.

The meaning of feedback

What decides success or failure in the field of professional work is not the way a person is, but the way he is perceived to be by others. If someone can become aware of the impression he makes on other people, it has two basic consequences: first, he understands other people's behavior toward him better than he did before; and secondly, he will be able to control his own behavior better – in a more deliberate way adapted to specific situations.

But the impression someone makes on other people usually remains hidden from the person concerned. Most people have inhibitions about telling other people openly and honestly what they notice and what they feel. The main reason for this is: fear of "hurting" others. Bosses are usually the last people to receive open feedback from their employees. Due to the hierarchical dependency involved, the boss's behavior becomes a taboo topic. Fear of punitive measures stands in the way of open criticism from the outset. But this means missing opportunities for developing the social competence that is so important, particularly for managers.

But what people have forgotten, they can certainly re-learn. The goal of personal feedback consists first in

> Sharpening the individual's self-perception

as a precondition for better control of one's own behavior. The second element consists of developing

> Openness, honesty, and trust in direct working, management, and cooperative relationships

as a precondition for a healthy emotional relationship structure, for fruitful collaboration – and thus for a high degree of effectiveness in the team as a whole.

Specific questions and answers

What does personal feedback mean?

Giving people openly stated reactions on the impression they make on others – i.e., the way their behavior is perceived by others.

What is the purpose of personal feedback in a team?

First: *personal development* for the individual concerned – particularly the development of social competence.

Secondly: *team development* – particularly the development of healthy emotional relationships as a precondition for effective collaboration.

Personal feedback is therefore an investment in the individual person, as well as an investment in the team as an organizational unit.

A genuinely open and team-oriented management culture can only really be established when views about management and collaboration are discussed openly within the individual team. Open feedback is one of the fundamental preconditions for teams to achieve self-organization and self-guidance inside lean structures.

Where is personal feedback practiced?

There is a basic distinction to be made between openness in a personal and private talk, and openness in a team. The individual learning effect and its benefits in everyday life are clearly highest when personal feedback is exchanged within

Figure 22. Personal feedback – extent of formalization

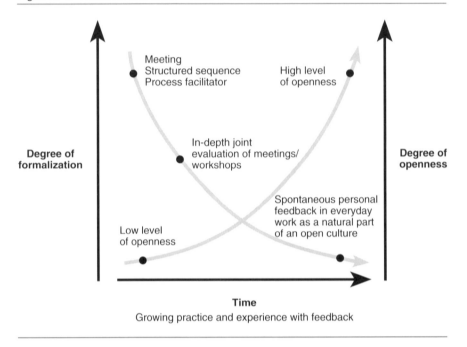

Degree of formalization

Meeting
Structured sequence
Process facilitator

High level
of openness

In-depth joint
evaluation of meetings/
workshops

Degree of openness

Spontaneous personal
feedback in everyday
work as a natural part
of an open culture

Low level
of openness

Time
Growing practice and experience with feedback

management itself, in a working group, in a project team – i.e., wherever several people have direct personal experience in dealing with one another.

How can personal feedback be introduced?

Both giving feedback and receiving it usually have to be learned and practiced. If there is absolutely no practical experience with feedback available, you have to start with structured and chaired forms of discussion, which can gradually turn into more spontaneous forms and finally become a natural part of an open and lively enterprise culture (see Figure 22: "Personal feedback – extent of formalization").

What does a structured feedback exercise in a team consist of?

It takes the form of a private meeting. Each member of the team is given a time allowance of an hour to ninety minutes in which the team concerns itself personally with him or her. This type of individual feedback round typically goes through four phases: first, positive feedback from the other members of the team; secondly, critical feedback; thirdly, requests and suggestions on collaboration afterward; fourthly, summing up and comments from the recipient (see Figure 23 : "Phases of a feedback session").

Figure 23. Phases of a feedback session

Phase 1   All the team members respond to the following questions:

- *What is it about you that I like?*
- *What is it that I think you do particularly well?*
- *What do I see as being your strengths?*

Phase 2   All the team members respond to the following questions:

- *What disturbs, annoys, confuses me, or makes me feel insecure sometimes?*
- *What is it that I think you don't do particularly well?*
- *Where is it that I think you stand in your own way?*

Phase 3   All the team members respond to the questions:

- *What would I pay particular attention to in your place?*
- *What is it that I think you might be able to do differently and better?*
- *What would I wish for in the future if I were you?*

The "recipient" listens carefully during each of these three phases, and asks questions if anything is unclear. He does not contradict, does not give explanations, and does not try to justify himself.

Phase 4   When the feedback is finished, the "recipient" makes his statement:

1 **Short summary**   ($\Rightarrow$ "acknowledgment")
  - *What are the most important points that I have grasped?*

2 **Comments**   ($\Rightarrow$ "shaving insight")
  - *How do I feel about this? What responses does it give rise to?*
  - *What was I already aware of? Which aspects have already been mentioned to me?*
  - *Which aspects are new to me? Which ones surprise me?*

3 **Evaluation**   ($\Rightarrow$ "setting priorities")
  - *Which points give me particular concern?*
  - *What do I want to think over specially?*

Is open feedback equivalent to "brainwashing" or "mental striptease"?

No. Someone who provides feedback does not have to expose his "innermost feelings." Personal privacy is not infringed. There are many personal matters that do not have to be brought up even in an open team discussion – e.g., salary matters, or personal career considerations. It is simply a matter of talking openly about the factual forms of communication, management and collaboration during everyday work. It is a matter of the way an individual appears, not of the very core of his personality (see Figure 25: "Areas of the individual").

Does feedback in a team mean the boss being appraised by his employees?

Yes and no. In the sense of an assessment, giving marks out of ten, commenting on abilities and qualifications: definitely not. In the sense of an exchange in a spirit of partnership concerning the personal impression made in the context of management and cooperative relationships: yes. Feedback makes hierarchical boundaries in a team softer, but it does not abolish them.

Does feedback replace institutionalized discussions with employees?

No. The only purpose of feedback is to create more openness and clarity in working relationships, supplementing the normal tools of management. It replaces neither target agreement discussions nor discussions concerning personnel appraisal and development.

What are the preconditions for constructive feedback?

Willingness on the part of all the members of the team – including the boss – to learn something new; a certain basic mutual acceptance of one another (sufficient trust that no one wants to "hurt" others); a calm working atmosphere; enough time; neutral process facilitating (at least on the first couple of occasions); and a few important rules of language (see Figure 26: "Guidelines for personal feedback").

Is feedback not based on completely subjective perceptions?

Yes, exactly. Feedback does not mean communicating "objective truth," but personal and thus subjective perceptions. One and the same form of behavior may be perceived and experienced completely differently by two different people.

What is the point of exchanging completely subjective perceptions?

If, as the boss, I am aware that employee X needs an hour of peace and quiet in the early morning before she warms up, and feels pressurized if I get her involved in discussions as soon as she comes into the office, whereas employee Y is an

Figure 24. Eight rules for personal feedback

- **"I'm OK – you're OK"**
  Feedback about your personal behavior is an opportunity to learn more about how other people perceive you. These perceptions are not objective truths, and are not value-judgments. In addition, they do not affect the core of the personality, but only how you come across.

- **Describe – don't evaluate**
  People giving feedback describe their own perceptions and observations – i.e., what they have noticed about the other person. And they describe how they respond to this: feelings, perceptions, questions, thoughts. They do not pass value-judgments, they do not make accusations, they do not moralize.

- **Always give positive feedback first**
  There should be either positive and critical feedback, or none at all – and the positive feedback should always be given first. It is important that both the "giver" and the "receiver" should consider both aspects. One-sidedness always leads to distortions. In addition, positive aspects help the "receiver" to accept critical remarks and "digest" them.

- **Feedback should be as specific as possible**
  Commonplaces and abstract ideas are no use to the "recipient." Feedback should be specific and comprehensible. It is best when practical examples from working with one another are used to underpin it. (Although single examples should never be "dramatized"!)

- **Everyone speaks for himself**
  Everyone uses the form "I" ("I feel ..., I find ...") and not "one" or you" ("you feel ..., one finds ..."). The feedback provider addresses the recipient directly and personally. Everyone refers to their own experiences and feelings.

- **Giving a signal when disturbances happen**
  If anyone feels hurt or insecure in the immediate situation, he should inform the others immediately so that it can be talked about.

- **Everyone is responsible for himself**
  Feedback is not a matter of passing a verdict and asserting obligations, but instead involves an opportunity to explore oneself. The "receiver" can decide for himself what he wants to take in and accept, and if appropriate try to change – as well as what he does not accept.

- **Strict confidentiality**
  Everything that is said in the context of personal feedback must remain exclusive to those who are present, and must not be communicated to outsiders.

Figure 25. Aereas of the individual

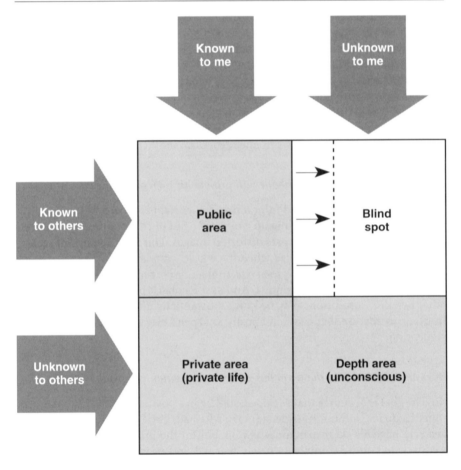

Feedback relates to personal presentation –
not the essence of character

early riser and appreciates it when I have time for him early in the morning because it means he can then plan his day properly – then I can make everybody's life easier if I start the day with Y. Or if I know that my occasional ironic remarks don't disturb most of my employees, but make a few of them feel completely insecure – then I can refrain from them now and then without any loss of self-respect. In short, open feedback makes situational management very much easier.

Is that all it involves: comparing subjective perceptions?

No. If most or even all of the team members say they have the impression that I am not representing our common interests strongly enough further up in the company; that my strict style of conducting meetings is felt to be obstructing open discussion in the whole team; that there is a substantial gap between target agreements or what is said in personnel development discussions and the reality that follows; or that my occasional criticism of conditions and shortcomings is perceived as giving a "public reprimand" to employees – then of course these are still just subjective perceptions. But it will be difficult for me to pretend that I don't need to change my ways in one respect or another.

Is there not a danger that someone will project his own problems onto others?

Yes, this is a basic danger, and in practice it does happen now and then. Giving people feedback means "holding up a mirror" – but of course mirrors may need cleaning, and they can also create distorted images. This is an important reason why feedback is best exchanged when the whole team is present. As a recipient of the feedback you learn how to assess subjective perceptions properly relative to their place in the overall context. And as a feedback provider, you learn that other people's perceptions may be quite substantially different from your own. In other words, feedback systematically sharpens everyone's faculty of social perception.

Does open feedback in the team basically require a neutral group leader?

No. The goal is of course that a team should be in a position to provide open personal feedback without outside support. After all, not everyone on a ski slope needs to have his ski instructor with him. But for the first two or three times, if feedback has to be completely newly learned and practiced, qualified expert assistance is strongly recommended. In the first place, the methods involved can be learned properly and much faster from the start. Secondly, the presence of a "neutral" person can give all the team members a sense of security as they enter this "fresh territory."

Figure 26. Guidelines for personal feedback

Goals

1 I learn more about the way that other people perceive me and my behavior.
2 I can learn and practice how to critically assess myself and my behavior.
3 I can learn and practice how to give other people both positive and critical feedback on their own behavior, in a constructive way.

Principles

- The essential point for my personal success at work is not the way I am, but the way that other people perceive me.
- The way that other people perceive me is normally hidden from me.
- Most people have inhibitions about telling other people openly and honestly about the way they perceive them.
- The main reason for a lack of openness in dealing with one another is fear – fear of being hurt and fear of punitive reactions.
- Partners at work know a great deal about the way I appear, and it would be extremely valuable for me to know this as well.
- If partners at work are sure it is what I really want, they will be willing to tell me what they see about the way I appear.
- If I know how other people perceive me, I will be able to understand their behavior toward me better than before.
- If I know what effects I have on other people, I will be able to steer my own behavior better.
- As an executive, I also am a "coach" to my employees – and one of a coach's most important tasks is to provide open feedback.
- As the "coach," I can only be genuinely effective if my employees tell me about the way they perceive my management behavior.

Individual preparation for personal feedback

We've now been working together for quite some time. I don't know my colleague (or boss) quite so well privately, but I've seen a lot of him/her at work and have gathered quite a few personal impressions. I have seen him/her in lots of different situations, and have had informal contact with him/her quite often.

Based on my experience with him so far, I wonder:

- What are the things I like about him? Which things does he do particularly well? What are his strengths?
- What disturbs, annoys, confuses me, or makes me feel insecure sometimes? Which things does he not do particularly well? In what ways does he sometimes stand in his own way?

I wonder ...

- Would I trust him to run a company that I had inherited and could not run myself for various reasons?
- Could I see him as my own personal boss?
- Would I like to have him as my direct employee in a team?
- Would I choose him as my partner to go on a difficult two-person expedition with?

I ask myself the following questions:

- *What positive thoughts and pleasant feelings do these images give rise to for me?*
- *What critical thoughts and unpleasant feelings do these images give rise to for me?*
- *What specific observations and experiences (statements or behavior of my colleague) probably gave rise to these perceptions?*

I will take quarter of an hour (alone, in peace and quiet, without disturbances) before our workshop meeting, for each member of our team. I will ask myself the above questions and try to discern my responses to them. I will make notes about my impressions, observations and feelings in keyword form – to provide the basis for the personal feedback I offer at the workshop.

Figure 27. Running a feedback session

Participants	All team members (management, working group, project team)
Place	Away from the office, in a quiet conference hotel venue (where everyone can stay overnight)
Time required	One and a half to two days (depending on the size of the team)
Introduction	First half hour for "warming up" and explaining the organization, time plan, and rules
Room	Quiet and well-lit, comfortable chairs, in a circle (without a table)
Materials	One flip chart, one or two pinboards (for visualizing the time plan, rules, main questions)
Principles	■ A feedback round for each team member (including the boss) ■ About one hour per feedback round (4–5 people) or ninety minutes (6–8 people) ■ A break of fifteen minutes to half an hour after each feedback round ■ The evening and at least an hour at the close are kept free as a time ■ margin for catching up ■ The first time: plan for no more than four feedback rounds per day

Sample timetable for a feedback meeting with seven team members

Day 1		Day 2	
8.30 a.m.	Introduction	8.30 a.m.	*Feedback round 5*
9 a.m.	*Feedback round 1*	10 a.m.	Break
10.30 a.m.	Break	10.30 a.m.	*Feedback round 6*
11.00 a.m.	*Feedback round 2*	12.00 a.m.	Break
12.30 a.m.	Break	1.30 p.m.	*Feedback round 7*
2 p.m.	*Feedback round 3*	3 p.m.	Break
3.30 p.m.	Break	3.30 p.m.	Time margin (option)
4 p.m.	*Feedback round 4*	4.30 p.m.	Review of meeting
5.30 p.m.	Quick review of meeting	5 p.m.	Close

Ideal format: everyone arrives the previous evening; joint discussion of the program followed by evening meal and informal get-together; program starts next morning with feedback round 1 straight away.
In general: informal contacts during the breaks and in the evening are extremely important for consolidating individual relationships and for the process as a whole.

Figure 28. Preparing for the first feedback meeting

Principles	■ Preparatory meeting with everyone in the team present
	■ Together with the facilitator
	■ At least four to six weeks ahead of time
	■ Time required: about two or three hours (if there is no previous experience)
	■ Aims and procedures to be discussed in detail
	■ If there are any serious reservations: discuss these calmly (if necessary allowing time for reflection and postponing the decision)
Agenda	▶ Goals (what the purpose of feedback is)
	▶ "Philosophy" (principles, model of the individual)
	▶ Sequence of events in a feedback session (phases and rules)
	▶ Time-table of the feedback meeting
	▶ Role assignments for the boss, employees, facilitator
	▶ Individual preparation
	▶ Organization (place and time)
Working papers	Handing out appropriate documentation

The question **"Who belongs to the team?"** is not always easy to answer in reality. In some teams, the secretary is part of the team, in others not. Or there are people representing central, specialized operations who regularly attend management meetings and therefore "half-belong." The decision depends on the situation. In general:

1) Those who really belong to the organizational "family": the boss, plus direct employees with core tasks.

2) At least at the beginning, additional participants should only be included if no one (including the boss) would feel inhibited by their presence in relation to openness toward other members of the core team.

3) In case of doubt, the size of the group should also be taken into account. Five or six people are ideal, seven or eight are still no problem. But larger groups already require more than two days. Communications become more difficult. The individual receives less attention.

Figure 29. When are feedback exercises not appropriate?

● *Lack of basic mutual acceptance*
Individual relationships, or all of the relationships in the "team," are hopelessly wrecked. People are associating with one another exclusively at the tactical level, but basically think little of each other. Feedback in the team would be nothing but an alibi exercise.

● *Completely new team*
People don't really know each other yet. There is a lack of practical experience in working together and dealing with each other. (On the other hand, if only one or two of the team members are new and they have all been working together for a couple of months already, personal feedback will be useful.)

● *Dissolving the team*
Restructuring is about to take place, and the team members are not going to be working together in the future. This by no means implies that personal feedback is not useful here. Each of the individuals could gain valuable information for themselves. But the "investment in the team" would be lacking.

● *The group has no team function whatsoever*
The team is not a real team: there are no common goals, no common tasks, no connections. They just happen to have the same boss. Feedback in the overall group is practically pointless. (However, independent

profit centers in one business area can certainly have strategic tasks in common!)

- *One of the team members is basically questionable*
  One member of the group is on the "blacklist." It is already known that he will soon be leaving for reasons of ability. Constructive feedback is not possible in this case. Feedback would degenerate either into a general "settling of accounts" or an insincere show. Plus: within the company, "feedback" would then be labeled "means of introducing sackings."

- *Acute conflicts or crises*
  There is an acute conflict between two or more people in the team that has not yet been resolved. This would superimpose itself on the personal feedback and at least partly obstruct constructive feedback.

- *High degree of openness in everyday work*
  Although this is rarely the case, it does happen: people already have a degree of openness in everyday work and an ability to work through conflicts that make it completely superfluous to carry out a feedback exercise as a special event.

The most important feedback rule: *describe, don't evaluate*

Why are most people afraid of "hurting" someone if they give them personal feedback? There is one good reason: the "filing cabinet" mechanism.

We can't see inside other people. All that we can make out are the factual forms of behavior. But we are simply not rational beings. We have a tendency to *interpret* what we perceive in others – and then *evaluate* the person on the basis of this interpretation. To make life easier for ourselves, we add two things to our observations: first, the *motives* for the behavior; and secondly the *characteristics* that these motives and forms of behavior are based on. And what we read into other people in this process is not always very flattering. What is involved here is not just a process of insinuation, but so-called *projection*.

Projections have effects.

First, it is insinuated that the other person "just is the way he is," and is therefore incapable of behaving any differently. He is branded, put in a specific pigeon-hole, and put away once and for all in the filing cabinet.

Secondly, a form of *selective perception* immediately comes into effect: from now on, you practically only notice things that confirm your own prejudices.

Thirdly, you assume – and quite rightly – that the other person would feel *hurt* if you gave him your honest opinion about him. The result is that feedback fails to happen – potential and necessary changes in behavior do not take place. And because they fail to happen, your own image of the person is constantly "confirmed" and strengthened.

When open feedback is carried out, it is a matter of converting this vicious circle into a positive effect – i. e., finding a form of communication that will allow important information to be passed on without causing injury. The most important rule is therefore: *describe, don't evaluate.*

What can be described?

1) Perceived behavior
⇨ What do I see, experience, observe …?

E.g.: *"You often ask to see me right away without any warning, without worrying about where I happen to be or what I am doing at the time."*

2) One's own feelings, perceptions, questions
⇨ What feelings does this trigger in me …?

E.g.: *"I feel like I'm your slave. I have the feeling I'm just at your disposal and that I'm not being taken seriously as a partner."*

3) Effects on practical work
⇨ What effects does this have on working processes …?

E.g.: *"My whole time plan gets messed up. But mainly: I get pulled out of meetings where a lot of other people are involved. Some of them have even traveled a long way to be there. In every single case, massive delays in working processes and decision-making processes are the result."*

What does evaluation mean?

1) Making sweeping value-judgments

E.g.: *"You are a tyrant."*
"You are completely chaotic."
"You are undisciplined and disorganized."

2) Making accusations

E.g.: *"You always think only about yourself and never about other people."*
"You abuse your power as the boss at my expense."
"You prevent efficient and productive work from being carried out here."

3) Making self-righteous insinuations

E.g.: *"You couldn't care less about the fact that you are completely ruining my work program."*
"You seem to enjoy pulling all the strings."
"All you're worried about is the impression you make further up – you don't care about anything else."

Consistently following this rule has two effects. First, the *feedback receiver* will also be able to accept critical feedback, because he does not feel that his personal integrity is being infringed on. This is a fundamental precondition for changing behavior. Secondly, the *feedback provider* learns how to question the distorted images he has of the people he is working with. He learns how to be more careful in his judgments. He learns how to give other people a chance.

Process-Oriented Project Management

There are several fundamental differences between process-oriented project management and conventional technocratic models. The main difference lies in the wholistic way of seeing things and proceeding, or – to put it another way – in the way it takes account of the *strategic and political dimensions of project work*. A project manager who thinks it is enough to use methodologically "clean" procedures to bring a large and complex project successfully to fruition is being naive, and will ultimately cause his or her company a massive loss of valuable resources. Two particular aspects – neither of which is mentioned in any of the existing handbooks – are largely decisive for the course of project work: *dynamics* and *networking*.

- *Energy*: Where does the "ownership" lie – who regards the project as his "own affair"? Which people are interested in the success of the project and prepared to give their personal commitment to it?
- *Power*: Who has how much influence on what happens? What are the "key hierarchies," who are the informal "opinion leaders," and how can they be won over?
- *Force field*: What are the overall influences promoting or obstructing things – and what are the effects of these force fields on the practicability of the measures being taken?
- *Networking*: What is the context that the project is embedded in? Who needs to be actively brought into it on which questions? What are the information and communication channels that need to be established to ensure low friction project work?

These and similar questions are in the foreground to begin with – and they will arise again and again during the further course of the project. Attention focuses on the people involved in the project and the individuals and groups affected by it – i.e., on the dynamic range of events in a field of high tension involving vested interests, needs, motivations, and power structures. The dynamic is ultimately based on the various driving energies and resistances present in each situation – with some elements always taking place on the surface, while others go on in the dark. Often, precisely what is most important takes place under "false colors."

A checklist

To help design specific projects, we have summed up the essential points in an initial checklist (Figure 30). In what follows, each point is briefly sketched in, with specific queries. Because in the end, everything depends on asking the right questions. If this is done, the steps to take in each specific case usually follow by themselves.

Questions to clear up ahead of time

> *"He who misses the first buttonhole*
> *will never manage to button up."*
> Goethe

A lot of the confusions and disturbances that develop in projects result from the fact that they were started on the basis of presuppositions that were not articulated. People more or less tumbled into the project by accident. The following points are intended to serve as test questions for a screening phase during which the weak points in a project can be recognized and rectified at an early stage. The important thing is to "tether the cow before you start milking it" (as they say in South Africa).

Reasons for the project and issues at stake

- Is the reason for the project as described a sensible one, or does it look like more of an excuse, with the real motive not being openly revealed?
- Has the situation occurred in this form for the first time? Or is there previous experience of it?
- Is a real analysis wanted, or are there diagnoses and possible solutions – spoken or unspoken – already available?
- Does the problem sound plausible? Is it important and complex enough to justify starting a project?

Client and contract partner

- How serious are the initiators of a project, or how serious do they seem to be, in their willingness to deal with the problem?
- Are they genuinely or only indirectly responsible for the topic?
- To what extent are they affected by the problem themselves at all?
- To what extent are they themselves part of the problem?
- To what extent are they reasonable enough and willing to contribute what they can to a solution in so far as they form part of the problem?
- Why have they not previously solved the problem themselves?

People concerned and people whose interests are affected

- Who does the problem directly concern?
- Who does it concern indirectly, so that they might have an interest either in perpetuating or altering existing conditions?
- To what extent can and should those concerned, and those with vested interests in the process of working through the problem, be involved – and do they want to be involved?

Figure 30. Checklist for project work

Points to clear up ahead of time:

- ❒ Reasons for the project and issues at stake
- ❒ Client/Contract partner
- ❒ People concerned and people whose interests are affected
- ❒ Inclusion of works council/personnel committee
- ❒ Goals and expectations
- ❒ Restrictions and taboos
- ❒ Planned procedure
- ❒ Time scale
- ❒ Criteria for success
- ❒ Reasons for the status quo
- ❒ Project liabilities
- ❒ Dependencies and networking
- ❒ Project culture and company culture
- ❒ Project management
- ❒ Project team
- ❒ Resources
- ❒ Inconsistencies and critical points

Decisive factors affecting the project:

- ❒ Guidelines for project work
- ❒ Project organization
- ❒ Decision-making structures
- ❒ Analyzing force fields
- ❒ The project's "underworld"
- ❒ Topography of the project
- ❒ Project supervision and team maintenance

Works council and personnel committees

- To what extent is the project subject to the legal requirements for workers' participation?
- Are there aspects of the problem that favor providing more participation than is legally required?

Goals and expectations

- What are the client's expectations? What is supposed to be different in one or two years' time from the way it is now?
- How specific and measurable are the goals described?
- Are there any signs that people are harboring concealed expectations?
- What are the declared or covert expectations of the other people who are affected, or who have vested interests?
- How plausible, realistic, and compatible are these expectations as a whole?

Restrictions and taboos

- What does the client, or what do the other people who are affected or who have vested interests, *not* want? What things should not be allowed to happen?
- Can these things be openly discussed?
- Are the reasons for these restrictions understandable and plausible?
- Are there taboo topics or questions?

Planned procedure

- Are there any particular ideas or constraints with regard to the methodological procedure?
- Do the planned or desired methods match the procedure that has to be selected with a view to the problem and the goals that have been set? If outside advisers are to be used:
- Can the client and those affected, or those who have vested interests, understand in detail the consultant's suggested ways of proceeding?
- Do they understand the consultant's concepts and the philosophy that lies behind them? Are they capable of judging what is in store for them?
- Do they feel competent enough to direct the project themselves – or would they prefer, for better or worse, to allow the outsiders to lead them by the hand?

Time scale

- How much time do the client and the others affected or interested think it is going to take?
- How realistic is this? Is it possible to push the project through in this amount of time?

Criteria for success

- What quantitative and qualitative criteria will be used to judge the success of the project?

Reasons for the status quo

- Why are things still the way they are – if so many people are allegedly suffering from these conditions? In other words, what is the "rationale" behind existing conditions?
- Who benefits from the status quo – who would benefit from the change?
- Are the contractpartner and those affected or interested unanimous in this assessment – or are there differences of opinion?

Project liabilities

- Is the topic a completely new one, or have people been working on it before? If they have, what was the outcome, what experience was gained, and what effects did it have?
- What is the "image" that the topic or project has in the company? Is it burdened in any way with bad associations from earlier on?
- What are the implications of this for the procedures that are planned?

Dependencies and networking

- Are there projects already in existence with similar tasks?
- Are there other current topics that can or must be linked to the questions involved here?
- Has the topic been approached previously from a different point of view?

Project culture and company culture

- How strongly is the company orientated around the division of labor principle, and how strong is its orientation toward hierarchy?
- How much experience and ability does the company have in controlling complex projects?
- To what extent is teamwork part of the company's existing culture?

Project management

- Is there enough *specialist ability* for the specialized questions that come up to be assessed correctly?
- Is there enough *methodological competence* for all the correct procedures, instruments, and processes to be chosen in this case?
- Is the required *social competence* available to deal actively with the various people, groups, and group-dynamic processes associated with the project – particularly in difficult, conflict-ridden situations?

- Is there enough *time* and *personal commitment* available for those concerned to devote themselves to the project to the extent that is, or could become, necessary?
- Have reserves been included in the planning to allow *team inspection* of the project groups and to resolve any unexpected disturbances that may arise in connection with the project?

Project team

- Has it been ensured that all of the envisaged members of the project group, in addition to all their other very welcome qualifications, definitely meet one fundamental requirement – that they can *work in a team*?
- Do the envisaged members of the project group as a whole have enough *specialist competence* to understand what it is all about and to be able to assess correctly the specialist questions that may come up?
- Is sufficient *methodological competence* available on the whole for the planned methods, instruments, and processes to be applied? If not: is there a willingness among the team members, and is it possible for them, to receive suitable training or use external resources?
- Is there enough *social competence* in the team as a whole for them to find constructive ways of dealing with the other people, groups, and group-dynamic processes within the framework of the project – particularly in difficult, conflict-ridden situations?
- Is the group able and willing to apply this ability to its own situation as well, and subject itself to a shared and critical *self-examination* at regular intervals?
- Is it clear to all the members of the group that the success of the project depends to a very great extent on their willingness to further develop their social skills?
- Are the *energy, commitment,* and *time available* among the planned members of the project group realistically in proportion to the probable demands that will be made of them?
- Is it clear to everyone that – in addition to the factual problems and questions of substance associated with the project – disturbances may, and probably will, arise in its surrounding circumstances, even including group-dynamic tensions among the project team itself – and that working through these difficulties is part of their "job"?

Resources

- Has a more or less sound and plausible assessment been made of the costs that are going to be necessary in addition to manpower – e.g., equipment and materials, rooms, finance, availability of people who may need to be interviewed or take part in workshops, and possible external support?
- Is this assessment more or less shared by all those entitled to pass judgment on it?

Inconsistencies and critical points

- What aspects seem to be contradictory overall, when everything so far known is put together?
- To what extent do the restrictions and taboos imposed call the project's goals or the procedures necessary for it into question?
- What do the prospects for success look like if the subject is approached in the way planned or suggested under these circumstances ?
- What are the critical questions or "bottleneck factors" that need to have an eye kept on them?

Decisive factors affecting the project

Guidelines for project work

What has generally proved its worth in the field of management and development can also be important for project work: orientation toward a clear model. Formulated and published as "rules" or "principles," the basic philosophy will give all of those involved a chance to orientate themselves better and if necessary protest about procedures and behavior deviating from these principles. "Participation by those affected," "open information for everyone," "support for self-help," "as much self-management as possible," "consistently keeping to deadlines and agreements"- principles such as these are examples of elements of the philosophy that may be essential.

Project organization

- *Duty book*: a so-called "duty book" can be used for the following:
  1. To describe the *targets* as specifically as possible, so that the future people are striving for can be imagined in as concrete a way as possible.
  2. To list the *tasks and activities* that need to be carried out to reach these goals.
  3. To present the *quantitative and qualitative criteria* by which success is to be measured.
  4. To produce a graphic representation on a time axis, showing the planned *procedural steps* in the form of a *project matrix,* including the necessary communication with those affected and those with vested interests – and with clearly marked *milestones:* starting point, end point, and all the essential interim points (see Figure 31: example of a project matrix).
  5. To take into account *disturbances in the project team and in the project's environments,* which are more difficult to plan for, but very likely to happen, so that enough of a *time cushion* is available (this time plan will need to be checked and updated at regular intervals).

Figure 31. Example of a project matrix

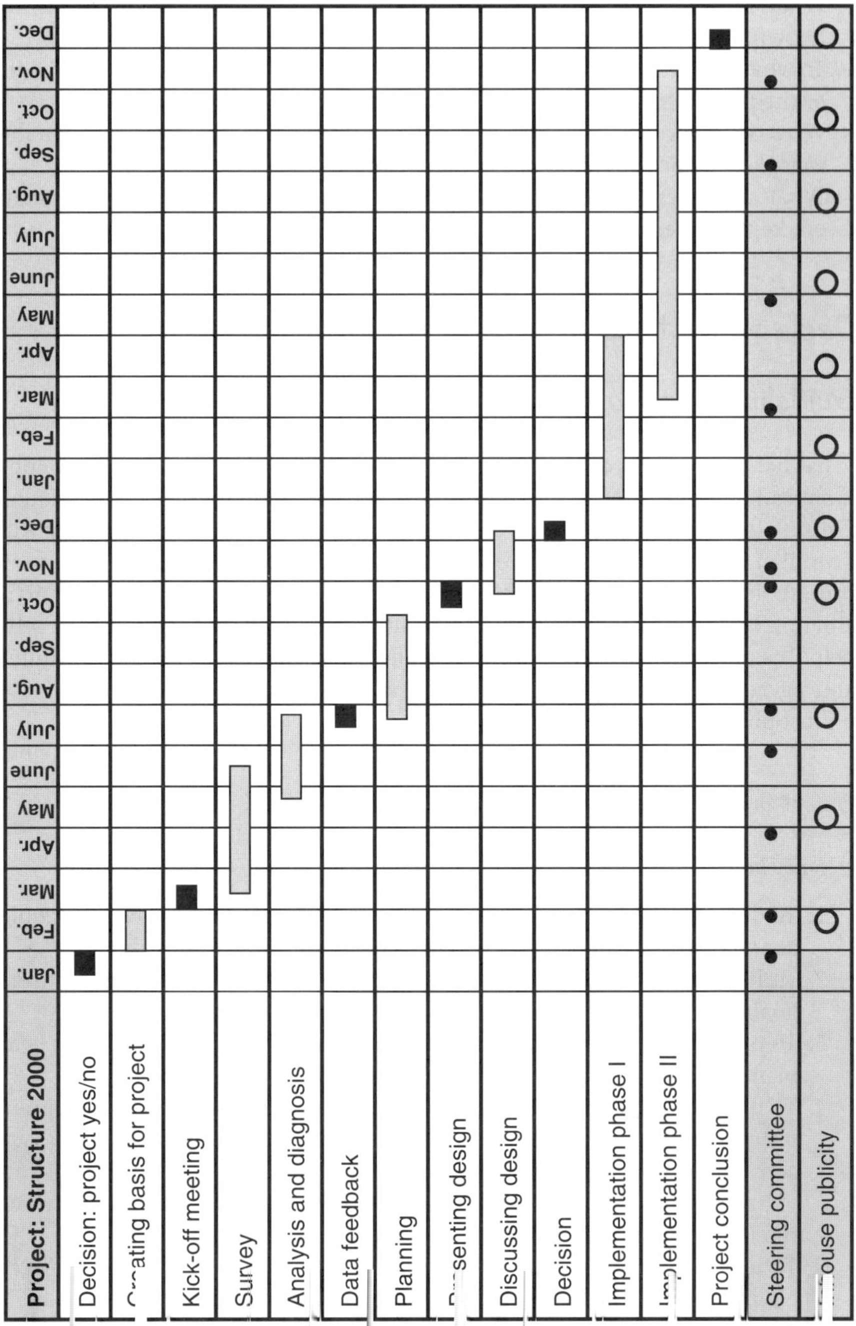

Project: Structure 2000

Activity	Jan.	Feb.	Mar.	Apr.	May	June	July	Aug.	Sep.	Oct.	Nov.	Dec.	Jan.	Feb.	Mar.	Apr.	May	June	July	Aug.	Sep.	Oct.	Nov.	Dec.
Decision: project yes/no	■																							
Creating basis for project		▯																						
Kick-off meeting			■																					
Survey			▯	▯	▯																			
Analysis and diagnosis						▯	▯																	
Data feedback							■																	
Planning								▯	▯															
Presenting design										■														
Discussing design											▯													
Decision												■												
Implementation phase I													▯	▯	▯									
Implementation phase II														▯	▯	▯	▯	▯	▯	▯	▯	▯	▯	
Project conclusion																								■
Steering committee	●	●		●	●	●	●				● ●	●		●		●					●		●	
...ouse publicity		○		○		○				○		○		○		○		○		○		○		○

- *Allotting tasks and roles*: In the course of an open discussion, tasks and roles are allotted to individual members on the basis of recognizable specialist and personal abilities in the team, so that everyone can see what is going on. As far as possible without affecting the project as whole, expectations for personal development and people's needs to make a mark are admissible and can be taken into account.
- *Working organization – project group or steering group*: Depending on the complexity of the tasks involved, the work can be done in a single project group, or in several teams under the direction of a control group.

  If the task is easily comprehensible factually, manageable in terms of its content, and if there are no other social or company policy aspects pointing to the inclusion of other persons and groups, we recommend commissioning a *project group* to work on the approach to the problem. Working groups with no less than five and no more than seven members have again and again proved to be the most efficient. If the group is too small, there is a danger that the range of ideas will be too narrow. If it gets too big, it uses up too much energy simply managing its internal group dynamics, and ends up spending more time on itself than on its tasks. In other words, the size and composition of such groups need to be decided solely on the basis of the *skills required* and the *functioning of the group,* and not, as so often happens, because various interest groups wish to have proportional representation. This type of desire to participate in shaping events can be taken into account in a wide variety of other ways – such as via questionnaires, permanent advisory committees, or regular hearings in which the current status of the project can be presented and ideas asked for.

  If the task is more complex, if the time expected to be available is relatively short, or there are other reasons to justify it, then several groups can be brought on board right from the start, and several project teams can be set up to work on various parts of the task simultaneously. But these satellite groups need to be commissioned and coordinated by a *steering group.* The sole and decisive criterion for selecting the members of the steering group is whether they have outstanding social and processing skills. Expert, detailed knowledge, or the fact that they belong to a specific department are, by contrast, of secondary importance here.
- *Project promoters*: If a project is subject to special disturbances and dangers from its environment that go beyond the project team's power to manage on its own, it may be advisable to appoint so-called *project promoters*. These are members of the organization who have enough insight and influence to provide appropriate protection when dangers threaten and to forcibly bring about the necessary breakthrough when blockages are attempted. This supportive and protective role can also be met by a correspondingly staffed *project advisory council.*
- *Time management and reporting*: The project leader will coordinate work on the project and the members of the project groups. This requires efficient time management: the availability of those taking part in the project has to be

coordinated with the necessary tasks and deadlines. It is vital for a *deadline framework* to be set up early enough, including all the anticipated meetings and other work demands that can be foreseen – including enough cushion time for things that can't be foreseen.

The project manager will provide an up-to-date form of *documentation* and *reporting* – to support the work of the project team and as a prerequisite for efficient *project control*. This will enable the project staff and the client to be kept informed at regular intervals of the project's progress and the quality of the work, so as to enable them to intervene promptly when there is any deviation from the set standards.

- **Communications concept and project marketing:** At the very start of work on the project, the project group or the control group should produce a special *communications concept* for it. Using a multidimensional matrix model, this will clarify when and how who is to be informed or involved on what by whom.

Depending on the importance of the project and the extent to which you need to win over allies and collaborators, the image of the project can be anchored and encouraged within its wider context using appropriate *project marketing*.

Decision-making structures

When you decide not to approach a problem within the framework of the normal hierarchical organization, often based on the principle of the division of labor, and instead to set up a project organization specially designed for the task, you create a special interface with the official decision-making system. If those with real decision-making power are not fully represented in the project group or steering group, with the necessary decisions already being made in the course of the project work itself, then you need to ensure that the officials or bodies who have formal responsibility are regularly informed or promptly involved – either directly or via an intermediate *steering committee*.

Analyzing force fields

Not just for work on the project, but also above all for the sake of later successful implementation of the project's results in practice, it is decisively important that the attitudes of all the interest groups affected by the project topic should be known:

- *Who is in favor of changing present conditions – and how much energy will they be prepared to put into it?*
- *Who is against change, and what strategies are they likely to use to obstruct or block it?*

- *Who is holding aloof for the moment, but under certain conditions could later become a "supporter" or "opponent"?*
- *What other topics and projects are linked to this project?*
- *What is the nature of the overall force field produced by these interactions for what is planned?*

The project's "underworld"

It is perfectly normal, and no real problem initially, for every project to have other aims that are being pursued alongside the official goals – subsidiary aims which are, of course, perfectly honorable in their way. This only becomes a problem when it is not recognized early enough and not included in the calculations. So the force field analysis needs to be supplemented with this *hidden dimension* as well. The general question is: *What is going on in this project under the surface?*

- *What are the hidden goals that the client is possibly pursuing? For example, using the reorganization to get rid of certain members of staff?*
- *Is it possible that important people affected by the project are remaining in the background and pulling the strings, so that the whole thing could end up as a kind of puppet theater?*
- *How much danger is there that people may be trying to use the project as camouflage to push forward older, previously unsuccessful goals, i. e., pouring old wine into new bottles?*
- *Are there any signs that the whole thing is just an alibi exercise purely intended to prove that it is impossible to achieve the target?*
- *What possible taboos are operating? Where and who are the "sacred cows" concealed?*
- *Does any member of the project team, or the project manager, have real interests, or suspected outside interests connected with the project, that might have an unfavorable influence on its course?*

Topography of the project

It can be highly instructive for the project team to take all the information derived from analyzing the force field and the project's "underworld" and present a description of the situation in visual form as a graphic. The graphic should clarify:

- Links with other topics and projects.
- Relevant environments and surrounding conditions.
- Open and concealed factors, individuals, or groups, that may encourage or hinder the project, and the resulting opportunities and dangers these may present in the short, medium, and longer terms.

Clarifying the dynamics and links in a single image in this way can be a valuable decision-making aid on whether or how the project should be started and run.

Project supervision and team maintenance

The project group – or in more large-scale projects, the steering group – subjects itself to examination at regular intervals (or on an unscheduled basis when there are signs of disturbances). Whether it carries out this examination itself or has it done by external advisors, the questions involved are the same:

- *To what extent is the force field in which the project is moving still comparable to that of the initial situation? In what ways may it be necessary to change the description of the situation?*
- *Are we still aiming for the right targets with this project?*
- *Have we got the right people on board?*
- *Are we working with the best possible methods?*
- *Are we allowing those affected to participate appropriately – as they see it?*
- *How well do decision-makers feel they are involved in the project?*
- *In the course of our practical work on the project, to what extent are we keeping to the original guidelines that we formulated?*
- *How well is our internal project organization working?*
- *How has our communications concept worked so far? What reactions have there been to it?*
- *How happy is each member of the project team with the role he or she is playing? How happy is each with the roles the others are playing, and with the interplay and atmosphere together?*
- *What other possible ways are there of making the work more efficient and satisfying?*

In Part II, Chapter 3, "Phases of the Process and their Pitfalls," we describe in detail the special risks that attend each phase of a project.

Dealing with Resistance

7

Resistance is a perfectly everyday phenomenon at work, and it is a normal accompaniment to every process of development. In practice, nothing can be learned and nothing can be changed without resistance. But resistance, whenever and wherever it appears, means you are forced to pause for thought. You have to give explanations and get involved in discussions, and now and then you even have to accept a change of course. When there is time pressure – and there nearly always is – resistance can seem extremely annoying, possibly even unbearable and unacceptable. You are tempted to dismiss it – but if you do, it is a mistake that you will live to regret bitterly later on. For the progress of any project aiming to implement change, it is decisively important that resistance – in no matter what form – should be recognized in time and responded to properly. If this is not done, serious delays follow, severe obstacles and blockages develop, and expensive mistakes are made. Dealing with resistance constructively is therefore one of the central factors for success in the process of managing change.

What is "resistance"?

> There can always be said to be resistance when planned decisions or agreed measures – which, even on careful examination, seem useful, "logical," or even urgently necessary – meet with vague antipathy, cause reservations that are not immediately comprehensible, or are passively evaded for reasons that are initially unclear, by individuals, groups, or even the whole staff.

Why does resistance arise?

If you seriously try to put yourself in the place of the people affected, the reasons for resistance are really quite obvious. In a slightly simplified form, there are three:

1. The people affected have *not understood* the goals, the background, or the motives for a step that is being taken.

2. The people affected understand what is involved, but *don't believe* what they are being told.
3. The people affected have understood it, and they also believe what they are being told, but *they don't want to cooperate,* because they do not expect any beneficial effects from the measures that are being planned.

The third and last point is the one most frequently encountered, and it is also the most difficult one. Because negative expectations cannot be overcome either by providing extra explanations or by simply affirming one's good intentions.

Resistance as a coded message

If people of normal intelligence who are not suffering from behavioral problems are resisting what seem to be useful measures, then they must have some kind of *doubts, anxieties,* or *fears.* In other words, it is not a matter of objective considerations and logical arguments, but of *emotions* – i.e., feelings.

Whenever there are feelings involved, however, it makes it more difficult to reach an understanding. In the first place, the measures that have been announced can seem somehow "suspicious" to the people who are affected by them, although they may not really know why. Consequently, when they are asked, they are unable to give an immediately plausible explanation, and instead (to avoid looking "stupid") they produce makeshift justifications of some sort.

On the other hand, it is possible that those who are affected do have quite specific anxieties, but through fear of either hurting others or placing themselves in a bad light, would find it embarrassing to talk about them. In this case, too, it is very difficult to find out by putting clear questions and getting direct answers what the real reasons for the problem are.

Both of these cases represent one and the same situation: there is a lack of logical connection between behavior and statements – the real "message" has been put in coded form, so to speak. What matters first is therefore to discover the deeper reasons for the behavior that has been identified, and to decode the hidden message – and it is only then that further steps appropriate to the situation can be decided on.

How to recognize resistance

It is not always easy to recognize resistance. The only thing that is usually clear is that something is not "right." The following are typical signs of resistance in individual people or smaller groups (see Figure 32):

⇨ Things suddenly stop "moving." Work only progresses with laborious effort. Meetings are conducted without any enthusiasm. Decision-making processes grind to a halt.

⇨ People fool about; they discuss trivial questions endlessly; they get tied up in details; no one listens to anybody else; they lose the thread.
⇨ Embarrassing silences occur. People have inhibited looks on their faces. Even employees who are otherwise committed noticeably keep to the background. There is a general sense of helplessness.
⇨ Clear questions are given unclear answers. One or two things seem apparently plausible, but when you listen closely there is a great deal that cannot be properly "pigeonholed."

At the company or corporate level, the following phenomena are typical of resistance:

▶ High numbers of staff off sick, high absence rates and staff fluctuation
▶ Unrest, intrigues, rumors
▶ Bureaucracy, internal communications using memos with page-long "copies to…" lists
▶ High manufacturing reject rates, wastage, breakdowns

These are typical signs of resistance: a vague problem situation – and difficulty in "localizing" what the problem really is.

Figure 32. General symptoms of resistance

	Verbal (spoken)	Nonverbal (behavior)
Active (fight)	**Contradiction**	**Agitation**
	Counterarguments	Unrest
	Accusations	Quarrels
	Threats	Intrigues
	Polemics	Rumors
	Stubborn formalism	Formation of cliques
Passive (flight)	**Evasion**	**Lack of enthusiasm**
	Silence	Carelessness
	Trivializing things	Tiredness
	Fooling about	Staying away
	Making things	Withdrawing into
	look ridiculous	oneself
	Debating unimportant	Going off sick
	matters	

Dealing with resistance constructively

Every employee – whether they are unskilled workers, secretaries, or executives – who is faced with planned changes first asks the following simple questions:

1. **"What is the point of the whole thing?"**
   - *What is the purpose of the exercise, and does it seem to me to be a plausible purpose?*
   - *Is management telling us everything, or are there purposes and background politics they are keeping quiet about?*
   - *Is what is involved really important, or are there maybe more urgent problems that management ought to be giving priority to?*
2. **"Will I be able to cope?"**
   - *Am I capable of coping with what is being planned for me?*
   - *Will I be able to carry out the new or extra tasks expected of me?*
   - *What are my chances of achieving good results in my work, and of achieving personal success?*
3. **"Is this what I want?"**
   - *What is there in it for me? Is the work interesting? Is it well respected within the firm? What sort of people will I be dealing with?*
   - *Is there a risk of losing anything: a safe job, part of my income, a good boss, pleasant colleagues, attractive career prospects?*

The spontaneous initial reaction to resistance is impatience, annoyance, or even personal dismay. The second reaction is to try to eliminate the problem by offering people further explanations. But usually it soon emerges that this is of no help, either. You run the risk of repeating yourself, and every further explanation gives the impression that you are only trying to justify yourself. At this point, it is clear that there must be deeper reasons for the problem.

There is now only one useful and constructive attitude to take: the analytical one. You have to speak to those affected in peace and quiet, either individually or in small groups. Only a calm discussion carried out without any time pressure or pressure for results, in which you can show a sincere interest in the situation of the people who are affected by the changes and in their personal opinions, can create the basis for trust that is needed before the more difficult ideas and feelings can come out. What matters is to put questions and to listen carefully:

- *What is particularly important to those who are affected? What are their interests, needs, and concerns?*
- *What might happen if you carried on as planned? What needs to be avoided, from the point of view of those who are affected?*
- *What are the alternatives, as those who are affected see it? In their view, what needs to be done to solve the problem to the satisfaction of all concerned?*

These kind of question lead step by step closer to the "coded message," and thus to the core of the problem.

The following points, which are relevant to the most important human needs in the working environment, always have to be given special attention:

Pay/salary   Are there direct losses of income, or other indirect financial disadvantages to be expected?

Job security   Is there any fear of a change of job or even losing a job – or are there other incalculable risks that are envisaged?

Contact   Is there a threat that good personal relations – with one's boss, colleagues, employees – may be lost? Is there a fear of being forced to work with particularly difficult or unpleasant people in the new situation?

Recognition   Are people afraid that the new work situation will require too much of them technically, or that they will no longer have the resources needed to carry out their tasks successfully? Does the new task or the new workplace have a bad reputation in the company?

Independence   Is there a risk of losing one's authority to take decisions, or personal scope for action? In the present situation, does one have some indirect influence due to personal relationships, which may be lost in the future?

Development   What training needs and career ambitions are present? What opportunities does the present situation provide – and what does the future structure look like in this regard?

Once it is clear what the main reasons for resistance are, the way is open to negotiate procedures that take the interests of those affected into account, without the goals of the project being questioned.

Example 1: semi-autonomous working groups

In a manufacturing and assembly plant, where work had traditionally been carried out at individual workplaces, it was planned to switch to semi-autonomous group work. The employees were carefully familiarized with the new approach and the advantages it offered: more varied work, more contact with other people, greater flexibility in the way in which work is organized, having a direct influence on organizing working processes. But the majority of them vehemently rejected the project. Initially, the company's management had not the slightest idea why there should be such resistance to the plan, since industrial psychologists had given descriptions painted in the brightest colors of the advantages of the new organizational approach for the employees. What was particularly confusing was that the various reasons for rejection given at works meetings and departmental meetings did not produce a comprehensible picture of what the problem really was. The company was faced with a puzzle. The resistance was so strong that management saw a serious threat to the project. It decided to get to the bottom of things. The following picture emerged from all the individual discussions they held: most of the employees had never worked in a team in their entire lives. They simply could not imagine being able to work productively in immediate dependence on their colleagues in a group, and being able to reach common decisions. They were afraid there would be a constant free-for-all in the group – ending up with poor work quality. "In the job I have today, I know what I have to do – and no one gets in my way in my own work." You cannot make something sound appealing when people know nothing about it. A bird in the hand is worth two in the bush. Once management had understood what employees' reservations were, they made the following agreement with them: to begin with, an experimental phase of six to eight months of group work would be introduced, so that everyone involved could get to know and experience the advantages and disadvantages of the new system. The experimental phase would then be evaluated jointly. If the majority of the employees afterwards still wanted to return to individual working, the experiment would be abandoned. All the employees were able to agree to this. The "experiment" proved extremely successful. After six months, almost no one wanted to go back to the old form of organization. Only one woman and one man felt distinctly uncomfortable working in a team; and it was possible to employ them outside of the teams without any problem.

Example 2: switching to computers

There were twelve switchboard operators working at an answering service, running a large number of phone stations. Each station belonged to a single client, who instead of using an answering machine or a secretary had rented an individual line at the service, which they could switch their calls to when they were away. The whole of the information flow was managed by hand. In front of each customer's line there were two boxes: one for the customer's instructions, and another for incoming messages. The office was one massive jumble of scraps of paper. From morning to night everyone was busy writing, shuffling paper, and filing or destroying handwritten notes. One day, the owner of the business discovered there was a fully developed computer system available abroad with standard software for processing the whole of this information flow on screen. No one would have to scribble any notes any more. There would be no more lost calls due to unreadable handwriting. The switchboard operators would have an immediate overview on their screens of all the messages coming in for each client. In addition, they would no longer have to rush back and forth from one client's line to the next. All the incoming calls, for any client, would automatically be switched to an operator who was free. In spite of the high investment the new system would involve, the firm's owner was very enthusiastic about the idea. He excitedly described this new prospect for the future to his staff – and found he was banging his head against a brick wall. All of the ladies, who had been working with him for many years, gave a thousand reasons why the whole thing was bound to be a flop from the very start, and why there could be no question of using the system "Machines always break down – and then the whole firm would grind to a halt." "Just think how much it would cost – we can't possibly earn enough to pay for all that equipment here." "We're switchboard operators and not data typists." Not one of them said, "I don't know how to use a computer – and I don't think I would be capable of learning." But this was precisely what slowly emerged from all the discussions as being the deeper reason for the opposition to the project. The company's owner made to his employees: "We'll all go to Paris together and have a good look at the company that is already using this system. We'll talk to the switchboard operators there about their experience with it. And then we'll have another discussion about what might be possible here." They went on the trip. Even just the quiet atmosphere and the tidy, clear workplaces at the other company worked miracles. Their French colleagues' experience completely convinced the Zurich switchboard operators. The firm switched to the new system – and no one today would want to go back to the old situation.

Example 3: job rotation for managers

Top management in a multinational corporation was complaining bitterly about its executives' lack of mobility. An urgent need for qualified managers in foreign subsidiaries kept coming up – but almost no one was prepared to transfer from headquarters and go abroad. Some of them said they had just finished building a house; for others, the problem was that the wife didn't want to live too far away from her parents; or the children didn't want to lose all their friends. The problem was examined in greater detail, and the following picture emerged from a large number of interviews:

Some of the wives concerned would actually even find it exciting to spend a couple of years abroad; true, the children did want to keep their friends, but you can't always arrange your life just to suit the kids – and anyway, it's no bad thing for children to get to know a completely new environment. On the other hand, in this company it is not very advisable to go abroad if you want to make a career. The few people who have dared over the years always had to stay there indefinitely. They never found their way back onto the promotion ladder at headquarters. "Anyone who goes away loses touch here. In this company you either make a career at headquarters, or not at all. The elevator only moves vertically. Look at the people at the top of the company. There are people who rose straight from central staff to company management without ever having to do a proper job on the line. But there's not a single person up there who was abroad even just for two years." All it really took was this one statement, along with a few similar ones, to show the company's management where the real problem lay. It was by no means impossible to get qualified managers interested in rotation to foreign branches. But you had to have individual personnel development plans – and clear agreements lasting more than the next couple of months. In short, if you wanted rotation to branches abroad, it had to be *rewarded* instead of being punished. These requirements have been met today – and suitable candidates all of a sudden appeared.

Figure 33. "Resistance" – four principles

1st principle:	***There is no change without resistance*** Resistance to change is a perfectly normal everyday pheno-menon. If resistance does not occur when a change is intro-duced, it means that from the very start no one believes it will work. → *It is not the emergence of resistance that should worry you, but its absence!*
2nd principle:	***Resistance always contains a "coded message"*** When people mount resistance to something that is useful or even necessary, it means they have reservations, anxie-ties, or fears. → *The causes for resistance are emotional by nature.*
3rd principle:	***Ignoring resistance leads to obstructions*** Resistance shows that the conditions required to proceed smoothly as planned are not present, or not yet. Increasing the pressure will only lead to increased counterpressure. → *Provide a pause for thought - take a fresh look at things*
4th principle:	***Move with the resistance, not against it*** The subliminal emotional energy has to be acknowledged – i.e., taken seriously first – and successfully channeled. → 1. *Remove the pressure* ⇒ *allow resistance to emerge* 2. *Put out feelers* ⇒ *enter into dialogue, investigate causes* 3. *Make shared agreements* ⇒ *re-arrange the proceedings*

It's the problem solver who is the problem

Resistance is always a signal. It indicates where there is an energy blockage. In other words, resistance shows where *energies can be released*. Resistance is therefore basically not a disruptive factor, but an opportunity – provided it is recognized and taken advantage of. The most dangerous obstacle is not re-sistance from those affected – it is the disturbed perception and impatience of those doing the planning and decision-making. It is too easy for them to forget how long they themselves took, how many debates and discussions they had, and how many doubts had to be overcome to achieve the new approach. But above all, they are not able to put themselves in the position of people whose job is not to develop a new approach for other people, but to carry it out. Once managers are convinced they have found the right way, they find it difficult to tolerate it when their employees do not show complete loyalty. Their annoyance, self-pity, indignation, and pressure for action are the most difficult obstacles – and ultimately the only really dangerous ones – on the way to reaching solutions by mutual consent. In other words, *the critical factor in dealing with resistance is in the end the way you deal with yourself.* What matters here is to overcome your own emotions, put yourself in other people's place, and investigate things you thought had long since been cleared up. Calling into question your own picture of a state of affairs – and therefore ultimately yourself – is the primary and most important obstacle that has to be avoided if you want to find a constructive way of dealing with resistance (see Figure 33).

Handling
Communication

8

Communication and change

Statistics show that executives spend 80% of their time communicating – in discussions, meetings, and conferences, as well as in analyzing, preparing, and passing on written information. Most of them also complain about this: "I'm stuck in meetings the whole time and never get any time to do the real work!" All that can be said to that is: wrong! Communication *is* the real work, communicating *is* management's job. If you have made sure the right information gets to the right place at the right time, and that the right people talk to each other about the right questions at the right time in the right way, then you have done your job as a manager in the best possible way. Because the communications infrastructure is a company's nervous system.

Depending on which nerve fibers are affected, functional disturbances in the human nervous system can cause a wide variety of symptoms: your hands can shake; minor or major paralysis can occur; you can go blind even though your eyes are healthy; you may suffer serious burns because the pain is not passed on; or you may become unable to walk because certain muscle areas are not responding to the control impulses from the brain – quite apart from severe and life-threatening disturbances to the metabolism.

And precisely the same applies in a company: its weal and woe depend on whether information from the environment is taken in precisely enough, passed on quickly enough internally, and processed properly. Even just everyday operational work requires effective coordination and control. And as soon as changes are planned, the need for communication increases massively: everyday business has to be able to continue undisturbed, but innovations need to be prepared and implemented at the same time alongside it. These processes have to be well coordinated with each another, and also carefully adjusted to ensure they match. This is only possible if everyone involved knows precisely what is supposed to happen when and why. Competent communication becomes the decisive factor for success.

In a period in which change is not the exception but the normal state of affairs, it is no exaggeration to say, quoting Peter Drucker, "management is communication."

What is really missing: understanding

"In fact, there are only very few political, social, or even personal problems that are caused by insufficient information of one sort or another. Nevertheless, at a time when inconceivable problems are piling up around us, when the concept of progress is decaying, and when even meaning itself is becoming suspect, the technopolist holds firmly to the hypothesis that what the world needs is more and more information – as in the joke about the man in the restaurant who complains the food is inedible, and apart from that the portions are too small."

Neil Postman

Normally, it is not a lack of information that we suffer from. On the contrary, we are usually plagued with an overwhelming flood of information. Instead, the real problem is that there is a *lack of communication.* Communication – exchanging information and debating matters with one another – is the fundamental precondition for interpersonal understanding. Underlying the request for better information that is often heard in companies there is almost always a more general concern: a wish for dialogue and participation. In fact, people have no desire, as is often feared, "to interfere with this, that, and the other," exerting influence and exercising power. What they do want – particularly in turbulent times – is not to be delivered up blindly to new developments and changes. They want to understand the goals and intentions involved, the background and the context. They want to know what is in store for them. They need to be able to communicate their concerns, and hope that these will be taken into account.

All of this can only be made possible by talking to people directly – in discussions and conferences that can sometimes be very time-consuming. However, the information strategies that are applied in practice often achieve precisely the opposite: people try to keep those who are affected out of what is happening for as long as possible. They try to keep them waiting, playing things down so that they can gain time. And when it can no longer be avoided, "communications" are provided in the form of official announcements, with the masses receiving information in writing. "Communiqués" of this sort not only hold the people they are addressed to at a distance, but also require them to have a high level of interpretative skills. Reading between the lines becomes the order of the day, fueling speculation – so that instead of communication problems being solved, they have actually been freshly created on a massive scale.

Formal communication in a company

Two things are therefore decisive at the outset. First, the difference between *distributing information in a one-way process* – and genuine human communication, which can ultimately only take place in a process of dialogue in *direct dis-*

cussions between people. At a time when the word "communication" is used for every kind of one-sided mass dumping of information – not least for product commercials in the mass media – this distinction cannot be emphasized too strongly. Secondly, *people learn and alter their behavior almost exclusively through direct communication.* Important though the media are in structuring the flow of information, the real art of management consists of organizing human communication properly within the company, with a view to *efficiency and quality.*

Numerous methods and procedures have been tested to help structure communications successfully in practice. We start with external communications in this book, since we believe in the principle that companies need to think and organize themselves from the outside in. In this chapter, however, the emphasis is clearly on internal communications, since these are usually where the fault lies if the overall guidance system fails.

The core element of internal company communications is a regulated management rhythm: usefully linked, regularly held team discussions at every level – a key function with regard to controlling and developing a company. We give special attention to this aspect here. The supplementary tools will be commented on in relation to the ways they can be applied in practice.

Communication between outside and inside

"Organizing from the outside in" can only be achieved by someone who – on the one hand – is constantly obtaining all the information needed from the outside, in order to recognize market demands, market movements, and his own degree of acceptance on the market quickly enough; and who on the other hand is continually and successfully communicating to that market his own performance and the image he desires.

The most important ways and means:

- Customer questionnaires, with various sections for the criteria thought to be currently relevant.
- Image studies.
- Analyses of markets and market trends.
- Comparisons with competitors.
- Customer care and customer information systems (e.g., customer service hotline, target group – specific catalogs, customer letters, customer newsletters).
- Image commercials and publicity work.
- Analyses of how effective commercials are.
- Systematic gathering and evaluation of information from all employees who have direct customer or market contacts (outside sales staff, technical customer service staff, orders department, complaints processing, phone).

But the information coming in from outside can only be used to its full potential if it is passed on internally and processed. Two things have to be ensured:

1. That information about customer needs and market trends should pass directly and without distortion or delay to the correct internal specialists, to be turned into solutions in the form of the corresponding products and services.
2. That the opinions and interests of other areas of the company – the hierarchy, headquarters departments, participatory bodies, etc. – should be coordinated in such a way that the processing sequence that is needed to operate in the market is supported and encouraged, instead of being disturbed or obstructed.

The reality is often quite different: valuable market information is not passed on, or not evaluated; at best, it first reaches headquarters staff, where it gets analyzed to death or talked away through internal politics; the development and marketing departments are at daggers drawn and not on speaking terms; expensive market research is consigned to outside contractors in order to gather data that one's own employees on the front line have long since already had; management is busy thinking about the year 2010; and no one feels responsible for the overall control.

These are the main causes usually responsible for friction, breakdowns, conflicts, and abortive developments: insufficient competence in internal company communications.

Network of regular management meetings

This is an indispensably vital part of the framework of internal company communications: a network of regular team discussions at every level – from the very top of the company right down to the grass roots. This network ensures the basic information supply. The relevant information can be passed from top to bottom and bottom to top as each step requires, and can be processed at every level in direct dialogue.

Regular executive meetings have long since become routine in many companies. However, there are two areas that often leave a great deal to be desired: the *efficiency* of meetings – i.e., their cost–benefit ratio; and the *quality of communication*. Efficiency can basically be measured by the dynamism of the innovative and decision-making processes, while the quality of communication can be judged by the enthusiasm or reluctance the participants have when they go into the meeting. If the executive meeting is referred to in company slang as the "morning service," the "snooze session," or the "muppet show," it can be assumed that much could be improved either in the structure of the meetings or in the participants' behavior – or both.

At the executive level, far too much is made of the mystery of human cooperation. It is usually comparatively simple rules that are being disregarded when executive discussions are creating dissatisfaction.

Separating everyday business and questions of principle

A tale from real life: one participant at a meeting is talking about a problem in everyday business, a second discovers that there is a question of principle involved, a third questions the company's long-term business strategy. The discussion runs back and forth – and by the end of the meeting the day-to-day problem has not been solved, no questions of principle have been discussed, nor has there been any real deliberation over strategy.

It is important to distinguish in advance between questions whose effects are short-term, medium-term, and long-term. It is usually extremely useful to arrange separate meetings for each of these three categories. In the first place, quite different types of preparation are necessary, and secondly it is easier to communicate when everyone is talking about the same thing. In many companies, the following pattern has proved its value: a weekly "at-home" day for controlling current business; once a month, a meeting exclusively for discussing principles and policy questions; twice a year, a strategy session to deal with the longer-term future; and once a year, a conference at which the team can devote its whole attention to discussing its own communications and cooperation.

In practically every company, there are subjects that become topical at certain times every year, so that based on the normal business rhythm you can predict almost to the week when they are going to come up – not just target agreements, planning rounds, budgeting meetings, but also important events such as conferences for foreign representatives and workforce meetings, which need to be properly prepared. It is a great advantage to schedule not only a fixed meetings plan down to the last detail for the whole year, but also to assign the most important predictable topics to the appropriate dates. The great advantage here is that everyone – particularly those who have to do the preparatory work – knows what has to be done when. The effect is that you no longer need to throw the whole company into a last-minute rush "suddenly and unexpectedly" year after year.

A few things have to be clarified in advance to ensure that an executive group can work as a genuine team instead of degenerating into a permanent circus:

- Executive discussions have priority, particularly policy and strategy meetings. Participation is obligatory.
- No deputies can be sent, certainly not to policy and strategy meetings.
- Employees can be invited to attend executive meetings in connection with specific specialist topics, but only when this is announced in advance and attendance is restricted to the relevant agenda item.

Establishing the agenda

A tale from real life: the meeting starts without an agenda, the discussion goes round and round in circles for hours on end, and finally nobody can remember why they came any more. Or: the agenda is a yard long, starts with trivial

matters, only a few discussion points get dealt with, and the rest of the items –
often the most important matters – are then postponed to the next session.

Introducing the topics for discussion is really the duty of all the participants. The job of coordinating topics usually belongs to the person chairing the meeting. And he should also ensure firstly, that the most important matters are at the very top of the list; secondly, that an objective is set for each item on the list (information, opinions, application, decision, etc.); and thirdly, that all the participants receive the agenda and documents with enough time before the meeting to allow them to read them and prepare for it.

At the start of the meeting, the agenda is carefully checked to see whether it needs to be added to or changed due to current events. Each discussion point then has a time slot assigned to it. It is only when this has been done, and when the facilitator ensures that the time plan is observed, that there is any guarantee that all the agenda items can be dealt with. Any items that can be postponed must be deleted from the agenda before the meeting starts its work, once the priorities are known.

Participants' preparatory work

A tale from real life: the head of department X urgently needs a decision from the group concerning an important question. But no one is familiar with the matter except for him. Some people use the meeting to ask intelligent-sounding questions. Others nervously shuffle their papers. Others again raise all sorts of reservations. And the ones who are really smart keep quiet and then propose adjourning the decision.

An executive discussion is not a promenade concert, not a sauna meeting and not a get-together with the regulars at the bar. Even in a good team of intelligent people, difficult specialist questions can only be effectively dealt with when all the participants ensure that they are well informed beforehand and have prepared themselves for the discussion. N.B. *you never read in meetings* – either individually or collectively! If files are distributed at all, then it should only be for later reading. Of course, it is always possible – and often necessary – to introduce complex questions and projects initially in the form of an oral and visual presentation. Providing information can thus certainly be the goal as one part of a meeting's agenda. However, as soon as it becomes a matter of common analysis, forming opinion, or even preparing to take a decision, having expertise is a matter of duty. In this respect, everyone shares responsibility for the whole team's ability to function.

Process of the meeting

A tale from real life: the meeting starts, but not everyone has arrived yet. The people who are present are in a hurry. They start working through the planned agenda points – as quickly as possible, so that they can get back to their desks. One person keeps getting notes passed to him from his secretary the whole time; another has to rush out quickly to make a phone call; a third is studying files to prepare for a different meeting. All of them keep looking at their watches. Some of their watches are also beeping every five minutes. By the time the last people have finally arrived, the first ones already have to go. Most of them are wary about saying anything, for fear the meeting might get even longer. The meeting finishes – and within seconds everyone has vanished from the room.

People are not machines. To be able to communicate properly, they need:

a) their discussion partners to be present
b) an atmosphere that is reasonably pleasant
c) the time and calm to listen and be able to speak.

A useful practice is to get together ten minutes before the work of the meeting starts, so that people can see each other without immediate work pressure and do a few things outside the agenda that are also important: passing on interesting information to one colleague, a quick query to another, arranging to meet with a third.

As described above, the meeting's work always starts with clearing up the agenda. But it can also be very useful to arrange a small, time-limited information round as the first regular agenda item, where everyone can briefly report about what the current hot topic is. For the main part of the meeting, however, the sequence of subjects and the length of the individual discussion points emerge automatically from the agenda.

Meetings that last more than one or two hours should on principle always be interrupted with a break in the middle. The practice of "interval training" in sports is now familiar, but not enough importance is given to this technique in the field of management:

Taking quick rests doesn't slow work down, it accelerates it.

A meeting should never close without the following points being discussed:

⇨ The most important items for the minutes
⇨ Important topics for the next meeting
⇨ Content, form, and addresses for outside information to be provided.

It may sometimes also be necessary to give brief consideration to the quality of the meeting:

– *What was good? What was not so good?*
– *What should we pay more attention to in the future?*

This means that the last fifteen minutes of a meeting should be reserved in advance for conclusions, process observations and future procedures.

Minutes of decisions

A tale from real life: important matters have been decided on, tasks have been assigned. People are now waiting for action, but nothing happens. Sooner or later, the problem that everyone thought had been solved comes up again. General consternation. Some people pretend to know nothing, others have only a very vague memory: "There was something said about that ..." No one is competent to decide, no one can be made responsible. New arrangements are made. Again nothing happens. Gradually, the subject becomes worn out. New, much more serious problems dominate the scene. And everyone enjoys having the freedom to hold to agreements or forget them, just at their own discretion. There is no one to check – and without check-ups, there can be no penalties.

Implementing and carrying through decisions is an essential part of the work of management. If decisions and agreements that have been made are dealt with in a careless fashion at management level, employees cannot be expected to take them seriously either. Keeping minutes is indispensable to ensure that individuals are able to organize themselves in all the turbulence and variety of different meetings and duties they have – and above all to ensure that the team can check the progress of its own work. In contrast to United Nations Security Council meetings, normal management discussions do not need to have every single word recorded verbatim in writing for the benefit of posterity. In terms of practical management, there is no time to read long minutes anyway. Instead, what is needed are *minutes of results,* briefly recording the content of what was decided and determined for future procedure: *who is to do what by when?*

Since the minutes are short, they can be written immediately after the meeting and sent to the participants as a working paper straight away. It is also immediately clear from this type of minute when – i.e., at which future meeting – which team member is to provide a progress or a completion report about which topic. The "law of reunion" is a form of guidance and control that is not only a particularly humane one, but also very effective.

Feedback and team development

A tale from real life: an important matter is being discussed by a group of executives. Several participants at the meeting are unprepared, as usual. People just issue statements. No one is listening to anyone else. There is no dialogue going on. Several people take no part in the discussion whatsoever. At the end, the facilitator gives a summary of what has been said, and records for the minutes what he regards as a "common decision." The decision is announced. But in the company, the controversy continues as if nothing had happened. Whole departments fail to observe the decision. Some members of the executive board say to anyone willing to listen, "I was always against it and I still am – but I was outvoted." The boss is annoyed, the atmosphere is terrible – and no one is willing to talk about it.

Even when a team has basically healthy internal conditions, there are always frictions, breakdowns, subliminal tensions, or even genuine conflicts when people work together in practice. In addition, the structure and organization of meetings have to be constantly adapted to changing conditions. It is absolutely necessary, therefore, to carry out an inspection at regular intervals and give the team's workings a critical check-up:

- *What is running well? What is not running so well?*
- *Is the way the meetings are organized still useful?*
- *Are we dealing with the things that really matter?*
- *How would we assess the style in which people communicate during the discussions?*
- *Are we open toward one another, or are people mainly behaving tactically at meetings?*
- *Does everyone observe the agreed rules?*
- *What do people feel about the working atmosphere? Do we usually look forward to our meetings together, or is everyone glad to get them over with?*
- *Is laughter sometimes possible at the meetings, or are they dominated by a mood of deadly seriousness, tension, and haste?*
- *How are the meetings chaired; what is helpful, what ought to be done differently?*
- *Are we satisfied with the way in which opinions are shaped and decisions are reached?*
- *Looking at the overall results, is the time we spend together well used?*
- *If not, why not? Who can do what to improve things?*

Questions like these have to be asked from time to time and discussed calmly. Openness and honesty have to be practiced and developed in the team. This is the only way in which the team can learn how to direct itself better – both with regard to its *effectiveness* and with regard to the *emotional atmosphere* and personal feelings of its members.

Teams that are completely unaccustomed to discussing their own interaction usually need several conferences, possibly even chaired by outsiders, in order to develop the required sensitivity about behavioral questions and the degree of openness needed in the full group. Teams that have already established these conditions can evaluate their meetings on the spot. Friction, disturbances, and emotional tensions can be constantly remedied. But the advanced techniques of openness and dynamism in a team involve the members spontaneously saying something at any time, even during the meeting, when they are particularly pleased or annoyed about something – no matter who or what. This is the best way of ensuring that problems in interaction are recognized early enough and solved. However, this presupposes a degree of openness and willingness to work through conflicts that is unfortunately only rarely seen at executive levels.

Two final remarks.

First, a usefully networked system of well-functioning executive meetings is the basic requirement not only for directing the company during normal operations, but particularly also for coping with organizational change, – i.e., for the overall control of innovative processes and the way in which they are linked with the normal organization. Company development cannot be carried out successfully without a well-functioning network of internal communications. This means: *company development often starts precisely with optimizing the communications infrastructure.*

Secondly, to ensure that the overall system can function properly, the individual teams have to be functioning properly. Often the initial tasks are not to do with questions of overall networking, but with *creating the conditions for open and honest communication within the individual teams.* This process often starts *at the very top.* The way things are done there sets an example that shapes communications and cooperation further down the hierarchy more than anything else can.

Additional tools

Special conference meetings and workshops

There are questions that in principle cannot be competently dealt with during meetings that are tied up with the rush of everyday business:

- Strategy development
- Detailed examination of the team's collaboration
- Working out tensions and conflicts
- Fundamental questions concerning management and collaboration
- Longer-term organization development

For working groups, project teams, and management groups, it is useful, when working through this type of topic, to spend one or two days in a closed conference out of range of phone interruptions. A project team that has been newly created should not even start its work without first having a closed conference to plan its work in peace and quiet and establish common guidelines for working together. And every management team should take at least two days every year for a review of the quality of its collaboration during the previous year – and for a preview of the medium-term future.

Dialogue meetings in larger groups

Regulated communications within the individual teams involved in the normal organization and in projects are not sufficient in periods of turbulence to ensure the flow of information and to coordinate activities – particularly in larger companies. Large-scale staff meetings are needed to guarantee that everyone gets the same message – as well as getting a reliable picture of the background and context.

The effects of meetings that are organized in a lively way in larger groups cannot be achieved in any other way. In the first place, there is *clarity*: things that have been explained in a large group will not subsequently be talked to death or misinterpreted. Secondly, there is *behavioral effectiveness*: dialogue in a large group has its own quality of persuasiveness, with a marked influence on people's behavior. Thirdly, there is a sense of identification – "us." There is virtually no other way of creating such a lasting sense of community.

However, the decisive factor in this is that a genuine dialogue must be established in which the quality of personal encounters is the priority. If work in a large group is not to degenerate into a mere podium performance, special small group forms of work need to be selected. In addition, there are special requirements with regard to visual presentation facilities, appropriate meeting rooms, and chairmanship. However, the effort and costs involved represent an investment that is more than justified by the effects achieved.

Listed below are four types of meetings in larger groups that have proved particularly effective in practice:

- *Closed strategy conference for the top two or three management levels*: when company management meets up with the directly subordinate heads of operational units once a year for a discussion about strategy, there are two things it can achieve. First, it will get extremely valuable ideas. Secondly, the motivational effects on the executives involved cannot be underestimated. You have the team genuinely "behind you." Sometimes it is even useful to include the third level of management – either right from the start, or during a second phase of the process. It is quite possible for this process to be organized into two phases: first of all, the second level of management meets separately – in large companies, they can be divided into groups with manageable numbers, in which dialogue is easier – in order to take stock of the current situation and develop ideas and methods for meeting new challenges. Based on this "material," you can then go on to the second phase, the actual discussion with company management.
- *"Kick-off meeting"*: larg-scale projects for change make severe demands on the communication process, particularly in the initial stages. The best way of clarifying things and creating a positive "fresh start" attitude is to hold an initial meeting to provide information to everyone directly involved or affected, about the goals, background, procedure, organization, and time plan, clearing up on the spot all the questions that come up in connection with the project.
- *Project information meeting*: In large, complex projects, it is necessary to gather together, at longer intervals, the whole group that is involved or directly affected for an intermediate stocktaking of the situation. These meetings are not only highly informative, they are in fact real tools for controlling the process, indispensable elements of a well-functioning early warning system.

- *Employee forums*: Alienation between top management and the grass roots is a problem in practically every large company. Each member of company management is only able to have direct contact with a very small number of employees, even when he is working on the principle of "management by wandering around." An employee forum is a helpful institution that fills the gap here: regular meetings between one or more management representatives and constantly changing larger groups of employees. However, employee forums are only useful when they are an established institution. It is only then that employees really come out of their shell, and only then that the meetings can be made genuinely interactive.

Appraisal and Progress Reviews

Regular talks with employees are an obligatory part of every communications strategy. There are two topics that require a personal discussion on fundamental matters at least once a year between each employee and his or her direct boss:

- *Target agreement and target checking*: a mutual critical assessment of target achievement during the preceding period. Agreement of quantitative and qualitative targets for the upcoming period. Establishing a mutual intermediate assessment. Agreement of provisions for timely consultation if the employee notices a deviation from target is likely.
- *Training and career development planning*: a critical review of a year's collaboration. Mutual open feedback: expertise and personal strengths and weaknesses of the employee from the boss's point of view; strengths and weaknesses of the boss from the employee's point of view. Agreements concerning future cooperation. Planning of training opportunities. Discussion of medium-term career development prospects for the employee at the company.

These interviews are not only an indispensable tool for guidance and control. They are also important opportunities to create motivation and identification with the company, and to spot potential and develop employees' abilities.

Project-specific communications plan

Projects are processes aimed at creating change. In practice, they almost always lead to internal information gaps, tensions, and conflicts. The slogan "communications are everything" is particularly applicable to project work. No project should be decided on unless a suitable communications plan has been prepared. Both communications within the framework of the project organization and also the information about the project within its immediate neighborhood have to be clearly regulated. Based on the planned phasing of the project, it can be predicted in advance when a batch of information is likely to be needed – and if supplying it is already an established part of the plan, it will firstly not be forgotten, and secondly it will be carefully prepared. In more comprehensive projects in larger companies, it may even be useful to produce a specific project newsletter at regular intervals. Given a lively format, this type of newsletter can make a vital contribution to keeping employees informed.

In the context of project management, communications are an indispensable tool for guidance and control. At the same time, however, communications about current projects help employees to identify with the company, and they help to develop an open and lively company culture (cf. Part II, Chapter 3, "Phases of the Process and Their Pitfalls").

Control systems

Maintaining control over results, processes, and quality is an indispensable tool of management in the context of a management cycle that involves establishing entrepreneurial goals, carrying out strategic planning, and implementing the consequent operational measures in various departmental areas and different places. However, controlling should be regarded as a *service,* and should provide those who are responsible for specific performance areas with all the relevant data they need to keep up to date with the current status and the way things are actually developing, so that they can intervene in time to correct matters when there are serious deviations from plan. This is often only possible with a substantial degree of conflict – particularly when the message the data provide is an uncomfortable one. But this process can only be turned into a fruitful dialogue if the controlling data are not (as so often happens!) used as a means of domination and turned into evidence for the prosecution.

Employee questionnaires

Seeking employees' opinions about their working situation, their view of things, their suggestions and proposals about organization, management, and collaboration within the company is a fundamental tool of communication within a company. If it is properly designed, a questionnaire alone can produce positive effects. But it is the results and what is made of them that are decisive. Questionnaire results provide an outstanding database for evaluating suggested improvements and ideas for change within individual organizational units together with the employees affected, and for implementing the appropriate measures. This process – living communication in the real sense – makes a vital contribution to optimizing performance and developing employees' motivation and identification with the company (cf. Part III, Chapter 2, "Organizational Diagnosis").

Workforce meetings

Workforce meetings are really intended to give all the employees an opportunity to receive relevant information at first hand, both from the labor union side and from the management side. They can be good opportunities for employees to get a "live" experience of the way in which disputes over fundamental matters can be conducted within a fair framework, and to participate in them.

In practice, however, this type of meeting runs the risk of degenerating into an election campaign arena, a show, or a public tribunal. Employees' representatives and company management line up for a populist exhibition fight, and the employees themselves are reduced to the role of mere spectators whose applause is being courted. Discussions about substantial matters, in which what matters is to present one's own position without any manipulative dramatization, accepting contrary positions and trying to understand them, generating processes of mutual opinion formation – none of this can take place, and is not even intended. By contrast, with a little goodwill on the part of everyone involved, genuinely careful preparation, and professional chairmanship if necessary, a workforce meeting can be made into a lively and impressive event that can make an important contribution to favorable internal conditions in the company.

Dialogue with employee representatives

Looked at over the long term, it is well worthwhile – for both sides- to invest sufficient time and energy in the interplay between company management and bodies representing personnel. Over and above the legal requirements, the following topics are the most important ones:

- The company's future
- Mood among staff, or in specific groups
- Untapped or frustrated potential
- Atmosphere and esteem in mutual dealings between management and labor unions
- Effectiveness of communication with one another, particularly with regard to identifying tricky problems and areas of tension soon enough and ensuring that they are dealt with.

Meetings of this type often require an additional informal framework to ensure that the dialogue will be successful. On the other hand, it is precisely this type of "carefully informal framework" that is used by some company managements to spoil the employee representatives and attempt to tame them – sometimes even to corrupt them. Nevertheless, those who retreat to the required legal minimum of formal information obligations, and then also interpret these too narrowly, need not be surprised about the effects. When genuine communication is not taking place, all that happens is an exchange of formal communiqués, meticulously prepared lists of demands, or even melodramatic indictments – as a prelude to workforce meetings and company meetings modeled on showtime, election campaigns, or public tribunals, as mentioned above.

The variety of contacts that labor union representatives have with the workforce can provide an inexhaustible source of information, which management is also capable of using. After all, it is usually also in the interest of these bodies to report about shortcomings and ensure that they are remedied.

The notice-board

The traditional type of notice-board is certainly not a very effective communications tool. But it can still serve to provide fast factual information. More up-to-date forms such as advertising pillars or screens at various intersection points in the company (entrance area, canteen, recreation areas) can make an important contribution to keeping everyone up to date and making the information lively. Here again, however, it needs to be ensured that the information is not given in the form of official announcements.

Company and staff newsletter

Company newsletters are nothing new – but the defects in newsletters that people complain about are as old as the idea itself: too much space given to statements by company management, barely concealed "royal circulars," material that sounds like sermons out of church newsletters, and other pious admonitions.

The decisive criteria for a lively company newsletter are:

⇨ It should be edited by employees, or at least with substantial participation from them.
⇨ There should be professional assistance with the journalistic design.
⇨ It should have a lively layout that is attractive because it suits the reading habits of its readership.
⇨ It should be taken straight out of real life, with photos, short reports, and interviews.
⇨ By far the majority of the reports and photos should be about people and events at the grass roots.

Media that are accepted by the workforce, that are irreverent and lively, are superb ways of communicating important company messages. But if they are perceived as one-sided "pastoral letters from the bishop," they are sure of one fate: they will only be read by very few – and usually the wrong people.

More and more companies are finding the courage to make room for the "virtue of irreverence," by encouraging this type of publication without trying to exercise any kind of censorship. However, it takes a bit of courage to be able to use this amount of freedom appropriately.

An up-to-date way of ensuring communications and encounters – particularly within each level of the hierarchy – is the information market model. Groups, responsibilities, or departments can introduce themselves in the form of "market stalls" and get talking to each other in this way. For example: project groups can provide information about the current state of their projects; company management can present its current strategy and be available to listen to visitors to its stall and answer their questions; the results of interesting questionnaires can be presented to a wider in-house "public." The whole market can be prepared and managed by a small interdisciplinary group. The main criteria for success with this kind of tool are: lively forms of stall presentation, enough opportunity to talk, and the ability to have a free discussion.

Informal communication

When you are intensively preoccupied with formalising communications in a company from the point of view of managing and influencing people, it is easy to forget that people cannot be prevented from communicating with each other – officially or unofficially, formally or informally, intentionally or unintentionally, openly or covertly. People are social by their very nature. Communicating with others is a basic human need, the basic precondition for psychological well-being. When lots of people start communicating with others, they can spread information, prejudices, and moods at astonishing speed. This is where the expressions "grapevine" and "rumor-mongering" come from.

Formal, official, regulated communications and informal, unofficial, unregulated communications are two different, but extremely important dimensions of the communications that take place within a company. In practice, however, the problem is whether the formal and informal channels are mutually complementary and are being usefully exploited – or whether they appear to be "two different worlds" that are constantly contradicting one another.

If you want to develop communications within your company, you have to take care of its informal communications channels as well. There are three principles that apply here:

⇨ Encouraging informal communication purposefully.
⇨ Ensuring that formal and informal communication channels are not contradicting one another.
⇨ Exploiting informal communication channels consistently.

There are a number of tried and tested procedures for achieving this as well:

- *Visiting sites – or "wandering around"*: the top bosses are usually the people who are least well informed in a company about what is going on further down the hierarchy in employees' minds and feelings – particularly at the grass roots. The alienation between the very top and the grass roots is simply

There are hardly any large companies that have not been through the follow-ing experience: on an important question, highly secret discussions are con-ducted within a small circle in top management, and preliminary decisions are taken. The various stages at which these decisions will be made known in the company are carefully planned; and the day beforehand, everything – most of it, unfortunately, well researched – already appears in the newspa-pers. The result: all the employees are annoyed about having to find out from the papers what is going on inside the company. Inside management: every-one is puzzled about who is responsible, and there are tacit mutual suspici-ons and distrust of one's own executives. And often no one ever finds out how it actually happened.

The facts are:

First: when a political matter such as an upcoming fusion or restructuring process is sufficiently plausible in itself, it does not have to be officially an-nounced before everyone starts talking about it.

Secondly: the top bosses usually have no idea about things that are already an open secret within the company.

Thirdly: in reality, no one at all ever consciously lets the cat out of the bag. But people like to communicate. One person maybe expressed a suspicion, another dropped a vague hint, a third maybe said nothing in response to a direct question. And anyone who is not dumb is soon going to be able to put two and two together.

Last, but not least: even company directors are only human. Two-thirds of the spectacular indiscretions seen in industry are due to chattering directors. Some of them just want to make themselves sound interesting somewhere; others may be deliberately spreading information as part of their political maneuvering.

The sixty-four thousand dollar question: who ends up as the target of mana-gement's resentment? Answer: the media, who are regarded as organizing a witch-hunt against the company out of sheer sensationalism and with no regard for the damage caused ...

a fact of life in every large company – unless the communications deficit is remedied by deliberate measures: by *direct, informal visits to the front line.* When this happens, the employees are playing a "home match." They are in their own accustomed working environment, and a visit from one of the top managers is welcome. If they can also see that the visitor just wants to find out what goes on there and what kinds of things affect people – then they will open up. In this way, the boss can find out things that even executives at the intermediate levels do not know. They can get a realistic picture of the situation in the company. Sometimes, of course, employees are reserved toward someone from further up the hierarchy, even when they are in their own workplace. But this is an important item of information too. You can then decide for yourself whether things should remain that way, or whether you want to do something about it.

- *Informal discussion sessions*: informal discussions with executives – for example, during spare moments at training meetings – are also rewarding, both as thermometers and as tools for communicating important messages. The relaxed setting and the opportunity for an easy-going exchange of views encourage employees to talk freely about what is really bothering them. These "fireside chats" are particularly productive when there are no large presentations involved – in which there is usually more form than content, anyway. The best way of getting dialogue going is for the boss not to start off by making formal statements himself, but to switch first to "receive" mode and at most put a couple of questions about the situation on the spot and how the people he is talking to feel about things. It is particularly beneficial if the commander-in-chief does not think he has to pretend to have a ready-made answer for every possible question put to him. Time to think has to be allowed – as well as admitting that you actually need to do some thinking before reaching definite conclusions. But what is important is to show that you intend to do something about a question that has been left open.

- *Phone calls with employees*: American Presidents, who are masters of the art of lobbying, have got into the habit of personally phoning up a whole series of senators, particularly the "opinion leaders," to hold discussions with them ahead of difficult legislative moves or controversial budget debates. It is an example that is also very apt for contacting employees in field sales, who are less well linked to internal communications. Management can personally call up a representative cross-section of employees – at home, if need be. In the process, you get not just a situation report and a number of fresh ideas, but you also show personal interest.

    Entering into direct communication with the lower levels, however, must not mean intervening all over the place like the lord of the manor and issuing assignments over the heads of people's direct bosses. Listening to the company, getting a picture of the situation, getting important messages directly to the front line, and documenting your own interest in things – these are the goals. If you play the big chief or pass out assignments left, right, and center over the heads of the responsible managers, you will find that direct contact with employees does not in the long run work out to be a blessing for you.

- *Parties, excursions*: many managers are literally trained compulsively to achieve efficiency, as defined by hard numbers. They work like computers: digitally. Everything human has been trained out of them during their careers. Every discussion that is not target-focussed is a useless waste of breath; emotions are regarded with horror; parties mean the onset of Sodom and Gomorrah. In reality, company parties and joint excursions are excellent opportunities for meeting people informally. When a boss takes part attentively and succeeds, at least to some extent, in being regarded as "one of us," he has a good chance of getting insights into the company's inner structure. At the same time, important messages can be taken directly to the people without distortion. This kind of natural meeting often leaves employees with a much longer-lasting impression than the most elaborate official events.

If you want to get a deeper insight into your company's underworld and listen to what "ordinary people" are saying, you often just need to say the word to find that employees are willing to put on a satirical revue show at a party. A revue show can bring into the open (sometimes with painful clarity, although entertainingly) lots of tricky issues that are no longer mentioned openly during everyday work, because people have simply accepted them – either with anger or resignation.

- *Communal rooms in the working environment*: these facilities are not used to their full potential in practice. Normal and natural contacts between people can be systematically encouraged by intentionally designing existing communal rooms to maximize their communication potential. It can start with installing a coffee corner where everyone who happens to turn up can meet during the break. And it is particularly important in the canteen – a vital opportunity for informal dialogue. In many companies, however, the top executives always eat in separate rooms. There is a two-class society, and communication within each class is almost the only kind that is encouraged. But even when the canteen is not shared, management behavior can encourage a tendency for more and more cliques to form at the tables. If there is not an open cafeteria where people are more or less obliged to get together informally, then a daily opportunity for spontaneous contacts and lively communication has been missed from the outset.

Laws of communication

In an up-to-date organization, communication plays a vital and central role. An essential aspect of organization and management basically consists entirely of structured communication. And there is no lack of specific tools and procedures – on the contrary: there is an embarrassment of choice. With regard to creative and competent communicative action, however, it is important in practice to note a few fundamental aspects – "laws," as it were – of communication.

- *Communication is the Siamese twin of every strategy for change*: any kind of strategy for change is only as good as the way it is communicated. Successful change in a company is only possible if it is accompanied by an open and lively communications policy.
- *The effectiveness of communication is based on lively dialogue*: as we have seen, there is no lack of tried and tested tools, methods, and procedures as

technical aids to communication. However, the more formal the communications format is, the less attractive, lively, and impressive it becomes. Therefore, the more drastic the effect of a message is intended to be, the more likely it is that the recipients' vital interests are going to be affected; and the more emotionally loaded the situation is – the better it is to select a procedure that allows lively dialogue. In plain terms, the more we are afraid of a direct encounter and argument in practice, the more need there is for it to take place.

- *"You can't not communicate"*: The communications expert Watzlawick formulated this axiom for interpersonal relations. But it can certainly be applied to larger organizational and social structures as well. Gaps in expected communication – silences, one-sided statements that leave no room for views to be exchanged – are filled up by imagined fantasies and interpretations. What is not said is *interpreted into* things – i.e., according to the recipient's prejudices. These "substitute messages," which are constructed by the recipients themselves, also have effects in the end, just as much as directly communicated messages do.

- *It's nearly always too late*: the speed with which changes are taking place is constantly increasing the urgency of the need for communication. If you want to communicate as completely as possible and all in a logical sequence, you will nearly always end up being too late in the whirl of events. Speculation rushes ahead of meticulously planned communications – following the same principle, that "you can't *not* communicate." So it is usually better to communicate incompletely, but on time and often, rather than to wait until precise and complete information is available. Everyone has to die some day – either with things unfinished, because it's too soon; or too late, but with everything finished. The only difference is whether you do it with a good conscience or a bad one.

- *People only hear what they want to hear*:

"What the heart resists, the head will not admit."
Schopenhauer.

The more emotionally loaded a situation is, the greater the danger of so-called "selective perception" on the part of the recipient. The message is not received in the sense in which it is intended. It is almost always understood as *something different* from what the originator sent out. Communicating in emotionally heated situations is like scattering seed in a storm …

Selective intake of information is mainly influenced by two factors: *the credibility of the originator* and the *prior experience of the recipient*. Depending on the context, point of view, prior experience, and assessment of credibility, completely different "truths" can be received – or attributed to the originator.

- *Proper communication requires careful investigation*: you can only communicate properly if you have previously sounded out what the inner attitudes of your intended audience are. It is only on the basis of this information that you can orient the communication precisely to the recipient and decide which method, which tool, what kind of "packaging" to use, and which person conveying the message has the best chances of "getting it through."

- *There is no such thing as pure communication*: communication is not an end in itself. Every communication is intended to achieve something – either openly or manipulatively. The more precisely it is planned and the more skillfully it is staged, the stronger the intention behind it is. One needs to be on one's guard against people who are out to conceal attempts to exert influence, or even deny that they are happening – because they are up to no good.

- *Fast communications demand direct routes*: if the effectiveness of a message depends on it reaching its intended audience quickly and without distortion, it has to reach the recipient:

  - By the shortest possible route.
  - Directly, i.e., without intermediate stops.
  - And allowing direct feedback (queries and comments).

And to do this, the cascade of the official hierarchical channels is usually not suitable from the very start. If you send out vital messages via intermediaries, you can be virtually certain that what the recipient gets will be something different.

Because no one will pass on a message that places him in a bad light himself; he will take out anything damaging to himself, or at least defuse it by relativizing it.

Everyone who has to pass on a message will, on the contrary, make sure that it is useful to him; so he will add his own special touches to it. In the same way, someone further up in the hierarchy has to assume on principle that everything reaching him from "down below" has passed through hierarchical intermediaries and was usually not sent out in precisely the same way.

But even when direct dialogue is possible, emotional overtones and misunderstandings can occur. Here, too, it is necessary to check the quality of the communication:

  - What reached the recipient, and how did he understand it?
  - What reactions did he have to the message?
  - Did the message received and the reaction correspond to the originator's intentions?

It is only this checking that allows one to see where and when corrections or additions are needed.

- *You can get too much of a good thing*: in larger and more complex companies and company groups, it is sometimes necessary to send out a particularly important message several times by different routes. In this kind of situation, careful attention needs to be given to ensure that employees do not start receiving stereotyped repetitions. Because repetition can quickly lead to immune reactions. People become blunted to the message and stop being receptive enough to new information in the future.

- *Appetite comes with eating*: only well-informed employees are committed employees. As the intensity and quality of communications increase, however, levels of expectation rise too. Employees become more critical, more self-confident, and more awkward. A "complaints culture" may even develop. But the question is what the goals are that one is pursuing. Regular and open communications can ensure that working processes and processes of change can take place with little friction. Motivation and identification with the company can be created. Competence can be developed. But no one should expect employees to become "more satisfied." On the contrary: people who are well informed have no choice but to be unsettled in view of all problems there are. Nowadays, calm and contentment are not meaningful goals anyway. A company that wants to survive needs employees who know when and why changes need to be carried out. And this cannot be achieved without a certain amount of disturbance. On the contrary: when calm and contentment are the order of the day, it would be cause for the greatest possible concern.
- *Communications do not mean "everyone has a say in everything"*: many bosses operate a form of secret diplomacy in important matters in which they have already formed their own opinion and perhaps already prejudged a decision – because they confuse dialogue with giving people a share in decision-making, or even with employee participation in management decisions. They are afraid employees might start fundamentally questioning what the boss intends to do and talking down his prior decision. This fear is based on insecurity. Either you have not done your homework and have not got arguments that are sufficiently watertight for what you intend to do. Or you do not have the confidence to stand in front of your employees and say, "This is what I intend to do. These are my reasons. These are what the consequences will be. What I want to do is talk to you about the best way that we can go about implementing this." If a plan is well thought through (and unfortunately this is not always the case in practice), it is not difficult to convince employees that changes are needed. They have no desire to reinvent the wheel. They appreciate management that has ideas and can create momentum. But they want to really understand the goals, the background and the consequences – and when they are directly affected, they want to be able to influence the way things are implemented. And all this is only possible through direct dialogue.
- *There is also such a thing as an "incommunicable message"*: in practice, far too little open, regular, and lively communication takes place. But we don't want to create the impression here that communication is a panacea, or that every kind of information can be communicated in any situation – if you just choose the right way of doing it. If communication is to be effective:

a) It has to be adapted to the target group.
b) It has to be timely.
c) An eye has to be kept on the overall picture.

There are situations in which open information may be either impossible or not useful from one or another of these points of view.

- Things that under no circumstances should reach the outside world cannot be discussed in larger groups.
- With an employee to whom no one – in all his long years with the company – has ever said that he did not meet expectations in any way, you cannot all at once put a general account of all his defects on the table and expect him to resign straight away with a sudden sense of deep insight.
- If a director who is not up to his management responsibilities is intended for early retirement, it is not possible to provide the whole company with open information about all the background circumstances.
- And if a situation needs to be turned around somewhere, it is not possible either to talk to everyone about the personnel and structural measures that are going to have to be taken, nor can you announce all sorts of possible intentions in advance. What really matters is to reach clear decisions and implement them as quickly as possible – and then get down to facing the challenges of the future together with the smaller team.

However, if the people who were responsible for creating such a situation in the first place are going to end up in prominent positions just as they were before, then it is hopeless to try and establish proper communications in the company, even using the best possible tools.

The Art of Designing Workshops

What is a "workshop"?

Workshops involve manageable numbers of people meeting together in a group – an executive group, a project team, or a specialist committee – to work on a specific topic that is too complex for the scope of a normal meeting. Workshops are particularly useful for strategic and planning tasks. Workshops are key events in the context of medium-term and long-term processes of change, as they allow a plan to be developed or an important phase of work to be planned as far as the implementation stage.

> ⇒ *Workshops are key events in the context of innovative processes.*
> ⇒ *Workshops always form part of a developmental process – i.e., there is always a "before" and "after."*
> ⇒ *Workshops take place outside the normal routine of meetings.*
> ⇒ *The goal of a workshop is to develop specific results that are capable of being implemented.*

Typical reasons for holding workshops

- *To update models, goals, strategies, and measures to be taken*: the environments that are significant to a company are constantly changing – almost faster than the planning figures can go through the rituals required in a company for internal agreement and approval. Consequently, a check has to be made at least once or twice a year – sometimes even more often – to see whether the strategy and the measures derived from it still match current conditions, or to what extent they need to be updated or even completely rethought. Sometimes it is even found that the goals and models themselves are outdated.
- *Working out conflicts*: bottlenecks at a vital point in a company – in the interplay within a department, or at the interfaces where different departments

collaborate – are one of the most frequent causes for people losing motivation, and for friction within companies. One of the central challenges for management is not just to "sit out" conflicts, but to deal with them professionally. Because of the importance of this aspect, we have given it a separate chapter to itself.

- *Team review and team development*: collaboration within a team has always been a key factor enabling it to fulfill complex tasks. With the growing importance of project organization and management models aimed at providing employees with the greatest possible "entrepreneurial scope," the importance of teamwork will increase even more. However, teams are extremely diverse and temperamental structures. We are usually quite happy about investing a lot of money in the maintenance and inspection of complex pieces of machinery – regarding that as perfectly natural and accepting that machines have to be regularly shut down with loss of production. But we usually assume that social systems – which are actually even more complex, and therefore in principle even more susceptible to faults and disturbances – should be able to run without maintenance and upkeep costs. Lots of teams remain far below their potential productivity because they are literally neglected. People are willing to find time for teams once practically everything has ground to a halt, and when a great deal of damage has already been done. But it would make better economic sense to take the necessary precautions for system maintenance: at regular intervals – at least once a year – a team can focus on itself. It can put itself to the test and give itself a proper check-up in every respect that is important for its continuance, its performance, and the degree of satisfaction its members feel.

- *Getting ahead of the need to adapt: sensing fresh developments …* But what if there are actually no problems at the moment – either on the market or within the organization, and not even in people's interpersonal relations? We would propose that in turbulent times such as we have today, the company with the best chances of succeeding and surviving is the one that is just that tiny bit ahead of its competitors. But how can you stay ahead of your competitors when they all have comparable products and similar organizations, as well as being just as customer-oriented as everyone else is? The only ones who can be sure of being ahead of the field are those who do not wait until all the customer's requirements are known down to the last detail. They have to be able to guess at future demand and adjust to it in advance. By contrast, the ones who are desperately rushing to adapt to a general trend when the clock is already showing five past twelve are going to be left empty-handed.

These and similar initial situations have the following aspects in common:

- They involve different, sometimes controversial opinions. Disputes are bound to happen.
- It takes time even just to create an awareness of the problem and achieve the internal discomfort required for changes to be put in motion – de-

stabilizing attitudes that may have gradually established themselves over years, and breaking through rigid structures.

■ In addition to "new thinking," you also need to have an attitude of welcoming fresh departures, an enhanced sense of community, and a group dynamic creating consensus, in order to get things moving.

Developing models and strategic targets, working through conflicts intensively, giving teams careful inspections, drafting visions for the future – these are fundamental ideas that cannot be just conjured up at a moment's notice. Topics like these require a different atmosphere, a different ambience, and a different style of management from ordinary discussions, meetings, and conferences, which usually have to fit into the requirements of fixed agendas and discussion times. Workshops – in the form of closed meetings, deliberately cut off from the rush of everyday operations and away from the normal meetings routine – provide a valuable alternative.

The starting-point comes before the beginning

A workshop is an expensive event to organize. It takes up the time of sometimes large numbers of highly qualified employees or highly-paid executives. In addition, events of this type create group-dynamic processes, and being able to exploit these skillfully is what decides the real atmospheric value and motivating effect of the meeting. Equally, neglecting such processes can have undesirable side effects and long-term consequences. It is all the more important, therefore, to carry out a conscientious check beforehand that an event of this type is actually appropriate, and if it is, to prepare for it carefully. This in turn requires fundamental prior investigations into the justification for the workshop, those affected by it, and its prospects of success (see Figure 34).

Particularly when one is brought in from outside as a consultant or chairperson, it is important to get a detailed picture about the following points:

– *Who is the real initiator of the workshop?*
– *Is the initiator actually capable of tackling this topic?*
– *Which interests and what goals are being pursued here?*
– *Do these goals appear to be clear and realistic?*

The publicized reason for the event and the official goals are, of course, always noble and high-minded. But there are often concealed interests at work as well – in fact, the concealed interests are sometimes the real reason behind the event. And if you fail to recognize them soon enough and unintentionally allow yourself to be manipulated, beware!

– *Who else is affected by the topic being dealt with, either directly or indirectly? How much energy do they have for tackling things?*
– *Who is benefiting from existing conditions, or is regarded by others as doing so?*

- *What do people agree on, and where are the differences or contradictions in their assessments of the initial situation, in their explanations about why things are the way they are?*
- *What are the chances of the venture succeeding in changing things? In what ways do the participants depend on one another? What effects might this have on the workshop?*
- *Is there any previous experience with this type of procedure and this topic? Have previous attempts been made to solve the problem? With what results? What positive or negative memories are associated with this?*
- *What views and expectations are there about the chairmanship and the organization of the event?*

A number of discussions have to be carried out to find out more about all these points.

What is absolutely decisive during this phase is to ensure that one-sided information is neither received nor given. At this point, you must not and cannot conduct any in-depth, detailed analysis; it is much more important to get a rough overview about who and what is involved in the topic. Once the discussions have been held, you will have an approximate picture of the force fields that are at work in connection with the planned workshop. You know who will probably cooperate and be in favor of it. And you know who is likely to create resistance.

Based on these exploratory talks, you can decide the following:

First, whether a workshop should be carried out at all, and whether it is useful to have it at the present time. It should be noted, however, that even just announcing this kind of event arouses expectations; but if there is little prospect of success, it is better not to initiate the plan at all rather than disappoint people's expectations unnecessarily.

Secondly, you can decide what the goals of the workshop are to be, who should take part in it, and who should chair it and be responsible for the details of the event.

The following mistakes are often made during this phase of exploratory talks and preparations for the basic decision on whether to hold a workshop:

▶ People do not really have any desire to clear up unpleasant aspects of the situation. Consequently, they leave existing conflicts unmentioned – in the false hope that they are likely to stay that way.
▶ People underestimate how familiar with the topic those affected are, and the effect this has on their willingness to tackle it. So there is a risk of finding yourself "giving mouth-to-mouth resuscitation to a corpse."
▶ People have no real desire to work out a common solution to the problem. They would prefer to dream up a ready-made solution in peace and quiet on their own, or just latch onto a solution offered by one of the people or groups affected – in their haste to be seen as someone who is able to grasp problems quickly and "come to the rescue."

Figure 34. Workshop – checklist for the exploratory phase

What needs to be clarified?

☐ Responsibilities and freedom of action of the initiator
☐ Incident for the question or problem arising
☐ Those directly and indirectly affected (as well as their dependency on one another and its potential consequences)
☐ Open and concealed goals and interests of those affected
☐ Prior experience of those affected with the topic, and its effects ("burdens of the past")
☐ Force fields related to the chances of getting things moving:
  ▪ *Energy for change*
  ▪ *Energy for resistance*
  ▪ *Beneficiaries of existing conditions*
☐ What is expected of those organizing and facilitating the workshop

What needs to be done?

☐ Holding discussions with representatives of the various groups and points of view.
☐ Deriving from that an overview of:
  ▪ *Goals*
  ▪ *People affected*
  ▪ *Chances for and risks involved in what is planned.*
☐ Making a preliminary decision about how to proceed.

What needs to be avoided?

☐ Taking a superficial view of the problem (usually due to fear of coming into conflict with people)
☐ Underestimating the "history" of the case and the power of the past burdens
☐ Having ready-made solutions in mind – and using the workshop as an alibi.

Design and planning

Creating a preparatory group

The exploratory phase has produced an initial, rough picture about who will be affected by the planned workshop or who might feel affected by it, whose interests are probably going to be touched on, and who expects to be included in the subsequent procedures. You know the range of expectations people have, and you have an impression of how many different points of view the topic will need to be approached from if a practical solution acceptable to everyone is going to be developed. Apart from that, you also know that getting people involved at an early stage, particularly during the preliminary phase, means that they will identify with the planned workshop more strongly and with the way in which it is arranged. Above all, it increases people's willingness to commit themselves more strongly even later on, during the implementation phase – after all, they have been "in on things" from the very start. From the outset, therefore, there is no scope for the "not invented here" syndrome that is often seen. Based on all this information, it can now be decided who should take part in the workshop and in the preparations for it.

Establishing the workshop's objectives and content

Together with this group, and against the background of the concerns and interests identified during the exploratory phase, the ultimate goals of the workshop can now be defined; the topics to be dealt with can be agreed; the sequence of the topics and depth in which they are to be dealt with can be determined; and finally, the "emotional charge" associated with the individual topics can be estimated, and you can assess the implications of this for the way in which topics are dealt with and the appropriate timing.

Selecting participants

The selection of participants must be based on the objectives to be achieved and on the topics to be dealt with, on the one hand. On the other, it must be ensured that the decisive matters do actually get dealt with, that the people who are really going to have to apply and implement plans in practice are adequately represented, and that no one feels seriously insulted if they are not included. In order to take account of all these different aspects, it may be necessary to select the participants without regard to purely hierarchical considerations.

In practice, the following situation is often seen: a group of employees who need to be substantially represented consists of 10, 20, or more people in all. A selection has to be made, since the workshop group would otherwise become far too big, and it would no longer be capable of functioning properly. In this situation, the most elegant solution consists of letting the group as a whole choose its own representatives. You can be sure that the selection will pick out colleagues who have both the expertise and the social abilities required. Employees – no matter at what level – have a very good sense of who will best represent their interests from the overall point of view. You have therefore killed two birds with a single stone: you get a well-qualified workshop team – and the most favorable conditions possible for the workshop's results to be accepted by the overall group.

Assessing the participants' initial situation

Now that you know who is going to be taking part in the workshop, which people are going to meet each other during it, and which topics are going to be dealt with, the following questions arise:

What kind of initial psychological situation should be expected?
Do those who are involved know what it is all really about?
Are they prepared and able to tackle matters openly – or are attitudes of caution and anxiety likely?

One of the fundamental aspects of a workshop meeting is being able to examine the problem from all the relevant perspectives together with those who are involved, agreeing on a common viewpoint and diagnosis and then working out a solution that everyone can support. To do this, people have to enter into dialogue with one another; but dialogue does not just develop at the drop of a hat.

The participants will usually be distanced in various ways both from the topic and from one another. In order to select the correct way of proceeding, you have to be aware of their psychological situation and their degree of willingness to tackle the issues. These will determine whether you can start from the deep end, or whether an "unfreezing" phase is needed to familiarize the participants with one another, with the topic, with the planned way of proceeding, and with the underlying aims of the meeting, in order to create sufficient motivation to deal with matters properly.

To be able to assess the participants' initial situation correctly, the preparatory team will need to get a picture of how clear the goal is, how well-informed about it the participants are in general, how aware they are of the problem and how much pressure they sense in relation to it, and how much trust they have in the workshop's initiators. Depending on the answers to these questions, it will also be clear how much or how little commitment or caution the participants are likely to show when the meeting starts. Which specific questions need to be put, and other points to watch out for, are described in detail in Part II, Chapter 2 and in Part III, Chapter 6.

If the preliminary investigation shows that important aspects of the participants' initial situation are unclear and unpredictable, or if it can even be safely assumed that there will be a difficult starting situation, then it is definitely clear that you cannot start by plunging straight into the main topic. Instead, the first step has to be designed in such a way that the participants are able to clarify things and establish trust – and through that, *a capacity to engage in dialogue and work together*. The way in which this can be achieved is described in more detail in the section on how to conduct the meeting.

Establishing working methods and procedures

Selecting the way in which the topic is dealt with is absolutely decisive for the workshop's success. There are topics that are more factual in nature, for which a knowledge of the subject involved is needed in order to deal with the problem. In these cases, it is necessary both to provide suitable documentation soon enough, and also to approach the subject with sufficient expertise available on the spot. On the other hand, there are psychological topics that affect attitudes and mutual cooperation. To approach these "hot" topics, it is normally useful to work without written documentation and attempt to achieve an open discussion as quickly as possible. It may be helpful, however, to clarify the basic matters being discussed using a few short visual presentations. The use of visual aids and the choice of working methods have to be decided on the basis of the type of topic involved, its complexity, the goal being aimed for in dealing with the topic, and particularly with regard to the group-dynamic background (for specific details, see Part III, Chapter 4 "Facilitating Processes").

Preparing the participants and the immediate environment

It is usually well worth making sure that all of the participants are properly pre-pared for the meeting – via informal study of the topic, a task list drawn up for the purpose, or by reading the documents beforehand. The shared time at the meeting is valuable, and must be kept clear for discussions and negotiations. It should not be used for studying documents or for long-winded introductions.

It is different when the topic involves emotional tensions. In these cases, pre-paratory work can even be damaging to constructive collaboration at the work-shop. The "opponents" may start collecting material for mutual "indictments," "sharpening their weapons" and attempting to win over allies. These prepara-tions tend to aggravate conditions for the discussion and make negotiations more difficult.

Whether or not they are given preparatory tasks, the invitation to the work-shop has to make it clear to the participants why something is being done, what it is expected to achieve, how one intends to proceed, and who all the other par-ticipants are going to be:

- Reason
- Objectives
- Contents
- Process (rough guide to procedures)
- Rules
- Participants

If it is possible without too much extra effort and cost, it is advisable for these aspects to be discussed in person with the participants at an in-house meeting beforehand.

Since workshops are intended to create a momentum that will often go far beyond the individual meeting itself, it is also advisable for the immediate en-vironment to be suitably drawn in. You will know from the exploratory discus-sions which people are affected by the workshop's goals, or which people think they are. You will also know who can affect the force field around the topic, and how much influence they have. Against this background, it can be decided who should be informed about the workshop by whom and in what way, and who needs be kept up to date with it and thus included in the overall process.

Length

Once the topic and methods have been established and the participants' state of mind is known, you can assess how much time should be allotted to the workshop.

There are three factors that should be taken into account here:

▶ An apparently harmless factual topic may be concealing unexpected dangers. It is only when a more detailed discussion is held with sufficient openness that the quite different topics really involved in it emerge.
▶ Some of the tensions associated with factual matters, or with the relationship structures involved, will only become capable of being discussed or perhaps even solved in an atmosphere in which enough time is allotted to informal contacts and to talking – often till late at night.
▶ There are always incalculable group-dynamic elements. Unexpected rivalries and trench warfare campaigns, as well as unpaid debts from earlier attempts to find a solution, can take up a lot of time – at least, much more time than was planned.

If you want to use workshops not only to deal with specific factual topics, but also to encourage team spirit and a mood of fresh departures, it is definitely useful to plan generous amounts of time. When there are emotionally charged issues involved, it is particularly valuable to include overnight stays so that the evenings can be used.

It is very useful in these cases to arrive early the previous evening and discuss the objectives, program, rules, and framework together, followed by an informal evening, and then start on the real work next morning fresh after a good night's rest. This is not only the best way of "warming up," it also has the advantage that unclear matters can be discussed early enough and in peace and quiet without the real program being affected. In addition, a great deal of information can be exchanged bilaterally and unfinished tasks can be completed, so that everyone can start on the shared topics with their minds clear.

Organization and role assignment

Decisions on where to hold the meeting, the choice of meeting rooms, and the specific time plan should be made not only on the basis of matter-of-fact considerations and costs; psychological factors should also be taken into account (see Figure 35: "Organizing Workshops" and Figure 36: "Design and preparation

Figure 35. Organizing workshops

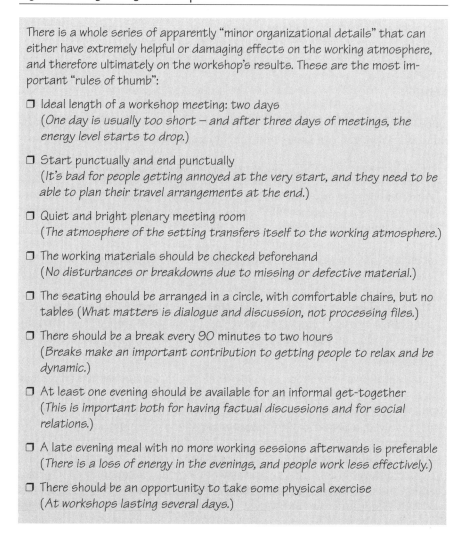

There is a whole series of apparently "minor organizational details" that can either have extremely helpful or damaging effects on the working atmosphere, and therefore ultimately on the workshop's results. These are the most important "rules of thumb":

❏ Ideal length of a workshop meeting: two days
(*One day is usually too short – and after three days of meetings, the energy level starts to drop.*)

❏ Start punctually and end punctually
(*It's bad for people getting annoyed at the very start, and they need to be able to plan their travel arrangements at the end.*)

❏ Quiet and bright plenary meeting room
(*The atmosphere of the setting transfers itself to the working atmosphere.*)

❏ The working materials should be checked beforehand
(*No disturbances or breakdowns due to missing or defective material.*)

❏ The seating should be arranged in a circle, with comfortable chairs, but no tables (*What matters is dialogue and discussion, not processing files.*)

❏ There should be a break every 90 minutes to two hours
(*Breaks make an important contribution to getting people to relax and be dynamic.*)

❏ At least one evening should be available for an informal get-together
(*This is important both for having factual discussions and for social relations.*)

❏ A late evening meal with no more working sessions afterwards is preferable
(*There is a loss of energy in the evenings, and people work less effectively.*)

❏ There should be an opportunity to take some physical exercise
(*At workshops lasting several days.*)

checklist"). The degree of effort shown and the organizational framework will also be interpreted by the participants as indicating the value of the event. It makes a difference whether you give the impression that you just want some matter-of-fact tasks carried out efficiently, or whether you make it clear that the time is intended for genuine encounters that encourage interpersonal relationships.

Finally, t needs to be clarified who is to have which tasks and roles:

– *Who is to be responsible for drawing up the design for the meeting? Who is to write the invitations, and who is to sign them and send them out?*

Figure 36. Workshop – design and preparation checklist

What needs to be done?

- Form a preparatory team
- Establish objectives and contents
- Select the participants
- Assess where the participants stand with regard to:
  - How clear are the goals
  - How much information do they have
  - Awareness of the problem
  - How much confidence do they have in what is planned
  - Openness
  - Motivation and commitment
- Decide on working methods
- Ensure that participants are sufficiently informed and prepared
- Decide on the length of the meeting
- Clarify the organizational framework
- Ensure that information is supplied to relevant outside bodies
- Clarify the distribution of tasks and roles between the responsible client, facilitator and any other officials required
- Draw up rules

What needs to be avoided?

- One-sided viewpoints and partiality
- False (too positive) assessment of the initial situation

- *What roles are to be assigned at the workshop: which tasks are to be carried out by the facilitator, and which belong to management?*
- *Are the usual privileges associated with higher status going to apply, particularly with regard to the frequency, length, and sequence of contributions to the discussion, or is this"pecking order" to be suspended during the meeting?*
- *Who is going to open the meeting? Who is going to arrange for any decisions to be taken if needed?*
- *Do minutes of the meeting need to be taken? If yes, what type: order of events, minutes of the content of discussions, minutes of results produced? Who will be responsible for writing and distributing the minutes?*

Clearing up these matters in advance will enable everyone involved to concentrate on the real job better.

Rules

To put the participants in the right mood for the type of work involved in a workshop, it may be helpful to list the important aspects in the form of "rules of the game" and agree on these as a *framework for behavior*. For example, the following aspects might be useful for guidance:

- *Principles of organizationl development, e. g.*: participation by those affected, systemic approach, helping people to help themselves, process-oriented approach, constantly adjusted planning.
- *Working on the subject matter and on the behavioral culture involved simultaneously*: this means keeping the specialist work in the foreground – but whenever atmospheric factors, personal attitudes and problems of mutual acceptance are involved, "turning the tables" and picking up these topics for careful discussion until the connections and interactions between the two aspects become clear.
- *Searching for solutions – if possible within one's own field of responsibility*: this means not being satisfied with just providing fresh descriptions for existing problems or complaining about them, but concentrating on solving them – with solutions that the people who are present can take responsibility for and implement.
- *Keeping an eye on the customer*: in all the analyses and solutions discussed, the points of view of other people who are not present, but are undoubtedly involved, need to be taken into account: employees, suppliers, internal and external customers.
- *Ensuring that matters are pursued further*: if it becomes clear that it will not be possible to deal with all the planned topics at the workshop, it needs to be clarified soon enough how the questions that have been left open will be followed up subsequently.

The phase of developing ideas and carrying out preparatory work also involves particular dangers and risks:

- ▶ Each of the parties involved may try to get the facilitator on its side. If he lets himself be too strongly influenced by the point of view and the arguments of one side or another, there is a risk that he will cease to be accepted.
- ▶ The participants' initial situation may have been evaluated too positively, since people dislike giving themselves a bad press. This can have the effect that a false procedural approach is taken – too objective, with too much focus on "efficiency" and with not enough time being allowed for "unfreezing."

Implementation

The basic idea underlying the meeting can provide valuable guidance to the organizer as well as to the participants and facilitator. It should therefore be made available in writing, if possible, instead of just being kept in the mind of the organizer or facilitator. However, putting it in writing by no means implies that everything has to run according to the plan. It has to be possible to react flexibly to dynamic developments – and in fact, this is where the real skill in running a meeting lies.

Special aspects of the start-up phase

Every situation involving a completely new group dynamic creates initial psychological difficulties for the participants. What stands out in the foreground for them at the beginning is not the questions listed on the invitation or the agenda, but usually concealed emotional questions:

– *What can I expect here?*
– *Who are the other participants, and how are they going to behave?*
– *Where can I take risks here, and where would it be better to be cautious?*
– *How am I going to cope here?*

Giving the right psychological structure to this type of start-up situation will have a decisive influence on the later success of the meeting. No matter how good the preparation for the workshop has been, and no matter how well those directly involved have familiarized themselves with the subject-matter and kept in touch with one another, it should not be forgotten that the participants are often facing a completely fresh start with this specific group of people, with the topic involved, and with the procedures being used. Particularly during the initial phase, our experience shows that serious mistakes are made – out of ignorance, uncertainty, sometimes even due to a lack of courage. We will therefore concentrate on these aspects here in particular, and provide tools mainly for the start-up phase.

The first step involves getting all the participants onto the same initial level, creating a common working basis. To do this, the organizer and facilitator first provide information about:

- Prior discussions that have taken place.
- Insights derived from those discussions.
- The idea for the meeting that has been developed from that.
- And what the organizer expects the workshop to achieve.

In addition, the rules for the meeting can be mentioned, including the role assignments between the manager responsible and the external facilitator who has been called in, when appropriate.

If the preparatory group has predicted that the initial situation is likely to be "normal," then it is the participants' turn immediately after this introduction to describe their expectations – using the following key questions, for example:

- *What do I think about the reason for this meeting, its goals, and the topics involved?*
- *What do I think about the way in which we are intending to approach the subject-matter here?*
- *What are the implications of that for my mood, my motivation, and my commitment in this workshop?*

If the group is larger than 10 – 12 people, it is best to discuss these questions in smaller subgroups and provide reports to the plenary session only about the main trends.

Everyone now has an initial impression of each another – objectively, as well as emotionally. The way in which the participants' expectations are described and presented provides further information about the initial situation – and therefore an opportunity to arrange the subsequent procedures accordingly and adjust the plan if necessary. If everything runs according to expectations, the process can go on using the existing agenda.

If it has already become clear, even during the preparatory phase, that the participants are likely to be in a tense or unpredictable situation to begin with, or if this introductory round shows that for one reason or another there is a "catch," then a "unfreezing" phase has to be introduced as a confidence-building measure.

Model for unfreezing

"Unfreezing" means that the analysis of the participants' initial state is expanded to become the actual first section of the workshop meeting. The focus is placed on the participants' current state of mind and the implications of this for their ability to work together and conduct a dialogue, and for their capacity to achieve something at the meeting. Together, everyone analyzes what has led to the current state and what would be required to change it. However, the major difficulty here consists of the fact that the vital aspects of the situation have been "swept under the carpet" and cannot be directly mentioned without difficulty. In cases like this, what are known as "projective methods" help – procedures that allow subliminal aspects to be brought to the surface not directly, but in a roundabout way and without anyone having to lose face.

Model 1: *Image without words*

1. *Forming groups*: in order to overcome inhibitions about making direct personal statements on delicate topics at an early stage when there is still uncertainty, the participants can be asked to form themselves into small groups of three to five people, with the choice being left completely open. The formation of "cliques" is actually desirable here, as it clarifies the informal network within the overall group.

The manager responsible, or the management team, should form a separate group, to ensure that the differing points of view of employees and management are not intermingled, or to prevent employees from anticipating and opportunistically agreeing to their boss's opinions and to prevent the bosses from being able to remain "under cover."

2. *Assigning tasks*: to begin with, everyone can make a quick personal note (about 10 minutes) about his or her thoughts on the following questions:

- *How do I feel about the current situation?*
- *What is this situation mainly determined by: e. g., people, positions, standards, atmosphere, interplay between people, conflicts?*
- *In what ways does this condition affect us, our feelings and our capacity for achievement?*

Each selected group can then meet with this starting material and discuss the various viewpoints listed in this way, working out what there is in common and where the differences lie, before finally preparing a group presentation. The group's results should reflect both the areas of agreement and the range of individual expectations (about 30 minutes).

After this, the group can then discuss how to represent its fundamental views in pictorial form using an agreed "*image without words*" – drawn on a flip-chart or on a screen – and can then create the image (about 30 minutes).

3. *Presenting the results*: the trick lies in getting the various groups only to display their images one after another to begin with – without making any comments on them at all. Everyone else who does not belong to the group concerned can then carry out free association about what they think each of the images is supposed to represent. This allows people to freely state what they have on their minds, without seeming to have any responsibility – after all, the picture is there in front of them! People can make jokes, exaggerate, make insinuations, be provocative – everything that is otherwise not permitted by normal conventions and manners. Once their colleagues' free flow of associations has dried up, the "artists" who produced the picture can then describe their own interpretation of it.

It is only very rarely that this exercise will fail to work properly. There are almost always a few objections to overcome at the beginning – "We're not artists! ... Why should we bother with this childish stuff?" But with a little skill and guidance, pointing out that "one picture can say more than a thousand words," this barrier is usually easily overcome.

Once all the images have been interpreted and commented on, a great deal of progress has already been made in analyzing the relationship structure and the overall emotional situation. The subliminal aspects involved are now more easily addressed. Usually, the "normal" clarification of people's expectations, as described above, can now proceed.

However, if it is found that the real problems actually lie in this subliminal, atmospheric area – either expressed openly or presented in the form of demonstrative "walls" and denials – then it is definitely still too soon for a start to be made with the planned agenda. Either the subliminal topic that has been touched on will have to be explored further, until the group is capable of working sufficiently well to go on to the main topics planned. Alternatively, you can decide spontaneously to change the planned agenda and make the "minor" topic into the *major* one.

Model 2: *what you think others are thinking …*

If the above method of using images is not appealing, verbal questions can also be used to sound out the participants' inner state. The decisive projective element in this method lies in not only asking for people's personal assessments of the situation, but also about *what they think other people are thinking …*

1. *Formulating the questions*: the questions should be aimed as precisely as possible at areas the preparatory investigations suggest are potentially emotional, but where things are being "swept under the carpet." These may be *objective* matters- e.g., identification with company strategy, structure and distribution of tasks, questions of management style on the part of bosses or colleagues, questions of cooperation and communication – but can also include more *emotional* questions about motivation, commitment, or openness and honesty in the meeting itself (see Figure 37).

2. *Explaining the questions, letting people fill out the questionnaire, and scoring.* The questions can be displayed where everyone can clearly read them – e.g., on screens or pin boards – and explained briefly. Everyone can anonymously write in their choices on a sheet of paper. The results are collected, scored, and displayed. It is important that not just the average, but the range of values given in the answers should be shown, e.g.:

N° 9 Openness and honesty at this meeting

a) I myself will say completely openly and honestly what I really think.

	1	2	3	4	5	6	I will be rather reserved and wait and see how things develop.	Ø 1.7
	x	x			x			
	x	x						
	x	x						
	x							
	x							
	x							

b) So far as I know my colleagues, I believe they will all give their genuine opinions completely openly and honestly.

	1	2	3	4	5	6	I suspect that a large number of people will be waiting to see what happens and will behave tactically.	Ø 3.6
		x	x	x		x		
		x	x	x		x		
			x					
			x					

Figure 37. Workshop – Strategy and Team Development.
Model of a questionnaire

1. *Identification with the scenario of company development and the planned strategy*

   a) I myself am completely in agreement. 1 2 3 4 5 6 I tend to take the view that things should not be so precisely fixed in advance.

   b) So far as I know the other people here personally, I am sure everyone is completely behind it. 1 2 3 4 5 6 I have some doubts about whether everyone is really completely behind it.

2. *Satisfaction with the new form of organization and the distribution of tasks*

   a) I myself am not really entirely happy with it. 1 2 3 4 5 6 I think the new form and distribution are a complete success.

   b) I believe some of my colleagues here may still regard the new situation as involving a few problems. 1 2 3 4 5 6 I am completely convinced that everyone here is fully behind it without any reservations.

3. *Management style practiced by those further up*

   a) The official guidelines make a committment to cooperative management style – but the reality is quite different, as I see it. 1 2 3 4 5 6 The last few months have completely convinced me that the concept is being given life from the top down, and is being consistently implemented.

   b) I suspect that my colleagues here are no longer really taking the official guidelines seriously, based on their experience so far. 1 2 3 4 5 6 I know that the others here are completely convinced by the idea, based on their experience of it in management practice so far.

4. *Management style at one's own level*

   a) In my own area of responsibility, I have completely implemented the cooperative management approach. 1 2 3 4 5 6 The goal and the reality are still far apart in my work.

b) I expect that my colleagues have already fully implemented the cooperative style.

1 2 3 4 5 6 In my opinion, my colleagues have still got a lot to do in this regard.

5. Cooperation with one another

a) In my view, the degree of cooperation in our management team leaves a lot to be desired.

1 2 3 4 5 6 I am completely and unreservedly satisfied with the cooperation we have.

b) Other people here probably think that we could make considerable improvements.

1 2 3 4 5 6 Other people here un-doubtedly have a completely positive impression of the way people cooperate.

6. Overall assessment of the way things have been done so far

a) I personally think what has been done so far and the steps planned next are good and successful.

1 2 3 4 5 6 I have serious reservations and am therefore rather skeptical at the moment.

b) So far as I know my colleagues here, I am certain that all of them unreservedly believe what has been done is good and successful.

1 2 3 4 5 6 I suspect that several people probably still have strong doubts.

7. Belief in the success of our strategy

a) I am firmly convinced that we will manage it.

1 2 3 4 5 6 We should wait and see how it works out in practice.

b) I am certain that everyone else is fully convinced of its success.

1 2 3 4 5 6 I suspect people still have substantial doubts and reservations.

8. Motivation and commitment to this workshop meeting

a) I myself am completely convinced that this meeting is valuable and am therefore fully motivated and committed.

1 2 3 4 5 6 It is not really clear to me what we are actually doing here, and I am waiting to see how it will turn out.

b) I am convinced that the other people here are fully motivated and committed.

1 2 3 4 5 6 I am pretty sure people here are inwardly rather detached from what is going on.

9. Openness and honesty at this meeting

a) I myself will say completely
openly and honestly what I
really think.

1 2 3 4 5 6   I will be rather reserved and
wait and see how things
develop.

b) So far as I know my
colleagues, I believe they
will all give their genuine
opinions completely openly
and honestly.

1 2 3 4 5 6   I suspect that a large
number of people will be
waiting to see what happens
and will behave tactically.

The risk of getting tied up in the details of various aspects can be avoided by adding an extra general question at the end, e. g.:

Overall need for repair work or further development required: when I look at the overall organization that we are dealing with here, I see a percentage overall need for "repair work," or a need for further development, of about:

100% 90% 80% 70% 60% 50% 40% 30% 20% 10% 0%

3. *Common analysis*: the scores usually speak for themselves, and do not need much comment. What is decisive is for people to talk to one another about them, about what they mean – and above all about what lies behind *their assumptions about their colleagues.*

This kind of topic focussed questionnaire is another way of getting people involved and making them feel they are affected, creating an awareness of the problem, bringing subliminal aspects to the surface, and exposing and activating the available motivations and resistance.

Once the psychological terrain has been sufficiently clarified and the necessary capacity for work and dialogue has been established, the real issues can be addressed. By contrast, if you go from a cold start and plunge straight into work on the real issues, there is a high probability that the meeting will fail. The psychological aspects that have not been worked through will interfere with work on the issues, and will distort it or obstruct it.

Setting priorities and finalizing the program

Now that the expectations of the organizers and of the participants have been openly laid out, the goals and subject areas for the meeting and the planned sequence and depth of work on them can be jointly checked, and if necessary supplemented or corrected. If things are more or less obvious, a brief discussion

Figure 38. Workshop – checklist: Conducting the Workshop

Phase I *Introduction*

- *Getting started, warming up*
  - Welcome and provision of information about events leading up to the workshop
  - Clarifying participants' expectations

- *Unfreezing*
  If the participants do not know each other, creating a basis for work and dialogue:
  - Image without words, or
  - Assessment of the initial situation for oneself and others

- *Program*
  - Overview of topics
  - Setting priorities and establishing a sequence
  - Assigning time quotas

Phase II *Working through the topics*

Example procedure:

1. Collecting data/describing symptoms
2. Analyzing the problem
3. Analyzing the force fields involved
4. Developing ideas for necessary changes
5. Plan of action
6. What will happen if nothing is done?
7. Prognosis for success

Continuous monitoring:

a) Progress of work on the subject-matter
b) Communication and cooperation in the overall team

Phase III *Recording results and planning follow-up and implementation*

- Summing up the conclusions and clearing up any points left open

- Establishing follow-up process:
  - Specific tasks with deadlines: who is to do what by when?
  - Preview: what happens afterwards?
  - Minutes: who/by when/to whom/in what form?
  - Information about the workshop: who/to whom/how/by when?

- Feedback (mutual appraisal of the social process)

Figure 39. Workshop – ensuring transfer

Points to remember:

- *Without minutes of the results and planning for implementation, transfer to practice is not guaranteed.*

- *Guaranteeing results and transferring them into practice is decisive for participants' motivation.*

- *A workshop is only as good as its planning for follow-up processes.*

- *Planning for implementation means making the effort to reach agreement through discussion.*

- *The time required to ensure that results will subsequently be transferred into practice is usually underestimated.*

- *Overrunning the time plan at the end causes restlessness and annoyance.*

Conclusion:

> **From the very start, sufficient time must be reserved at the end of the workshop to ensure that results will subsequently be transferred into practice!**
> *Rule of thumb: one hour per day of the workshop (excluding feedback)*

will be enough to clarify matters. If the situation is not so clear, appropriate aids should be used to demonstrate the various points of view and wishes involved, in order to avoid any suspicion of manipulation. The simplest way is for each participant to be given a certain number of score points, which can then be assigned to the topics that seem most important.

Pattern for working through issues

The following procedure has proved its value for working through a given set of issues – either in plenary sessions or in subgroups:

1. **Collecting data and describing the symptoms**
   What is it all about? What is the actual reason why we are dealing with this topic?
   Where is the shoe pinching? What symptoms have appeared?
   What problems are likely as a consequence?

2. **Analyzing the problem**
   What lies behind it? What are the possible causes of it?
   What does the real problem consist of? What else is it connected with?

3. **Analyzing the force field**
   a) *What is it that has made the current situation so attractive that it was capable of arising in the first place, or has been able to persist? Who is benefiting from this situation? Who might have an interest in everything remaining the way it is (even though he may be loudly complaining about it at the same time)?*
   b) *Who is genuinely dissatisfied? Who is really interested in changing things?*
   c) *What is the overall balance of forces between the energies that are maintaining things the way they are and the energies that are aiming to change things?*

4. **Plan for change**
   Taking into account the range of different interests that have been identified, what could the potential changes look like? How can the expected resistance to these changes be dealt with? What alternatives are there with regard to specific ways of proceeding?

5. **Plan of action**
   How can the planned change be specifically implemented? What resources are available and how much effort is needed? Who needs to do what by when?

6. **Final check**
   What will happen if nothing is done?
   (Dealing with this scenario serves, on the one hand, to allow reassessment of the "cost of change" – sometimes it is "cheaper" in the end just to live with certain problems; on the other hand, discussing this question can also release the final momentum necessary for change to be implemented.)

7. **Prognosis**
   How strongly do people believe that the planned change is going to succeed?
   (A final examination of whether people will just routinely go through the motions, or whether there are real chances for success – a fundamental criterion for the final decision as to whether or not the problem should really be tackled.)

The two-level principle

Whenever people get together, relationships develop. The type of relation involved has a substantial effect on the efficiency of work – either positive or negative. So attention must be given not only to the objective procedure and the content of what is discussed, but also to the way people relate to one another. As soon as things start to get stuck, the only solution is to take a break from working on the issues and have a look "backstage" to see what is going on in the area of interpersonal relations – and what effect it is currently having on the work.

Progress and process reviews

To ensure that potential disturbances are recognized early enough, it is a good idea – in addition to dealing on the spot with any disturbances or obstructions that come up – to carry out a regular preventative check on the group's internal state – e. g., using the following questions:

- *Are we dealing with the right questions here?*
- *How satisfied are we with the results so far?*
- *How would we assess the process we are using?*
- *What do we feel about the way we are relating to one another?*

This pause for thought, making an interim appraisal either for a specific reason or just prophylactically, or putting together a current picture of the group's mood, can open people's eyes to important subliminal trends in relationships and behavior. What these interim reviews reveal can allow you to decide whether you should go on dealing with the selected matters without any second thoughts, or whether it would be advisable to change the subject for a time in order to remove any disturbances that may have accumulated. Genuinely skillful facilitation involves keeping an eye on both aspects – the issues of substance one is concerned with, and the relationships between the participants, i.e. both the *what* and the *how* – relating them to one another and working on whichever side of the stage is currently the decisive one.

The end is by no means the close …

Workshops are not one-off events that occur in isolation. As we have pointed out above, workshops are meant instead to create the decisive momentum needed for long-term processes of development – often going far beyond the meeting itself. With a view to all that will come after the workshop, you have to finish or interrupt work on the subject matter early enough to ensure that enough time is left to clarify subsequent procedures:

- *What tasks have we completed, and how are we going to ensure that results are implemented in practice?*
- *Which points are still open, and what is going to be done about them?*
- *Who needs to be informed about the results, by whom and in what way?*
- *Who will be in charge of managing the follow-up of the process?*

Implementation and the remainder of the development process can ultimately only be ensured by reaching clear agreements about who needs to do what by when, and who is to have overall responsibility for the process.

After completing a final appraisal and carrying out planning for the follow-up, a short joint appraisal of the emotional aspects should take place at the end as well. "Joint" in this case means that all the participants should speak, at least briefly.

Main questions:

- *How do I assess the results?*
- *What do I think about the way the workshop has gone?*
- *How satisfied or dissatisfied am I with the role I have played at this workshop?*
- *What is my mood now that I'm on my way home?*

This final feedback session should not take place under time pressure. It provides a last opportunity for imbalances in the social structure, or imponderable aspects involved in subsequent procedures, to be identified and discussed.

Frequently encountered dangers

▶ *Excessive objectivity*: even when everyone has recognized the importance of interpersonal relations when working on issues, and fully intends to bear this in mind during the meeting, it is still far too tempting to make the workshop as objective as possible. Human relations are a delicate topic. Not surprisingly, therefore, people usually try to avoid them as much as possible in every day work. They only start talking about it when it becomes unavoidable – i.e., once discussion of the subject matter has ground to a complete halt. Valuable time is wasted. Earlier, it might still have been possible to control the potential disturbance to the meeting's work. By contrast, dealing with fully developed disturbances in social relations is not only extremely laborious, but also much more unpredictable.

▶ *Concentrating on solutions*: *"I've got a terrific solution – all that's missing is a problem to go with it…"* The statement is, of course, completely true to life – perhaps because it is better for people's personal prestige to offer quick patent solutions, and ones that are as spectacular as possible, than to get involved in an unobtrusive, laborious search for background and context. If things are not nipped in the bud, people can start racing each other up the pass lane to produce ideal solutions. The atmosphere becomes hectic, and everyone starts worrying about making a strong enough impression. When this happens, there is only one thing to do: turn the stage round, explicitly discuss the behavioral pattern causing the disturbance, and thus create space for a calmer atmosphere in which mutual searching, care, and "hastening slowly" are required.

▶ *Overzealous facilitation*: the chairman or facilitator feels he is the one with the main responsibility for the meeting actually producing results. He wants to be able to prove something – to his clients, and above all to himself. He pushes the system forward, behaves like a "better-quality manager," and makes himself the real standard-bearer. Imperceptibly, the participants are allowed to escape their own responsibility for supporting the meeting. Any resistance that occurs is either overlooked or skillfully maneuvered out of the way by the facilitator.

▶ *Deliberate confusion tactics by the participants: behaving "as if"*: every state of affairs must have some attractiveness for people, since it would otherwise not exist – and this should not be underestimated. Complaining about a state of affairs by no means implies a genuine desire to change it. If this type of vested interest – which is well concealed for good reasons – is not recognized, then an external facilitator, in particular, runs the risk of being taken in by the clientele's tricks. And one of the most sophisticated forms of protest and resistance consists in people behaving as if they were totally dedicated to the workshop and involved in it. Everyone hides behind a front of hectic activity, busily producing materials. There are yard-long lists of problems and suggested changes. Visual aids are exploited to desperation point. At the same time, everyone knows – and this is the goal they are all aiming for – that nothing is going to change after the workshop. However, they are well practiced in maintaining appearances enough to ensure that no suspicions are aroused. The complaints that are often still heard about the ineffectiveness of workshop meetings suggest that these alibi exercises take place much more frequently than you would expect. The more the facilitator concentrates on the subject-matter involved, the less he will be able to expose this game. On the contrary, he will mistake the participants' enthusiasm for genuine commitment – and will probably think it was his skillful facilitation that gave rise to it.

▶ *Protective design*: the great advantage of meetings held as closed special events lies in the invaluable (if difficult to control) *group dynamic* that they create. Processes suddenly become possible that were previously inconceivable. Understandably, some organizers or facilitators feel rather uncertain and anxious in the face of this potential dynamic at the meeting. And to control their own insecurity, they try to structure the event as precisely and narrowly as possible with regard to its content, methods, and timing, leaving no room for maneuver – in the hope that nothing will happen that they won't have under their control, as if the only point of the agenda and planning was to make the facilitator's life easier.

But this type of overstructuring is an inappropriate straitjacket, in view of the important goals involved in this type of meeting. Because – among other things – a workshop is meant to allow genuine encounters, creating space for learning and personal development, a momentum that can produce a sense of community. In addition, practice shows that a suppressed emotional dynamic will sooner or later burst its bonds in one way or another, despite every precaution that is taken. The more tightly a meeting is structured without sufficient reason, the more you will need to be prepared for unpleasant surprises. Of course, it is just as out of place to make desperate efforts to allow group-dynamic topics to boil over. The workshop's objective results must always remain the primary goal. Instead, it is a matter of sensing, according to the situation, when there are subliminal emotional processes going on that are interfering with the work and obstructing it in the background. Exposing and discussing these processes has only one purpose: to restore the capacity for dialogue and work – on the familiar principle that "disturbances take priority."

▶ *Failure to ensure that results will be transferred into practice*: often, workshops that have, in principle, gone very well finish with a disproportionate amount of rush, with no clear agreements being made on subsequent actions, and with correspondingly mixed feelings on the part of the participants about the cost – benefit ratio. To begin with, not enough time has been allotted at the very outset to ensure that results will be implemented and that subsequent actions and feedback can be discussed. Secondly, toward the end you happen to be in the middle of an important topic and you want to "round it off" at all costs. Thirdly, everyone starts to feel restless, because they have booked their travel arrangements according to the program and are afraid the meeting is going to overrun it time. The result: the closing section of the workshop turns into an undignified botch, or is just left out completely. The mutual working process is abruptly broken off, and subsequent activities bear no relation to the value of what has been achieved at the workshop. This clearly belongs in the category of "wasting valuable resources." It is always possible to continue work later on unfinished topics – provided it is jointly planned at an early enough stage. The final part of a workshop therefore has to be allotted sufficient time in the program, and this time must under no circumstances be encroached on.

Figure 40. Workshop – the main risks

▶ Rationalising emotional topics

▶ Concentrating too much on solutions

▶ Overzealous facilitation

▶ Confusion tactics by participants *(pretend "as if ... ")*

▶ Protective design

▶ Failure to ensure that results will be transferred into practice

Conflict Management

10

Conflicts are normal

Conflicts are actually a completely normal and everyday part of human life. There is no such thing as a relationship that is permanently free of conflict. Wherever people act together, different points of view, needs, and interests collide – sometimes between individuals, sometimes between smaller groups, and sometimes also between large organizations. And when changes of some sort need to be made, conflicts are already pre-programmed – because there are always some people who want to create something new, and others who want to preserve the status quo. There can never be change without conflict.

Most conflicts are resolved in everyday life in a completely undramatic way. Sometimes one person gives in, sometimes the other, and sometimes a compromise acceptable to both sides is worked out – and next day, no one can remember any more that a conflict situation arose at all. From time to time, however – suddenly and unexpectedly – things take a completely different course. Dialogue develops into a dispute, which in turn becomes an argument. Emotions start to heat up: outrage and anger, hate and contempt. The opposing parties become locked together in an exchange of attacks and counterattacks. People get hurt – and before you know it, there is a war going on and the main aim is to annihilate the opponent. When it is all over, there are either a winner or a loser – or rather, there are two losers. All that is left is the damage that has been done – at best, wrecked interpersonal relationships; at worst, deaths, physical injuries and psychologically damaged people, ruined villages, scorched earth.

To prevent things taking this course – in the community of nations, in family life, or at work – is one of life's primary goals, from both the ethical and the economic point of view. The ability to recognize conflict situations quickly enough and control them in such a way that change is possible, while at the same time damage is limited, is one of the most important things a manager can do nowadays in exercising his profession successfully.

The dynamics of conflict development

If you want to repair a bicycle or an automobile, you first have to understand how it works. So we can give a quick review here of the most important aspects of the dynamics of conflict.

An uncontrolled conflict typically has four clearly distinguishable phases:

1. Discussion

As a longer-term conflict process develops, the events it causes can become so strongly superimposed over the original issue that in the end no one can remember that the original conflict itself ever existed. At the very beginning, however, there is always something at *issue* – the subject which, during what was a quite friendly dialogue to begin with, gave rise to differing opinions or showed that differing interests had to be asserted.

Example: *in an open-plan office where conditions are rather cramped, Department X asks its neighboring Department Y whether it might agree to transfer four square yards of extra floor space to it, to make room for a new item of specialized equipment that Department X has had to buy. However, Department Y points out that it is short of space itself, and is not in a position to give away any of its office space.*

The issue is a perfectly everyday matter. To begin with, there is no reason for a severe conflict to develop. Similar problems have often come up at this particular office. And so far, a solution has always been found.

2. Superimposed events

During the discussion, a critical situation develops: one side's arguments cease to be accepted by the other. What the other side says is called into question. The other side is accused of being self-interested, behaving tactically, and therefore of being insincere. At this point, the dispute rises to the moral level. The actual issue has questions of value, relationships, and personal matters superimposed on it. Emotions come into play.

Example: *Department X believes that Department Y is not nearly as short of space as it is itself. In addition, working with the new equipment will require a high degree of concentration, and constant disturbances will not be possible. Department Y, on the other hand, considers that Department X is using a perfectly ordinary piece of working equipment as an excuse to make itself more comfortable at other people's expense.*

Fairness and justice become the central issue. In addition, Department X feels that its professional importance is not being taken seriously. It feels belittled. Department Y, on the other hand, is afraid of being exploited and outmaneuvered. Value judgments and personal issues start to be at stake.

3. Escalation

As soon as one side starts to believe that the other is not taking it seriously, and that its dignity or integrity is being infringed or even that it is being lied to or abused, it reacts with anger and outrage. It thinks the gauntlet has been thrown down, and – justifiably, in its own eyes – moves onto the counterattack. And exactly the same happens on the other side.

Communications between the partners are interrupted. Attempts are made to isolate the opposing side and injure it. Allies are sought in the vicinity. The conflict moves into the *hot* phase. What is known as *symmetrical escalation* develops. This is based on three mechanisms:

- *First*: emotions on both sides supply massive amounts of energy, with people becoming more committed than ever before.
- *Secondly*: events no longer take place on the basis of the logic of the issue involved; the process has *escaped rational control*.
- *Thirdly*: both sides start suffering from *selective perception*. They only notice whatever confirms their own prejudices about the opposing party – and systematically ignore whatever contradicts these prejudices. The effect of this is that every step taken by one side makes the other feel justified in hitting back even more heavily.

It is no longer the original issue that is in the foreground, but the *current behavior* of each side. The struggle has become self-perpetuating.

Example: an unpleasant encounter takes place between representatives of Departments X and Y, during which both sides hurl at the other's head everything they think about each other. Both sides make personal reproaches and hurtful accusations. After this, the atmosphere is ruined. People stop talking to one another. Both sides make representations further up the hierarchy. Sharply-worded documents are formulated. People and departments in the vicinity are drawn in and polarized. The open-plan office splits into two "camps."

Emotions now dominate the scene. The issue about the office space has not been forgotten. But the foreground is now dominated by questions of fairness and justice, the importance or unimportance of specific duties and tasks, and – last, but not least – the credibility of specific individuals.

4. Hardening of attitudes

No conflict can remain permanently in the hot phase. Sooner or later, a cooling-off period occurs – either because one side has won and imposed its own interests, or because the balance of power has created a stalemate situation that develops into a state of delicate balance. In the latter case, it is a "cold war" that dominates the picture, and the conflict has become "chronic." In the working world, this is quite a frequently encountered situation. It can go on for years, or even decades. Real or perceived injustices are not forgotten, however, and a constant potential for future conflict remains.

Example: in view of the crisis, management has decided to cut the Gordian knot and issue a judgment of Solomon: Department Y will transfer two square yards of office space to Department X. This decision is final, there is to be no further discussion, and conditions become more cramped in both departments. The neighboring departments go back to their normal routine, but the atmosphere between these two departments is still disturbed. They never talk to each other, and certainly no one ever cooperates with people from the other department. People systematically avoid one another.

Maintaining conditions like this – and particularly the *lack of communication and cooperation between two task areas* – takes up phenomenal amounts of time, money, and nerves. In addition, the danger of open hostilities breaking out is never entirely banished. But the environment has learned how to stabilize the situation to some extent, at least in the cold state.

Prerequisites for conflict resolution

Every conflict has its own history. It is not just a sudden event, and certainly not an accidental one; it is the result of a very specific process of development. A conflict is "learned" – and if you want to eliminate it, you have to make sure it is "unlearned" again. An understanding of what has happened needs to be acquired, mistrust has to be broken down step by step, and trust has to be gradually built up again. The steps that led everyone astray have to be retraced for some distance before a new course for the future can be charted without any danger of a relapse.

In concrete terms, what has to be done?

- *Establishing direct communications*
  A conflict can only be solved by the conflicting parties themselves, if at all. However, direct communications between them were broken off at an early stage of the conflict process. The first and most important task is therefore to reestablish a situation of direct dialogue – i.e., getting the adversaries round a table.
- *Monitoring the dialogue*
  The two parties to the conflict are not initially capable of genuinely communicating with one another. Without outside assistance, the continued effect of selective perception would mean that in no time at all they would misunderstand each other again and get tangled up in an argument. Particularly during the initial phase, a neutral third party is needed to carefully monitor the interactions between the two parties , and ensure at every step that what is said is not understood differently from the way in which it was intended.
- *Exposing emotions*
  There is no hope of solving the conflict if the subjective perceptions, disappointed expectations, feelings of offense and injury on each side cannot be openly articulated. It is only when this is done that the pressure of pent-up emotions can be reduced and the conflict can be reduced to the level of its origin – i.e., genuine needs and interests.

- *Coming to terms with the past*
  It is not enough simply for people to express their feelings. Both partners have to get the other side to understand the circumstances, situations, or events that caused them frustration, disappointment or fury – and why. It is only when this is done that each party can recognize its own – intentional or un-intentional – contribution to the process of conflict. This in turn is a precondition for ceasing to regard the other party as the only guilty one.
- *Negotiating a mutually acceptable solution*
  Once the rubble has been cleared away, what matters is working out a lasting solution to the problem. The decisive aspect here is that no one must be seen as a "loser" (see Figure 41, "Modes of human conflict behavior"). It has to be genuinely rewarding for both partners to break with the past and enter into negotiations. The solution has to take the interests of both parties into account. But the solution is only one aspect; negotiating it on a basis of part-nership is another. Practicing ways of working together is in itself an impor-tant step in resolving conflict. It is only here that a real farewell to conflict actually takes place. So far, people have just been talking. Now they have to *do* something together. A *new situation* is created.

Figure 41. Modes of human conflict behavior

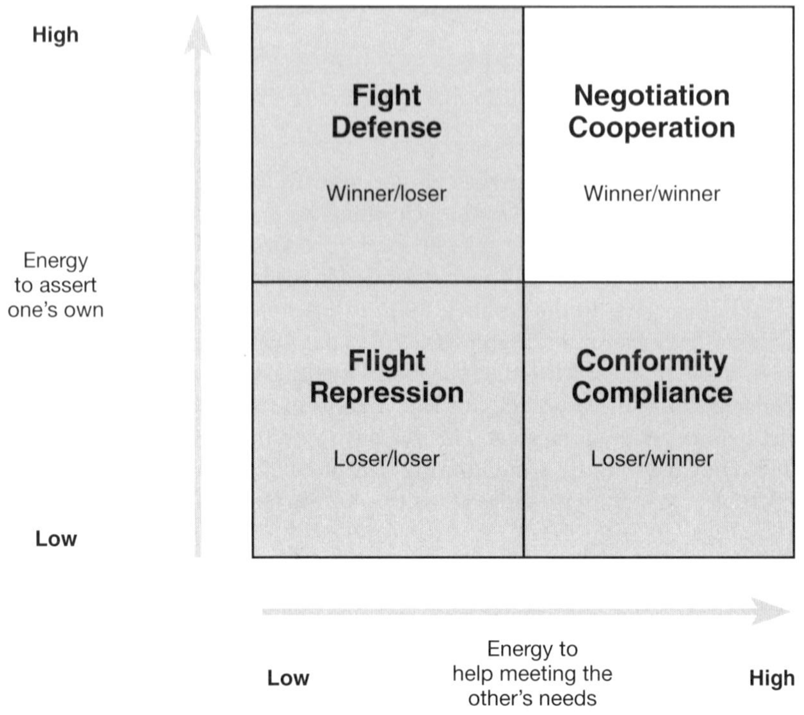

Phases of conflict resolution

Based on the above preconditions, a purposeful and planned process of conflict resolution between two parties – whether individuals or groups – takes place in six phases. This "process architecture" is not arbitrarily chosen. Each phase builds on the previous one, and none of the steps can be omitted.

Phase 1: *Preparation*

This is the phase of the neutral third party, the mediator and conflict manager. He has access to both parties to the conflict, and at the outset forms the only link between them. During this phase, he has two aims. First, *understanding the background to the conflict*: learning the history as seen from the point of view of each of the parties; identifying the interests and sensitivities of each side. Secondly, *creating the preconditions for genuine talks*: indicating perspectives; questioning the "hopelessness" of the situation; giving people courage; and suggesting rules and procedural steps for a direct meeting. The mediator has to carry out shuttle diplomacy during this phase – perhaps even for an extended period – going back and forth between the two parties to the conflict. He represents the first, indirect and auxiliary form of communication between two parties who are formally incommunicado. "*Kissinger diplomacy*" has become a term often used for this.

Phase 2: *Opening up*

When things get this far, a great deal has already been achieved: people can actually sit at the same table with each other once again. However, the atmosphere is tense, and there is a high level of distrust. What matters now is confirming everything that has been promised in the bilateral contacts in the presence of both parties to the conflict: the *starting-point;* the *purpose* of the exercise; the individual *procedural steps;* the *rules;* the *role of the mediator;* the *role of the two parties to the conflict;* the *time plan*. Usually, no queries or corrections are needed regarding these points. But it is a good idea to mention these matters explicitly once again at the start. The two parties to the conflict are emotionally excited. They may not be remembering half of what has been agreed and promised. A clear structure provides security – for the mediator as well.

Phase 3: *Confrontation*

It is now a matter of the two partners openly presenting their view of matters, their specific experiences and perceptions, and the feelings associated with them. By far the best way of doing this is in a structured fashion: first the one side, then the other. If both sides talk at the same time chaotically, genuine communication and understanding is not possible, and the task for the moderator will become too difficult. There are two decisive aspects. First, both reports have to be listened to in full, must not be interrupted, and should not initially be discussed or dismissed. Secondly, openness. The people presenting the reports should just say exactly what they think and speak quite freely. Questions can be asked if something has not been understood, but every other kind of interruption must be immediately silenced by the facilitator.

Phase 4: *Evaluation*

Once all the experiences and feelings the partners to the conflict have brought with them are out in the open, the material has to be mutually inspected, arranged, and evaluated. There are issues that are still open and have to be clarified; there are important new recognitions, things one had not been aware of or may have interpreted falsely, and there are matters one does not wish to leave as they are – points that have to be made more specific, pictures that have to be straightened out, wounds that need to be licked. During this phase, care is the number one priority. This, if anywhere, is where aggression, distrust and prejudices must be broken down; here, if anywhere, is where the conditions for creating fresh trust can be created. It may be necessary to go back into the past for a bit in order to understand what happened properly – and see it as an unfortunate process-related event, instead of as an act of unilateral aggression that one has been the victim of. Moral indignation can be cleared away, and the issue of guilt can be abandoned – that is the fundamental aim here.

Phase 5: *Negotiation*

What are the genuine concerns? What objective interests are present – and what emotional needs? These matters have to be clarified by both sides. It is only when both sides have genuinely understood the other's priorities that negotiating a solution can start with any prospect of success. Generally, there is no lack of ideas. But what is important is that the solution should be carefully safeguarded on each side. A single brilliant inspiration capable of making everyone happy is rarely found. The solution will have to be a compromise for both sides – but it must never be a cheap, shabby, or hasty compromise. Both partners have to explicitly confirm that the solution that has been found appears to them to be fair and acceptable. Otherwise, negotiations will have to continue. Other aspects of a lasting solution include not only specific measures relating to the issue in question. There have to be additional agreements: on rules for dealing with one another and communicating properly during everyday work; provisions for dealing with any breakdowns in mutual relations; and a deadline for a joint provisional appraisal and assessment of the current position.

Pennies do not just drop from heaven; you have to earn them. The quality of the solution reached will be measured by the way it is implemented – and some hard work has to go into that. The open discussion has led to mutual relief. There is a certain amount of euphoria, and people may be tempted to think everything is fine. But everyday work has its hidden dangers. Despite goodwill on both sides, breakdowns can still happen in everyday life. Both partners are then going to have their nerve tested to see whether they really mean seriously what they have been saying about working together. Only strict observance of the agreed rules will help overcome new critical situations that arise, without conflict arising once again. The new system of cooperation will require maintenance. As time goes on, however, both sides will learn how to deal with each other. Relationships will become normal again – and sooner or later, everyone will have forgotten the conflict that there was. That is when it will finally have been overcome.

Resolving a conflict between two groups

In companies and institutions, conflict between two groups is one of the most frequent and costly problem situations. For example, the following conflict patterns are very often encountered in practice:

- Marketing ⇔ development
- Central controlling ⇔ production line
- Central computing service ⇔ production line
- Central personnel department ⇔ production line
- Works council ⇔ management
- Holding company staff ⇔ corporate companies

But tensions and conflicts can arise even between adjoining groups or departments, between committees, between project groups and production line areas. The complexity of these situations often means they have to be approached in a specific, systematic way: by preparing and implementing a *confrontation* or *conflict resolution meeting* (see Figure 42). This method has proved highly successful in practice, and is therefore briefly described below.

An overview of the procedure:

1) *Preparation*
   Both parties to the conflict prepare a presentation (see Figure 45, "Conflict resolution meeting – main questions in preparing the presentation") concerning their view of the conflict situation – their image of their partner in the conflict, their self-image, and the image they suspect the other party has of them.
2) *Conflict resolution meeting*
   In the framework of a joint meeting with a clearly structured program (see Figure 43: "Conflict resolution meeting – program") and clear rules (see

Figure 44: "Conflict resolution meeting – rules of the game"), the two sides initially present their conclusions. Then the material is arranged and worked through together. The aim is to identify possible openings toward a solution during the meeting itself, and to firmly establish a common method of developing more specific ideas.

3) *Follow-up*

In mixed working groups, specific suggestions for solving the problems identified are initially developed. In a second joint conference meeting, the results can be adjusted and adopted.

It is useful to ensure that no one directly involved should be used as moderator or chairman during the preparation and conduct of the meeting. The moderator's role must be clear from the very start, and must be accepted by everyone involved. In addition to a well-developed ability to communicate, the role of conflict manager demands an ability to observe very specific rules of behavior (see Figure 46: "Ten golden rules of behavior for conflict managers/mediators").

Figure 42. Conflict resolution meeting – questions and answers

What is a conflict resolution meeting?
A method of achieving structured, mediated conflict resolution between two parties.

What is the aim of a conflict resolution meeting?
To initiate a process of conflict regulation:
⇒ Creating transparency with regard to the issue for those directly affected by the conflict.
⇒ De-escalating emotions and reducing the conflict to the objective, factual differences of opinion and conflicts of interest.
⇒ Negotiating potential approaches to a solution and specific procedures to implement these.

How many participants should there be?
Ideally, there should be two groups of five to eight people each (plus one or two mediators).

How long should a conflict resolution meeting last?
One or two days (if the problem is complex and obdurate, preferably two days).

What are the benefits of a conflict resolution meeting?
● High efficiency: the most important things can be mooted and made discussible in a short time and in a concentrated fashion.
● Lively way of working: you can for once "let it all out" without a constant danger of drifting away into bickering.

What is the drawback of a conflict resolution meeting?

With problems involving large departments, only a selected group of those directly affected can participate, since the groups would otherwise get so large they would no longer be able to communicate at the meeting.

When is a conflict resolution meeting useful?

When an acute or latent conflict of a highly explosive nature has become long overdue for discussion – and when attitudinal and behavioral problems are obscuring the objective issues involved.

What are the most important requirements for good results?

1) Careful selection of participants: only those directly affected who have a vested interest in the issue.
2) Careful preparation: the two initial presentations provide the basis for the whole of the meeting's work.
3) Tight chairmanship: keeping to the program, the time plan, and the rules agreed at the outset.
4) Careful follow-up: safeguarding the results by consistent further work and regular common appraisals and "de-briefing."

Figure 43. Conflict resolution meeting – program

1) Plenary session	**Introduction**
	■ Short review of prior history
	■ Aims and program of the meeting
	■ Rules
2) Plenary session	**Presentation by party A**
	Clarifying questions (*no discussion!*)
3) Plenary session	**Presentation by party B**
	Clarifying questions (*no discussion!*)
4) Group work (A & B separately)	**Processing**
	■ Most important messages we have grasped …
	■ What is new to us, or even surprising?
	■ Most important topics for joint discussion
5) Plenary session	**Presentations**
	plus clarifying questions
	Creation of a joint list of topics with the help of the mediator (*with a time slot allotted to each topic*)

6) Plenary session	**Discussion of the most important topics** with mediator (*keeping to time limits, so that none of the important topics is missed out!*)
7) Group work (3 mixed groups)	**How to proceed further** ▪ What immediate measures can be taken? ▪ What topics need to be dealt with in more detail? ▪ How should this be done (who with whom by when)?
8) Plenary session	**Presentation of suggestions** Short discussion strictly chaired
9) Plenary session	**Setting up of working organization and time plan** Joint agreement: who is to do what by when? ▪ Photographed minutes of meeting to all participants ▪ Form and content of information about the meeting ▪ Arrangements of next joint meeting
10) Plenary session	**Feedback** Short personal statements: ▪ How satisfied/dissatisfied am I with the results? ▪ How would I describe my mood now going home?

Figure 44. Conflict resolution meeting – rules of the game

Equal rights
Party A and party B are two independent partners with equal rights.

Topic: working together
The subject of the meeting is the ability and form of cooperation between party A and party B – we are not here to discuss specific factual topics from everyday business.

Openness and honesty
Problems must be clearly and directly described – no beating about the bush!

> **Describe, don't "moralize"**
> Status, situations and behavior must be described, facts and opinions should be presented – with no accusations and no reproaches.

> **Listen and understand**
> Listen, don't interrupt – ask questions, don't try to justify yourself.

> **Practical examples**
> Use examples from everyday work to illustrate things
> (but never dramatize individual cases).

> **Address people directly**
> People who are present should be addressed directly
> (but forms of behavior and their effects should be described,
> instead of motives being interpreted into them).

Figure 45. Conflict resolution meeting – main questions in preparing the presentation

1. *Image of the other party*

   ■ *How do we regard or perceive the others? How do they carry out their tasks? How do they behave toward us?*
   ■ *What is (or appears to be) particularly important to them? What is their main motivation? What are they particularly interested in, or less interested in?*
   ■ *What do we particularly like about them and the way they behave? What works well in what we do together? What are their strengths?*
   ■ *Where is there a problem? What are the points that bother us? What do we see as deficiencies, friction, sources of conflict – i.e., constantly recurring problems in everyday work together?*
   ■ *What are the questions we have long wanted an answer to – or that we would like to talk about with them at last?*

2. **Self-image**

   ■ *How do we see ourselves and our own role? How would we assess our own behavior in our work together with the others?*
   ■ *What is our own main motivation? What is important to us in the way we carry out our tasks?*

- What do we achieve? What do we contribute to good collaboration at work?
- What internal problems do we have that may affect the way we work with others? What are our own deficiencies?

3. Assumed image the other side has of us

- How do we think the others see us? What do we suspect is the general image people have of us?
- What are the most important points the others will probably "rebuke" us with?

Presentation: max. 45 minutes – most important statements in keyword form on flip-charts
(Made specific with practical examples, naming the people involved, describing typical forms of behavior – but avoiding accusations and insinuations!)

Wanted: the capacity for conflict

Effective methods of managing conflict are a very good thing. However, nine times out of ten, conflicts would not have got as far as needing this kind of costly campaign to resolve them – if only someone had drawn attention to the existence of divergent interests early enough, pointed out the danger of fruitless disputes, and got the parties to the conflict to sit down and talk about it. Often, it is enough for the problem to be discussed openly and brought to the attention of those involved – and the issue resolves itself automatically.

In practice, however, the existence of obvious divergences between needs, interests, and values is systematically repressed and played down – not only by those directly involved themselves, but also by everyone around them. And sooner or later, they find that relationships are hopelessly ruined. The higher you rise in the hierarchy, the more neurotic the approach to conflict behavior often is. While ordinary people generally still just say what they think and feel, for many managers tactical maneuvering has already become second nature. These are the real world champions – both in repressing the existence of conflicts and in tactical *Star Wars* and karate moves.

One of the truisms of management, however, is that "*prophylaxis is better than treatment.*" The abilities:

- To recognize conflict quickly enough
- To talk about conflict openly and without prejudice
- To conduct conflict in a constructive way as one of the participants
- To help manage conflict as an outside onlooker

Figure 46. Ten golden rules of behavior for conflict managers/mediators

1. **Carry out a careful diagnosis**
   Get a good picture of the background and context of the conflict. Try to grasp the dynamic of what has happened.

2. **Proceed according to a plan**
   Draw up a plan of how you are going to proceed. Never work without having a plan in mind. If you just set off on a mystery tour you will never reach your destination.

3. **Ensure that roles are clear**
   Make it clear to yourself and your partners what your role is and how they should carry out their own tasks – and uphold these roles consistently.

4. **Create acceptance**
   Take both parties to the conflict seriously. Try to put yourself in the place of each of them.

5. **Encourage communication**
   Keep communication going with and between the two parties to the conflict, and encourage rapprochement between them.

6. **Allow emotions**
   Don't make desperate efforts to put emotional events on an objective basis. Feelings are realities as well – the most important ones, in fact!

7. **Maintain neutrality**
   Under no circumstances take sides with one party or the other. Do not let yourself be manipulated. Preserve your independence and your impartiality.

8. **Be open and honest**
   Always remain transparent and credible to both partners. Never behave differently at joint meetings from the way you do in bilateral talks.

9. **Have patience**
   Don't expect quick progress or results. Keep an eye out for small steps in the right direction.

10. **Maintain humility**
    You should never feel you alone are responsible for success. If one partner or the other does not want to resolve the conflict, it will persist (it was Freud who described the phenomenon of "secondary benefit of the disease"). You are not a magician.

are among the greatest skills that people in responsible positions in organizations can have. However, there is a universal dearth of these skills. It is one thing for people in management to have sharp elbows, a lack of sensitivity and a good right hook they can use to lash out all round them regardless of the consequences. But why is it that so many people almost compulsively avoid conflicts from the outset – appearing to completely overlook the fact that there is any conflict, even when it is positively forcing itself to their attention?

Human beings, just like animals, not only have the natural instincts of aggression that are necessary for personal survival and the preservation of the species, but also instinctive behavioral programs that reduce the level of aggression or suspend the mechanism altogether when required for reproduction, social coexistence, or targeted cooperation in complex tasks.

Practical life shows how difficult it is to establish a trusting working relationship with new partners – bosses, colleagues, or employees. But once this relationship has been achieved and people have started to deal with one another as genuine colleagues, as partners, and perhaps even on a basis of friendship, the cross-bar that has to be leaped over for any mutual injury to be caused is raised higher and higher. Sooner or later, it gets so high that any kind of dispute is out of the question from the very beginning. The result is that people, just like animals, become "muzzled."

But while healthy animals are always ready to dispute with each other, even "inside the family" if necessary, human beings tend to lose this ability altogether. Differences of opinion stop being mentioned, open disputes are carefully avoided, and the awareness that opposing interests exist is simply "repressed," to use Freud's term. The standards that apply – tacitly, of course – are the following: "*it is bad manners to be critical*"; "*grown adults never argue*"; "*being emotional is a sign of immaturity*"; "*conflicts are damaging*." The result: a management culture based on the so-called "harmony model": joy, love, and pancakes. And this is precisely where the problem lies – the company's activities are placed out of the range of constant critical examination, tensions cannot be released, and the organization becomes incapable of self-renewal and becomes ossified.

If a standard has ceased to be useful, it should be changed. This is the first and most important step toward a flexible, lively and innovative organization – developing a behavioral standard that says criticism is not "bad manners," arguments are not "nasty," conflict cannot be assumed to be "bad" from the very start. A standard that says exposing differences in opinion and conflicts of interest is the precondition for mutual success; that it is not some kind of impossible "harmony" that is needed, but a *constructive argumentation culture* – a world in which conflict is not repressed, but taken as an opportunity to discover fresh solutions by conducting disputes on a basis of partnership (see Figure 41: "Modes of human conflict behavior").

Changing
a Company's Culture

11

Culture as a guidance system

Corporate culture can be defined as the *entirety of the standards and values* that constitute a company's spirit and personality. What is the function of these?

Standards and values are constants that serve for guidance. They channel people's behavior. The ultimate goal is *to reduce complexity*: they create clarity for all the members of a social group regarding what the organization regards as "good" or "not good," what is "allowed" or "not allowed", what is to be "rewarded" and what is to be "punished." Knowing this not only helps the individuals in the group to adapt to their environment, exist more or less without conflict, and meet with acceptance from those around them. In addition, it provides them with guidance regarding the behavior of others: they know what they can expect from the people around them and what they need not expect, and consequently what attitude they should take to specific situations. Their social surroundings become comprehensible, transparent, and predictable. Human societies, of every type, would be completely incapable of functioning without these "rules" – standards that provide orientation internally and cohesion toward the outside.

Each standard and every value guides the behavior of individuals and groups in a very specific direction that is important to the survival and success of the group as a whole – "customer orientation," for example, "cost awareness," or "teamwork" (see Figure 49). This is also the deeper reason why "company culture" was hardly ever heard of in business even just ten years ago. In the old, classically hierarchical organizations based on the division of labor, people were guided by command, with narrowly restricted working tasks, and through the direct managerial authority of their boss. In the networked organizations of the future, in the era of the decentralized, self-guiding organization, employees at all levels have immense scope for independent action. They can carry out complex and demanding tasks – without hierarchical supervision, in the context of an organization that exists in a state of constant flux. In this situation, the external structure can no longer provide orientation and security. Instead, *transparent and stable standards and values* are increasingly taking its place. It is these that carry out the decisive functions of creating order. They give the community its identity and create a framework within which individuals and groups can largely organize themselves, without losing sight of their common goal.

In the final analysis, there is no form of guidance that is more efficient than a distinctive, consistent company culture. Because if the common goal is right, the rest can be confidently left to the decentralized, self-guiding organization. Costly coordination and control systems are no longer needed. This is the main reason why "corporate culture" has now become so important that it is one of the principal factors for success.

Forms of expression

Difficult to define, and ultimately incapable of being fully objectivized, a company's culture is the result of a complex social process that lasts many years. It is not expressed in hard facts and figures, but in *emotional qualities.* In the end, its essence can only be experienced, not measured or calculated. How do you recognize a company's culture? How does it communicate itself?

The ways in which it expresses itself broadly fall into the following categories:

- *Communication*: what is communicated in writing, and what is communicated by word of mouth? What kind of things do people write and speak about? What style of language is used? What is not discussed, what is treated as taboo?
- *Behavior*: how does management behave? How are decisions taken? What kinds of behavior are rewarded, and what types of people are encouraged? How are communications and collaboration conducted in the company? How do people treat one another?
- *Structures*: what kinds of building, facilities, and room arrangements dominate the scene? What forms of organization and regulation are given preference? What type of management apparatus is there, and how is it used?
- *Social events*: what kinds of events and rituals take place, alongside everyday work? Who gets together with whom, on what occasions? How well do large events run, what is their value as an experience?

All of these channels communicate to the outsider the spirit that has developed in the company in the course of its history. Unmistakable "laws" and "rules" that guide social life from within can be recognized as "characteristics" distinguishing the company's personality. What is known in management jargon as "corporate identity" is very closely related to the predominant culture in a company.

Insiders may often be quite unaware of the culture (or anti-culture) of the company they work in. They are directly affected by it, have never experienced anything else, and take the "lifestyle" familiar to them in their everyday work for granted. Sometimes people only find out how good or bad things are for them when they meet with colleagues from other companies at outside events.

Influential factors

The culture of a company or an institution may be strong or weak; it may have been consciously cultivated, or may have developed historically; and it may be based on clear basic values, or may contain its own contradictions. But in every organization that is more than a couple of months old, specific standards and values develop. What are the main factors that influence these?

To begin with, a company is shaped by a whole range of *fundamental factors* – to begin with the sector of the economy it belongs to (see Figure 47). The products it manufactures, the kind of customer it deals with every day, the capital equipment it operates with, and the personnel structure necessarily developing from the company's operations – all of these factors create a very specific framework that shapes its common life. The cultures of a steel foundry, an engineering office, a fashion store or a large bank are therefore not comparable. For example, a company in which large numbers of women work will be much more lively and vivacious than one where there are only men.

In public administration, the burden of regulations that have to be observed creates conditions from the outset that encourage bureaucratic working processes and over-cautious behavior. And in an international airline, there are bound

Figure 47. *Corporate culture – basic factors (hard to influence)*

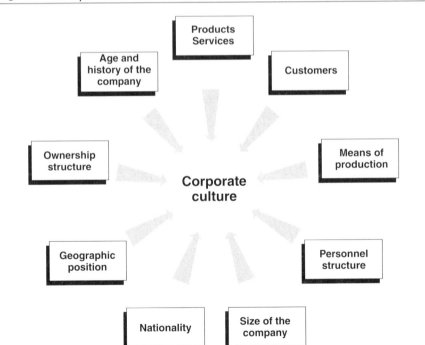

to be much more cosmopolitan attitudes than in a local building firm. But the size of the company, its country of origin, its geographical position, its age, and its ownership structure play an important part. A completely different culture develops in a small family company than in a large multinational corporation.

In addition, however, there are a great many *company-specific factors* that can create completely different conditions for the development of internal social coexistence between one company and another – even within one and the same branch of industry (see Figure 48). If top management behaves in an elitist, distant, and hierarchical manner, you can hardly expect a cooperative culture of partnership to develop in the company. If the whole management system is aimed at cultivating and rewarding individual performance, and if management is busily demonstrating every day how to wage departmental war, it will be difficult to develop a team spirit in cross-departmental project groups. If the top directors deal with one another by sending memos, if executives and office staff all live behind closed doors in individual offices, and if it is well known that it is the boss's job and his alone to think about any changes needed, then the company's capacity for innovation is bound to be limited from the outset.

Figure 48. Corporate culture – corporate-specific factors (easy to influence)

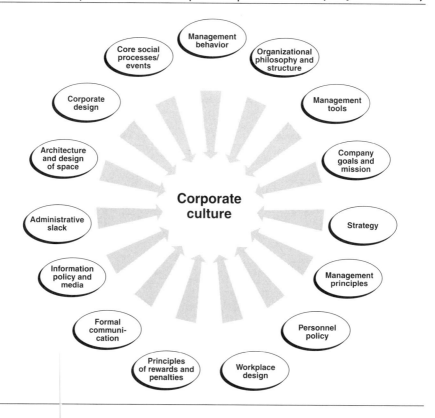

Changing a Company's Culture

However, we do not mean to give the impression that archaic conditions are prevalent throughout the business world – or that there is any such thing as a single, correct form of company culture. The reality is much more complex. On the one hand, what can be regarded as useful and desirable in terms of culture in any specific case may depend heavily on the overall situation, particularly the company's *strategy* and *structure*. On the other hand, in practice – and particularly in large companies or institutions – it is very rare for there to be a universally clear and unambiguous culture. On the contrary, the problem is usually that there is not a uniform culture, and sometimes even that glaringly contradictory standards and values are at work. In these cases, complexity is not being reduced, but actually increased – with a consequent lack of guidance. Cautiousness becomes the basis for successful behavior. Tactical maneuvering dominates the scene.

Example: teamwork in a company

On the one hand ...
In management's newly formulated principles, particular emphasis is given to the importance of teamwork for the company's success. Interdisciplinary, cross-departmental project teams are to be set up. Quality circles are to be established. Semi-autonomous groups are planned in the production area. Employees and executives are to be trained in group dynamics. Internal facilitators are to be trained.

On the other hand ...
The top director makes speeches glorifying outstanding individual performances. The financial director writes in newspaper articles, "There is no such thing as collective responsibility." The board of directors is a living demonstration of unadulterated hierarchical behavior. There are countless managers who regard "the whole fuss about teams" as downright nonsense. The wages and salary system is only capable of rewarding individual performance, and group performance rewards are taboo.

Effect ...
Endless debates are conducted about the usefulness or otherwise of group work; opinions become polarized; the productivity of the groups that have actually been set up remains far below expectations.

This is often the real problem: impetus that is put in at one point is counteracted by a contradictory impetus coming from somewhere else – simply through the lack of a clear approach and a consistent line at top management level. The chaos of different standards and values predominating within one and the same company recalls the Bible phrase, "for they know not what they do ... " People with the reputation of being tough calculators, in particular, take no account whatsoever of how much these internal contradictions within a company are actually costing at the end of the day. Something that cannot be measured cannot appear in the accounts.

Actual and target values

Success in any strategic reorganization nowadays depends, among other things, on whether or not the cultural preconditions are in place for the new structural model to work. If you just tinker with the organization chart, you are risking a flop from the start. A profit-center organization in which all the specialist functions are left centralized and the controlling department regards itself simply as an extension of the supreme command will never be capable of working properly; managers who have never learned how to think in networks and delegate responsibility are from the outset incapable of managing successfully in shallow structures. And if a public body has been managed like a "state within the state" for long enough, structural measures alone are utterly incapable of converting it into an efficient, user-friendly and service-oriented organization.

When a company is intending to change its strategic direction, it is therefore not only a question of finding suitable structures, but also a suitable culture. The "target state" has to be defined and compared with the "actual" situation. A manager entering a company from the outside for the first time usually has no trouble describing the actual situation. But someone who has made his career in the organization is usually blind to its weaknesses and practically incapable of recognizing the dominant culture with all its specific strengths, deficiencies, and contradictions – least of all when he himself has had a strong influence on the company's destiny.

But there is a tried and tested method of obtaining a specific and realistic picture of the "actual situation": getting employees to assess the culture. A special catalogue of questions can be developed for the purpose. Usually, however, it is sufficient to ask employees to consider a list of points referred to in the company's mission statement and management principles, or a list of general success factors like the one given in Figure 49. Once everyone involved has stated which of these points they think have actually been achieved in the company, which have not, and how this is demonstrated in everyday practice, the main strengths and deficiencies of the current situation are already established.

However, the main problem does not lie either in analyzing the actual situation or in defining the target state that is to be reached, but rather in the implementation process – the question of how the company's culture can be changed in everyday working practice.

The road of change

There is no great skill involved in changing a company's structures. But if you want to change people's behavior, you can easily find yourself biting on granite. Before you seriously attempt, as an entrepreneur or executive, to alter the culture in your area of responsibility, you will need to take one thing into account: that behavior is learned – and learning one culture also means unlearning the previous culture, which may have developed and consolidated itself over a period of decades.

We are not saying this to discourage you and keep you from undertaking a project of change that may even be necessary for survival, but simply to call attention to the scale of the venture you are embarking on.

There is a whole range of ways of influencing a culture:

- *Describe the target culture in specific terms*
- *Carefully justify the necessity for change*
- *Establish standards by serving as a model yourself*
- *Working together on changing the culture*
- *Changing course through personnel appointments to key positions*
- *Rewards and penalties in the management process*
- *Consistent project management*

This is not a menu you can just pick and choose from, however. If you want to see results before your great-grandchildren do, you will need to exploit all of these aspects simultaneously and with a high degree of consistency. And even then, you are not going to be able to change your world overnight. In the medium term, however, you can be sure of lasting success.

---

1. Describe the target culture in specific terms

If you want to develop a new culture, you first have to say what it is going to look like. You have to describe it and its core elements – the standards and values on which it is based. But this is not enough. Initially, standards and values are nothing but slogans, empty phrases. If employees are to understand what is meant, these abstract concepts will have to be supplemented and filled out by comprehensible specific examples; they will have to have some "meat" put on them.

For example:

"Customer orientation"

is an abstract concept initially.

Specific examples:

- ➡ *Everyone should know who his customer is.*
- ➡ *Customers and their wishes are to be taken seriously.*

- *Internal partners will also be regarded and treated as customers.*
- *A highly developed sense of pride in providing a service will dominate, both internally and toward the outside world.*
- *Relations with customers will be lively, friendly and personal.*
- *Internal and external customers will actively participate in the development of new products and in improving service.*
- *Attitudes and actions of employees and executives will be consistently aimed at enhancing benefits to the customer.*

There will be plenty of resistance during the process of change. But if there is a lack of guidance about the destination at the very outset, you will never even get off the starting blocks.

---

2. Carefully justify the necessity for change

If they do not understand the necessity for it, people are incapable of altering their behavior. Understanding it is still by no means a guarantee, but it is an indispensable prerequisite. In a company, you have to explain to employees and executives that it is time for changes to be made. It is not necessary here to paint the existing culture black, and with it the common history that everyone shares. You should be loyal to your own past. After all, the existing culture was quite successful under the conditions that prevailed in the past. But conditions have changed – and this has to be made unmistakably clear to everyone involved.

Culture is not an end in itself. In exactly the same way that a specific form of organization can be useful or obstructive in various specific conditions, values and behavioral norms can also be either suitable or unsuitable for coping with the common tasks of the future. In other words, it is not simply a question of company folklore here. The new values and behavioral standards that are being sought are *strategic factors for success.*

Providing a specific – and therefore credible and plausible – justification is what first establishes the preconditions for the changed awareness that is needed in the company. This, if anywhere, is where management based on providing meaning and purpose is needed. Because there will be some people who have never given the slightest thought to matters such as "culture," "basic values," or "behavioral norms." Most people simply accept prevailing conditions as if they were just a matter of fate. The fact that something like "culture" so much as exists, let alone the idea that people might be capable of designing it and changing it, is a completely new idea for some people.

3. Establish standards by serving as a model yourself

Even in an era when managerial authority and leadership have fallen into disrepute in many fields, it is still the case that the most effective way of influencing people's attitudes and behavior in organizations consists of credibly representing certain standards and values oneself in top management, and serving as a model. More than ever today, people are seeking and need figures with whom they can identify, people who can convince them – not only through what they say, but also and above all through what they do and the way they do it. If there are values that management regards as important, it must stand by them, state what they are – and act accordingly! What matters is setting an example by taking actions that will attract lots of attention. Forms of behavior that support the planned development must be rewarded, and conditions favoring movement in the opposite direction must be openly criticized. In addition, you need some healthy skepticism about your direct subordinates. They have to be checked to see whether or not they in turn are passing on the ideas and helping to implement them consistently. Even top managers will willingly accept an open, team-oriented and participatory management style from their direct boss – without it ever crossing their minds to check how they treat their own staff. Only direct contact with people at the levels below your own immediate staff will show you how much has got through to them – and what has not. Some people who have made it into the higher levels of the hierarchy may say, "I'm not a missionary!" No, a manager is not a missionary – but one thing is certain: cultural change cannot simply be administered from your desktop. And who is going to make a start if the top director does not? Whose behavior has the best chances of influencing that of others? And who is it who is being paid to create the best possible conditions to enable the company to meet the challenges of the future?

4. Working together on changing the culture

The first step toward developing the culture is achieving sensitivity to it – in yourself and others. People need to be made aware of the company culture that is currently predominant, with all its strengths and weaknesses – and ideas about how to change it need to be developed. The boss does not need to invent everything himself – and he certainly does not need to do everything himself. Things move fastest when employees themselves become active. Management's task is to ensure that this happens – a mutual critical appraisal and stocktaking of the actual situation; a description of the desired target state; ideas about how to get there; specific steps that need to be taken. It is surprising how much imagination and commitment employees can develop when it is a matter of critically questioning and redesigning the culture of the company's shared life and work. But it is also important to make sure that the employees do not simply stew in their own juice. You have to send them outside their own walls as well, for example to visit companies that already have several years' experience with new forms of organization, management, and company culture. This will give them new ideas, in the first place. Secondly, it ensures that no one can say, "This is all pie in the sky. Something like that could never work in practice." And getting all the employees involved in working on the company's culture is not merely a means to an end. In itself, it already represents living, practical experience of the new, lively culture.

---

5. Changing course through personnel appointments to key positions

---

As mentioned above, the most effective methods of guiding and accelerating change are via people. Nothing gets things moving in an organization faster than having the right man or the right woman at the top. Initially, this makes the development of the new generation of top managers extremely important – the selection criteria, the assessment procedures and the conditions for promotion. But no matter how important these systems are for the long-term future of the company, they only take effect very slowly. With today's competition for time, however, fast reactions and fast action are needed. Management posts have to be suitably filled, and replacements made if necessary, much faster and much more flexibly than used to be possible. And it is not just positions in the production line that company management needs to keep an eye on here. Leading positions in project groups are becoming increasingly important for companies' overall development. The time is long past when it was possible to assign project management positions as a playground for executives who were of no use anywhere else.

Two things have to happen to get things moving in a company. First, unconventional *promotions to key positions* – targeting people whose behavior shows particularly clearly that they stand for the values that need to be developed. This means altering the selection criteria. Secondly, those with official positions who are not willing or able to represent the new culture in a credible way have to be just as unconventionally *removed from key positions*. Difficult though this might seem, there is no alternative. Even a few people in key positions with their foot on the brake are enough to call into question the credibility of the whole project. By contrast, if action is taken in a way that everyone can see, the sluice-gates will open over a wide front. It is then – and only then – that people will get the message: *they mean it seriously.*

---

6. Rewards and penalties in the management process

Important though individual personnel decisions are, re-appointments cannot just be carried out at will in every position in a company. The personnel resources to do it are just not available. But you can and must consistently exploit every tool offering rewards and penalties in the management process. The two most important control tools: *target agreements* and *employee appraisal.* Here, too, it is not simply a matter of using the tools available, but specifically of applying the desired culture consistently as a yardstick of management behavior.

It is only when individuals sense that it is not just all talk, and that action is really being taken – that behavior is being observed and assessed, and that behaving as if nothing had changed is going to have consequences for people – that the seriousness of what is planned will be grasped. This does not mean taking a pessimistic view of human nature, it is simply a question of people's mechanisms for learning and unlearning behavior throughout their lives.

7. Consistent project management

If you have enough time, you can of course take a completely relaxed approach to changing the company's culture as an open, unstructured process – just "letting things grow" would be a nice way of putting it. But if you need a different culture within a comparatively short time – usually meaning within two or three years – so that the new, lean organizational forms that are vital to survival will be able to work at all, then you need to approach cultural change as a key project and manage it in a consistent fashion. And when you do this – just like building a new administration building, launching a new product line, or creating a new corporate structure – all the same issues arise that are described above under the heading "target-based management" (principle no. 1 in our "Charter for Managing Change" – Part II, Chapter 6).

Some may find it surprising to talk about target-based management even when it is changing the "soft factors" that is involved: clearly set targets, criteria for success, a project organization capable of functioning properly, a realistic schedule for phases and deadlines, an efficient project control system, and appropriate forms of communication. Some important projects for introducing change in a company's culture have come to nothing due to a lack of consistent management.

The above gives an outline of the strategic approach. The rest is more or less just getting on with the job: selecting the specific measures needed on the way to a changed culture. Here, too, management has a leading role. In the search for factors capable of having a strong influence on the culture, employees and executives always first think about:

- The model or vision
- Management style
- Common events and meetings

While these are actually important, living and working together in a company is decisively affected by things that are much more tangible:

- Organizational structure
- Formalized processes
- Management tools

- Promotion practices
- Management rhythm and running meetings
- Information policy and information media
- Wages and salary system
- Training and development

All of these items should be investigated regarding the extent to which they support the desired culture, or whether they are diametrically opposed to it in their existing forms.

Incidentally, the phenomenon of "culture" cannot be attained with systematic measures alone. *Imagination, creativity,* and *zest for life* are needed. Keep an eye out for women and younger candidates, both male and female. They are not as set in the (wrong) ways as the so-called "seasoned" men, and they can provide particularly good support in designing the culture in your company or organizational unit.

In this connection, one final personal recommendation: make sure you keep some critical distance from yourself! It is quite possible that you are not a particularly gifted person when it comes to questions of culture. It is quite possible that your employees have a much better feeling for the ways in which the culture is capable of being developed in the area you are responsible for. This does not really matter. Not every brilliant idea has to come from you, by any means. It won't hurt you to let your employees take you by the hand for once. But the one thing you should never do is follow the "not invented here" principle! Never dismiss an idea from your employees hastily, just because it seems strange to you. You can risk doing something that has never been done before in your company. After all, this is exactly what you want – for things to be different. Isn't it?

Figure 49. Corporate culture – norms and values

Examples of norms and values as strategic factors for success, which can be more or less strongly pronounced in a company:

Customer orientation
Thinking and acting by executives and employees is directed toward the customer and the customer's benefit. Both internally and toward the outside world, there is a marked sense of pride in providing a service. Social Relations with external and internal customers are lively, friendly, and personal.

Employee orientation
Management behavior and management tools are directed toward the needs of employees. An atmosphere of partnership that is free of anxiety predominates. Employees are actively integrated into decision-making processes. Individuals and groups are trusted and have responsibility delegated to them. A lack of "ability" is rarely complained of.

Quality

The quality of products and services is given a high value throughout the whole company. Everyone feels personally responsible for the quality of the work he produces. Professionalism — in no matter what field of activity — is highly regarded in the company, and is appropriately rewarded. Investments are made in working materials and in training and further education for employees and executives.

Performance orientation

At all levels, everyone works toward targets and results. Efficient management and personal commitment are part of the company's style. Executives and employees act with an awareness of both costs and profitability. People are aware of where money can be earned and where things are costing money. Modern information systems and control instruments are available — and they are fully used.

Willingness to be innovative

The atmosphere is one that welcomes change. Optimizing products, production equipment and the working organization is always at the forefront of people's minds. New ideas and criticism of existing conditions are accepted. Lateral thinking is not excluded. Discussion and collaboration extend beyond the boundaries of each group or area of responsibility. A willingness to learn is regarded as a virtue, right up to top management level. Mistakes are regarded as opportunities to learn. People experiment with unusual ideas and have the courage to risk investing in new approaches.

Bias for action

Executives and employees have broad scope for independent action — and they exploit it to the full. Decisions are not delayed. A distinction is made between "important" and "urgent." Groups that operate without any hierarchy are equally capable of taking action. Squabbling over areas of responsibility and all the rituals involved in covering one's own back are unknown. When somebody faces a problem, he acts spontaneously on the spot whenever possible.

Open communications

Openness and honesty are the distinctive characteristics of the information and communications style in bilateral relationships, meetings, and conferences, as well as in the institutional media. Delicate questions, poor results and criticism of management are not taboo. Management provides information not only in writing, but also orally whenever possible, and appears in person to take part in controversial discussions, even at larger meetings. Informal communication is highly valued. Every important or interesting piece of news runs through the company like wildfire — one of the main reasons why all the employees are always extremely well informed.

Teamwork

There is a good team spirit, both in management groups and work groups. Groupwork is used systematically both for operational and for innovative tasks. Facilitation skills, use of visual media, and team development are highly valued as parts of the training program for both executives and employees. The ability to work in a team is consistently checked and encouraged in the company.

Overcoming conflicts

Problems – including interpersonal ones – are openly discussed. It is not harmony that prevails – but a constructive confrontation culture. Differences of opinion and conflicts of interest are openly disclosed, mooted for discussion, and the substance of them is toughly argued out. A great deal of time and energy is invested in cleanly negotiated solutions that are not based on shabby compromise. Quite serious grievances can develop – but the decisions negotiated are supported by all.

Security of employment

The principle applies that no one has a right to a specific job; everyone must expect to be transferred or have to take on a different task. However, the company will do everything in its power to ensure that no one has to be dismissed for economic reasons. When business is going badly, then in addition to cost savings and use of reserves, everyone working in the company will accept income cuts on a basis of solidarity.

A sense of community in the company

Executives and employees identify with the company and show personal commitment to the "common cause." They stand up not only for their own interests or those of their organizational unit, but act with an eye to the whole company. There is a sense of belonging that goes beyond the boundaries of hierarchy and departments. And this sense of belonging is also seen in an ability to take part in celebrations and parties together. Everyone likes to get together in a big group at festive occasions.

Performance Improvement 12

Reducing costs and assessing potential benefits

Most companies today are facing two problems: *costs that are too high* and *declining profits*. Some of the world's strongest corporations, whose prosperity would have been regarded as a law of nature only a few years ago, have run into difficulties and have been forced to carry out profound restructuring measures. Companies that for far too long never gave a thought to the future are vanishing completely. But even healthy and basically successful companies are also having to optimize costs and profits in order to survive.

In many companies, however, cost-structure analyses are carried out in the form of dramatic crisis interventions – as one-off, conflict-laden shows of strength that break over the company like a tidal wave, sweeping away practically all of the management culture that had previously been built up over many years. The main reason for this is that people have waited too long – and now believe they are forced to reduce costs dramatically at a single stroke as part of a crash program. And the job can only be done with a hatchet.

But not all of the companies in which this approach is taken actually need radical measures to restore them to profitability. All that is really involved in some basically healthy companies is a perfectly normal cost-structure analysis. However, it is usually connected with high-profile projects for which funds have often already been advanced on the stock market. Management and consultants practically always come under immense pressure for success in such cases – mostly of their own making. Far too often, the result is methods that certainly achieve clear cost reductions, but at the same time involve a scorched-earth policy that leaves the company internally devastated.

Seven deadly sins

To begin with, a list of the most frequent and also the most flagrant mistakes that are made in practice when cost-structure analyses and cost reduction measures are the order of the day. If you can avoid these "deadly sins," you have already gained a great deal.

Deadly sin no. 1: *Across-the-board cuts*

This is probably the most frequent management mistake: across-the-board cuts in personnel or materials costs by a percentage of X, ordained from above. The justification is always the same "equal sacrifices." No one should be favorodized or disadvantaged. But appearances are deceptive. In fact, "equal sacrifices" involve the greatest possible injustice – because the ones who have already slimmed their departments into shape in the past have to give just as much blood as their colleague next door who operates on the principle "There's lots to do – let's wait and see what happens!" and who has accumulated the most fat over the course of the years. Across-the-board cuts are from the very outset incapable of being in the company's broader interests. Not all the activities that go on can be measured by a single standard. There are only two criteria that are ultimately decisive:

1. *Who creates what productive added value today?*
2. *Who needs what resources to guarantee the productive added value he creates and that is required of him?*

"Equal sacrifices" have got nothing to do with the matter. Across-the-board cuts say most about the person who orders them: he obviously has no confidence in his own ability to use documents and critical discussions to judge where slimming measures can be made without causing damage to the company as a whole, and where they cannot. In addition, he does not have the self-confidence to face his employees and take responsibility for more nuanced decisions. Some people may not like to hear this – but across-the-board cuts are ultimately just a sign of incompetent management.

Deadly sin no. 2: *One-sided focus on savings*

Important though it is to reduce costs, it is just as important to optimize profits. In the first place, increasing profits and performance are urgently needed to increase the company's scope for action, or at least to maintain it. Secondly, employees find it much easier to carry out defensive measures when offensive ones are being taken at the same time. Thirdly, everyone involved learns to think and act with a sense of cost-awareness *and* a sense of profit orientation – a vitally important attitude if the company is to have any future at all. By contrast, when people merely start hunting for potential savings, it is easy for a cost-cutting mentality to develop that has lost its real function and can sometimes even be dangerous. Management – particularly the nitpickers in charge of checking costs (beware of letting them loose!) – becomes capable of thinking and talking only in terms of "reducing costs." The whole company gets sucked into a euphoria of delirious cost-cutting. People forget to think in terms of the strategic context and simply take decisions on the figures based on the criterion, "cost reduction: yes/no." Important investments, even small ones, fall victim to the savings epidemic, which sucks everything costing any money into itself, like a black hole. Future-oriented thinking is out, longer-term opportunities are missed pointlessly. Management's credibility sinks to zero – and rightly so, because if you first sleep through and miss a vital development, and then charge about like a bull in a china shop when things are already too late, then you have no business to be in top management.

Deadly sin no. 3: *Unrealistic targets*

There is a rule of thumb that says that in every company or administrative body in which a structural analysis has not been carried out for five years, costs can be cut by 10–20% without affecting overall performance in the slightest. And there is a second rule that says that nine out of ten executives are neither able nor willing to point out potential cost reductions in their own area of responsibility – unable because they have developed professional blinkers, and unwilling because if any potential rationalization could be identified the question would arise of why it had not long since been recognized and carried out. To break through this mental block, during cost-structure analyses line managers are often instructed to propose cost reductions on an almost grotesque scale – 40%, for example. Instructions like that lead in practice not only to severe undercurrents of resistance, but also sometimes to quite absurd suggestions – which in turn cause disturbed relations between the investigating units and the decision-making level. The psychological damage caused by this type of exercise ends up being completely out of proportion to the objective results. Adults with whom you want to continue working in the future should not be treated like dumb kids – particularly since there are other ways of overcoming mental barriers than the one described above.

Deadly sin no. 4: *Suspending responsibility*

A lack of trust in one's own staff often has a further consequence: forms of project organization are chosen that put the line manager of an organizational unit under the microscope, and force him into a powerless position in the face of a committee of superiors, colleagues, and outsiders. The investigation's inquisition-like methods, and the existence of decision-making mechanisms that are opaque to the executives affected, provoke patterns of conflict based on attack and defense, making any kind of fruitful discussion impossible, and ultimately relieving the executive concerned of his share in responsibility for decisions affecting his department. Even in the most distinguished companies, this can suddenly lead to decision-making meetings that are conducted like court-martials. You would think you were in a second-rate provincial theater. Some of the company bosses involved would get the fright of their lives if they were later shown a video of one of these meetings that they had taken part in. It is an event at which virtually irreparable damage to the atmosphere can be caused in the space of a single half hour. Above all, however, the learning effect that is so vital for the future is not achieved: *practicing consistent cost management on one's own initiative.* In addition, this kind of approach makes it far too easy for a weak manager to avoid responsibility for the changes introduced in his department. Once everyone in the building knows how this kind of project operates, everyone can take refuge behind the decision-making bodies that have been set up. And last, but not least: since no genuine dialogue takes place, there is also a risk that those who have good arguments to defend themselves against drastic cuts will be denigrated as "uncooperative" elements. By contrast, the real weak points in the company's personnel will be overlooked, and will become a serious handicap in everyday operations when genuine management is needed once again.

Deadly sin no. 5: *Taboo on the hierarchy*

It is quite normal in business for top management to limit its role in organizational and profit-optimizing projects to commissioning them, supervising them, and taking decisions. The individual organizational units are all given a critical examination – but the big chiefs themselves remain untouchable. Structures and processes, communications and collaboration are examined everywhere except where they have the greatest effects on the company as a whole – namely, at the very top. The first thing to suffer from this is management's credibility. But there are also other, *structural effects.*

First, weaknesses in top management become further entrenched, and are bequeathed to posterity as sacred monuments. But it is precisely here that there is often substantial potential that could have been tapped.

Secondly, headquarters staff – who in practice are usually world champions in creating indirect costs – are automatically also excluded from critical examination, or merely looked at superficially, on the grounds that they are "management tools." Only top management is regarded as the clientele – but not all the points further down the line in the company, which are affected every day by what headquarters staff do. If the people who have cocooned themselves with staff are the same ones now deciding on the cuts to be made, then their staff will not only have a good life, but even an eternal one.

Thirdly, leveling out the hierarchy, one of the decisive ways of achieving cost reductions, is either not even considered or is restricted to the lower levels – leading to the florid organization charts that one occasionally encounters in practice.

Deadly sin no. 6: *Overlooking important partners*

A cost-structure analysis is always a highly explosive project – not because of the analysis, but because what is inevitably going to follow unless the project comes to nothing: restructuring measures, and consequently personnel implications. It is extremely tempting for management to conceal these intentions for as long as possible and only to inform personnel representatives, the works council and co-determination bodies when there is no longer any way of avoiding it. This approach takes a bitter toll in practice. On the one hand, these institutions will feel they are not being treated as serious partners, or even that they have been deceived, when they find that ready-packaged and complete projects are being presented to them from which it is obvious that management must have been busy with every detail for as much as six months or a year already. At best, this causes severe irritation; normally, it leads to the affected bodies retreating to take a distant and critical "supervisory" role in the project; in the worst case, which is often still seen, it leads to open obstructiveness. And there is another aspect as well: all of these bodies have a completely different access to important sections of the employees, and have valuable information channels available to them. These can be actively integrated into the preparation of a project of this type, and can make extremely valuable contributions – not only with regard to the analysis of the actual situation, but also concerning the way procedures for the project are designed. But the absolutely decisive element is this: if it eventually emerges that drastic personnel measures are unavoidable, then you will need the assistance of everyone who can help to make the painful steps required socially acceptable – as informed, capable, and responsible allies. This does not mean to imply that the works council should be informed and actively involved the moment that management has its very first thoughts about a project of this type. But we would say this: it is in the company's own interest for the works council to be involved before legal requirements make it inevitable anyway, and particularly before the planned measures are more or less finalized. The rule of thumb is: *in case of doubt, earlier rather than later.* If you have a good conscience, good arguments, and your relations with the relevant bodies are not hopelessly ruined, there is no reason to be afraid of entering into dialogue at an early stage. Because what you invest in a discussion based on partnership will pay for itself ten times over later on, when the project's difficult implications begin to be felt.

Deadly sin no. 7: *Lack of implementation*

This is the seventh and last of the cardinal sins: an inability or unwillingness on the part of top management to take the necessary decisions. Whether it is because there is no one who wants to answer to employees to unpopular decisions; whether it is because management itself cannot agree on "equal sacrifices"; or whether it is because of the sudden shock of discovering that it is not actually all that easy to realize the existing potential. You cannot just do without 100% of this or that job, make an employee here or there 100% redundant or scrap an individual organization unit here or there without replacing it. There is plenty of potential. But it is extremely widely spread, and can only be exploited without damage to the overall system by carrying out complex organizational changes – a task that requires the highest possible skill in networked thinking and process-oriented action. And some people simply feel the job is too much for them. In any case, at the end of this type of project what often happens is that a series of conjuring tricks have to be carried out, and a whole lot of juggling with numbers, to avoid final comments in the press such as: "a waste of time and effort." Public administrative bodies are particularly at risk here. Party-political structures in management committees often stand in the way of a tight, efficient decision-making process. Comprehensive analyses consequently often conclude with embarrassing "horse-trading" at the level of the lowest common denominator, and the results of the project are completely out of proportion to the total effort and costs involved. In companies, when the results of long and painful discussions can be summed up in the phrase "the mountain gave birth to a mouse" – then you can forget about motivation and goodwill on the part of the employees. The first thing, therefore, that needs to be clarified and ensured *before the start* of a cost-structure analysis is the *ability* and *willingness* of those responsible to carry out genuine change and, if necessary, take painful decisions. Because no analysis is better than an analysis that is left without concrete results.

A constructive approach

If you choose a strategy of mistrust toward your employees in connection with a cost-structure analysis or a project aimed at optimizing results, you will be missing a tremendous opportunity to develop the "entrepreneurial thinking" in your company that is so often propagated nowadays. In this book, we argue for a *participatory* and *development-oriented* approach. This is based on the following principles:

- Project work takes place *as a line responsibility.* Responsibility for examining a specific organizational unit lies with its director, and the project is controlled within the framework of the regular management group.
  For examining interdepartmental questions, special *cross-section projects* can be defined and provided with the appropriate project organization.
  The *management organization* is the subject of a separate sub-project.
- Both *potential cost reductions* and *potential profits* or *performance contributions* must be investigated.
- The management group in each organizational unit investigated is supplemented during the project by *at least one external.* However, responsibility for any suggestions made remains with the line.
- To provide an adequate basis for decision-making with regard to potential cost reductions, two scenarios are used: *10% cost reductions and 20% cost reductions.*

- *Internal and external customers* are *involved in the project work* in an appropriate form. Individual customer representatives can actively participate in the framework of the project.
- *Employees* are not only openly informed about the goals and process of the project, but *actively participate in project work.*
- *Support from one's own specialist services* or *external consultants* is made available in a suitable form, so that individual organizational units are able to call on it.
- The heads of the organizational units being investigated communicate their suggestions to *the steering committee responsible for taking decisions,* or to the *management board.*
- After *detailed discussions with the responsible heads of department further down the line,* decisions are taken at top management level in accordance with the company's overriding interests.
- An *open information policy* is followed. The entire staff receives detailed information about the actual situation, goals, content, and process of the investigation before the project starts, as well as receiving regular information on its current status and each of the next steps coming up.

What is the function of the external member?

Every project team needs someone who is not professionally blinkered – someone capable of seeing things without distortion. His task consists of asking so-called "stupid questions" as an outsider, critically questioning everything as a "lateral thinker," and contributing his perceptions, views and ideas as someone who is not directly involved. He provides important supplementary expertise to that of the internal members – and in addition, often serves an important function in catalyzing communication and cooperation in the team.

Who is a suitable "external"?

Basically, anyone who is himself involved in practical management, but who has no "investments" of his own in the area affecting the project. In large companies and corporations, it may even be possible to use a colleague whose ordinary job is sufficiently distanced from the project. Capable executives from firms that are colleagues, customers, or suppliers, are very suitable for the job.

Of course, professional consultants can also be used as externals. This is particularly appropriate when the relevant team has little experience in project management, or when the area being dealt with is particularly large and problematic. A professional consultant can also be used more flexibly. In addition to serving as a neutral external member, he can also take on a number of duties involving methodological advice and support, which an external line manager would not be capable of.

What type of support has to be made available?

In the first place, there has to be a central project management that is always accessible to provide information to those involved in the project when questions of what to do or how to proceed come up. Secondly, the expertise of controlling, information technology, or personnel departments or operation services may be needed. Thirdly, not everybody all the way down the line has the necessary experience with regard to methodology in problem-solving processes, designing workshops, or managing conflict in a team. They need support with regard to chairmanship, visualization, and team development. Suitably qualified specialists can usually be found in the educational and training system.

As mentioned earlier, external consultants can also be used to provide all of these forms of support. In many cases, this is valuable or even necessary. But before a professional consultant is used, it must be carefully clarified what the specific need is – and whether it might be possible to find someone in-house to meet it. The slogan should be, "*Do what you can do yourself – don't do what you can't.*"

Why two scenarios – 10 % and 20 % reductions?

The aim of the exercise is to produce a competent basis for decision-making allowing company management to decide with an awareness of all the possible consequences where slimming-down measures can be taken and where they cannot. Decision-makers must be able to judge where "fat" stops and where "muscle" starts. Experience shows that this usually lies in the range between 10 % and 20 %. Using these two "probes" makes it very much easier to assess the situation.

Of course, there are firms and companies with a fat content very much greater than 20 %. In these cases, however, it is seriously questionable whether a cost-reduction analysis is the right method to use at all. It is usually an overall strategic reorganization that is needed in these cases – a project with a methodological approach that is quite different and involves much more profound structural change.

There are also individual organizational units or departments in almost every large company in which the cost-reduction potentials are much greater than 20 % – whether because the unit's strategic importance has declined, or because it has succeeded in finding a niche in which Parkinson's law applies without restriction. But in these cases, the question is: what is wrong with a management board that hits the whole company with a blanket 40 % reduction exercise, simply because it is incapable of seeing the areas in which disproportionately high potential cuts can be made?

Ways of improving results

There are basically four ways of improving results in the final analysis:

1. *Reducing products, services and tasks that have an unfavorable cost-benefit ratio*
   Total abandonment, tightening up the range, reduced performance, reduced quality, reduced frequency, etc.

2. **Expanding products, services, and tasks that have a favorable cost–benefit ratio**
   Additional services for existing customers, acquiring new customers, charging for previously free services, offering internally available services to third parties at a charge, etc.

3. **Achieving increased efficiency through a more rationalized organization**
   ⇨ *Optimizing the structure:*
   Amalgamation, centralization, decentralization, outsourcing, incorporating other elements, reducing administrative staff, shallower hierarchy, customer-focussed and target group-focussed organization, project organization, self-organization in semi-autonomous teams, etc.
   ⇨ *Optimizing processes:*
   Simplifying, standardizing, deregulating, etc.
   ⇨ *Optimizing the infrastructure:*
   Production equipment, space available and layout, computing, management information system, management tools, etc.

4. *Increasing efficiency through improved communications and cooperation*
   Information flow, decision-making, team formation and team development, interdepartmental collaboration, etc.

All of these possible ways of improving results have to be systematically tested – both within individual departments and at the level of the company as a whole. Particularly in connection with the fourth point – increasing efficiency through improved communications and collaboration – there is often a massive potential. However, the effects of soft factors are difficult to quantify from the business management standpoint. When there are nitpickers in charge, potentials of this type are almost always culpably neglected, or not even considered at the outset.

Example: *a company is suffering from a drastic excess of committees. Far too many groups and committees are working on far too many topics. Due to a mistaken approach to "participation" and "networking," everyone who might ever have had the slightest connection with the topic is included in every newly formed group. The effect: too many people are trying to be in too many places at once; everyone ends up just sitting around in meetings; too many people feel they have to say something about too many topics; all the groups include people who are basically only observing and obstructing, with no willingness to make constructive contributions. Result: no progress is made; the company loses sight of the overall priorities; the "output" is completely disproportionate to the effort put in.*

Of course, it is simply not possible to train hundreds of executives in group dynamics for long enough for them all to become willing and able to work efficiently and constructively in groups. But what you can do is to introduce one perfectly simple rule:

Project teams, task forces and committees can as of now have no more than five members. Exceptions – six or seven people – will need to be justified and will require official approval. Committees of eight or more people will no longer be tolerated on principle.

Effect: within an extremely short time, the energy being lost to meetings is substantially reduced and the efficiency of the groups is dramatically increased. But this effect is not a measurable one. A single successful project may in some circumstances bring in millions – and the productive benefit of the overall acceleration in the working and decision-making processes will be impossible to overestimate. But none of this can be put into hard figures down to the last penny, and it is impossible to provide cast-iron proof that it is connected with the new committee rule.

Particularly when the department involved is not too large, some cost-structure analyses and studies of potential profits can be carried out on a do-it-yourself basis and with limited external consultancy costs. But it should be remembered that many executives have no experience whatsoever in this area. They need a certain amount of advice on the methods involved. Here again the rule that applies is: *clearly described tasks are half the battle.*

We have drawn up appropriate model task instructions for you:

- *Identifying the potential*   → Figure 50
- *Getting customers involved*   → Figure 51
- *Involving employees*   → Figure 52
- *Presenting project results*   → Figure 53
- *Milestones and deadlines*   → Figure 54

Figure 50. Performance improvement – identifying the potential

All existing products, services and tasks are to be systematically investigated and analyzed from the following points of view:

1) *Reduction (when there are high costs)*
   - ☐ Total abandonment (cancellation without replacement)
   - ☐ Partial abandonment (tightening the range of products and services offered)
   - ☐ Reduced quality, reduced frequency, longer reaction time

2) *Expansion (when there is a favorable cost–benefit ratio)*
   - ☐ Additional offers for existing customers
   - ☐ Identifying new customers
   - ☐ Charging for previously free services
   - ☐ Offering internally available services to third parties at a charge

3) *Increasing efficiency by optimizing the structure*
   - ☐ Amalgamation/centralization
   - ☐ Decentralization
   - ☐ Outsourcing
   - ☐ Incorporating outside elements or differently
   - ☐ Reducing staff positions
   - ☐ Reducing the hierarchy or flattening it
   - ☐ Customer-oriented and target group-oriented organization
   - ☐ Project organization
   - ☐ Self-organization in semi-autonomous teams, etc.

4) *Increasing efficiency by optimizing processes*
   - ☐ Simplifying processes
   - ☐ Standardizing processes
   - ☐ Working more toward full capacity
   - ☐ Deregulation

5) *Increasing efficiency by optimizing the infrastructure*
   - ☐ Production equipment
   - ☐ Computing/management information system
   - ☐ Management tools

6) *Increasing efficiency by improving communications and cooperation*
   - ☐ Decision-making
   - ☐ Teamwork
   - ☐ Interdepartmental collaboration

Figure 51. Performance improvement – getting customers involved

- Defining the most important external and internal customers.

- Clarifying specific interests and needs; establishing the customer image of oneself (strengths and weaknesses as perceived from outside); common stocktaking and analysis of cooperation.

- Discussion of specific consequences of abandoning specific tasks or services; gathering existing ideas with regard to cost reductions.

- Discussion of one's own ideas about increasing profits or profitable performance; gathering the customer's ideas and suggestions.

Competently conducted discussions with external and internal customers are not only useful in gathering information, but also involve real-life customer orientation and create an aspect of "corporate identity"!

Figure 52. Performance improvement – involving employees

- Open and comprehensive information about the actual situation, goals, content and course of the project.

- Participation appropriate to each level concerned, both in the analysis and in the development of ideas and suggestions for reducing costs and activating potential profits and performance.

- Regular information about the current state of project work and the next steps coming up.

- Active participation in implementing mutually developed measures that have been approved by a management decision.

Active participation by the employees affected is carried out not only with an eye on motivation and identification with the company, but also with the aim of developing cost awareness and profit orientation – i.e., entrepreneurial thinking and action – at every level!

Figure 53. Performance improvement – presenting project results

The heads of the organizational units investigated, and of interdepartmental projects, present their suggestions to the management committee or to company management in the framework of a visual presentation lasting 45 minutes, based on the following aspects:

1) Measures to be taken if total costs (personnel and materials costs) have to be reduced by 10 %.
2) Measures to be taken if total costs (personnel and materials costs) have to be reduced by 20 %.
3) Measures to be taken to activate potential profits.
4) Measures to be taken to activate potential performance.
5) Investments that are necessary to be able to carry out existing core tasks more effectively or manage new tasks in addition.

The suggestions should be specifically broken down in relation to:

a) One's own organizational unit
b) Other organizational units or departments
c) Overall structures and processes (company as a whole)

The following specific points need to be mentioned:

- Extent of budget effects of a cost reduction, a profit increase, per-formance increase, or investment.

- Qualitative advantages and disadvantages (opportunities and risks) of a suggested measure.

- Effects of a suggested measure:
  ▶ Within the organizational unit
  ▶ On other organizational units or departments
  ▶ On outside partners and bodies

- Implementation of a suggested measure:
  ▶ Preconditions required
  ▶ Procedure
  ▶ Schedule

Figure 54. Performance improvement – milestones and deadlines

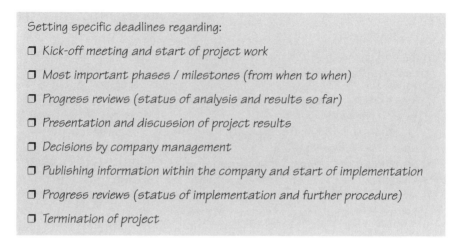

Setting specific deadlines regarding:

❑ Kick-off meeting and start of project work

❑ Most important phases / milestones (from when to when)

❑ Progress reviews (status of analysis and results so far)

❑ Presentation and discussion of project results

❑ Decisions by company management

❑ Publishing information within the company and start of implementation

❑ Progress reviews (status of implementation and further procedure)

❑ Termination of project

But anyone who wants to undertake this type of project within his own field of responsibility should first make sure that its goals are clear:

- *Does the goal involve reducing costs by X percent as a one-off campaign within a time-limited project?*
- *Or does it consist of getting executives and employees sufficiently motivated and competent that they are able to continuously optimize costs and profits in the future on their own initiative, and are familiar with methods of doing this?*

The answer to these questions will determine the approach chosen.

Coaching 13

Old wine in new skins?

An older term has come into increasingly frequent use in recent years: "coaching." Some people may regard this just as a passing fashion that will vanish as quickly as it came. But in fact there is a bit more to it than that. In the first place, there has been a fundamental change in the general view of what management involves. Providing consultancy and support is increasingly being regarded as a central function of management: the manager serves as the "coach" for his employees. This is what has brought the term into widespread use in the field of business management. Secondly, the tasks of management have become more difficult. There is a high degree of complexity involved. Even competent and well-qualified executives no longer have everything "at their fingertips" – and the less competent ones are just hopelessly out of their depth. Coping with this degree of complexity requires thought and consultation to be carried out in mutual dialogue – but not everyone has the right internal partner to talk to about his most difficult problems. And this has in fact led to an increasing demand for professional coaching. Wherever there is a demand, a supplier will emerge – although not always the right one. There is hardly a single consultancy firm that does not also offer management coaching.

To get straight to the point: coaching can be an extremely successful operation. But coaching is not, as many people think, a panacea for every ill. Some people despairing of the behavior of their boss or employee advise him to go for "coaching" – in the hope that his character neurosis or the fact that he is out of his depth will all dissolve into goodwill and benevolence. But coaching is not a form of therapy. And if a manager is in the wrong place, even therapy is not going to help. Instead, whether or not coaching is indicated needs to be clarified according to each situation and on an individual basis. If there is a rule of thumb at all, it is that *it is the best managers who benefit most from coaching* – and they only need it in specific situations, in the context of specially demanding tasks.

Questions and answers

- *What is coaching?*
  Personal advice and support.

- *What is involved in coaching?*
  It involves discussing specific questions and current problems of management in one's own field of responsibility; critical checking of one's own management actions in dialogue with a neutral and competent partner.

  In contrast to specialist consultancy, this does not involve passing on methodological expertise, but is concerned with optimizing behavior and management action within a highly complex and highly networked social and political environment. Among other things, it means recognizing and solving one's own emotional involvements. The most dangerous stumbling-blocks are of course the ones that lie within oneself. These are usually the ones that are not recognized soon enough.

- *Why and for what purpose is coaching offered to executives?*
  Management tasks have become much more complex and demanding at every level in recent years. In addition to everyday operations, there are difficult structural and personnel changes to cope with. People in management are in a constant field of tension between a variety of opposing interests. One's own behavior can have a decisive influence on whether things succeed or fail. Critical reflection and personal feedback can be decisively important in developing the right way to proceed or in overcoming "blind spots."

  However, one's direct partners at work – bosses, colleagues, and employees – are practically never completely impartial. Their own interests, prejudices, and hierarchical dependencies limit the extent to which they can be open. In addition, it is often tensions precisely in the individual executive's immediate environment that need to be clarified. In particularly turbulent periods, difficult projects, and acute conflict or crisis situations, a competent and neutral "sparring partner" can make a vital contribution to the development of adequate ways of proceeding – in the interests both of the individual concerned and of the company.

- *What forms of coaching are available?*
  In the first place, there is *individual coaching*. This involves a very personal and individual form of consultancy, the form and frequency of which can be chosen according to the situation. However, a certain amount of regularity is a prerequisite for success.

  Secondly, there is *team coaching*. This is based on a systematic exchange of experiences, collegial advice and personal feedback in a small team of employees with more or less comparable management responsibilities, but who are not linked by direct working relationships in their everyday business. The team gets together at regular intervals for working meetings directed or attended by a facilitator. Each participant has a time allowance made available at each meeting to work together with the rest of the team on the questions that are preoccupying him.

Team coaching means "coaching in the team." By contrast, when a team (management group, project team, expert committee) uses consultancy services in order to improve its style of internal collaboration, that is an activity belonging to "team development."

- *Does team coaching obstruct the development of formal teams?*
  No. A coaching team is a learning platform for individuals. Everything the individual learns will be of benefit in everyday work and collaboration.

- *Can experiences not be shared and feedback passed on in the framework of formal teams?*
  Yes, this not only can but should take place. But to begin with, it happens far too rarely in practice, because it is not part of the normal management culture. In the good times, something like this is regarded as "unnecessary," and in the bad times there is just "no time" for it due to chronic overwork. Secondly, there are certain natural boundaries to the amount of openness you can have in formal teams. The problems that involve real "pickles" are at least easier to approach when the people you are discussing them with are not the same as the ones you work with every day.

  It should be emphasized once again that coaching is not supposed either to replace or obstruct the exchange of experience and feedback in formal teams, and particularly not between bosses and employees, but on the contrary is meant to stimulate it and support it. Someone who tries to use coaching sessions to set up an "alternative world" to what happens in practice is not a professional "coach."

- *When should there be individual coaching, and when should there be team coaching?*
  Individual coaching can be a very powerful tool to support those in positions of responsibility who have to cope with critical situations or guide companies through difficult processes of change. However, the effort and cost are relatively high, and the numbers of competent consultants available are relatively limited. From the outset, therefore, individual coaching cannot be a blanket solution, and can only be used in isolation.

  It is a different matter with team coaching. The emphasis here is on mutual, collegial advice. Five or six participants can be assigned to one team coach – who can be an internal company coach if there is someone with the right training available. This tool can therefore be used on a broad basis in a large company.

- *Who can be used as a management coach?*
  Particularly experienced and socially talented executives, consultants, or management trainers.

- *What are the most important prerequisites for successful coaching?*
  First, it has to be *voluntary*. Only those who are themselves interested in taking part in a common consultancy process with others can be effectively advised. Secondly, *those involved must be neutral*. Those who are linked to one another in everyday working relationships can never be completely impartial advisers. Thirdly, *openness* and *trust*. Without openness, tricky questions cannot be dealt with, and without personal trust the degree of openness needed cannot be achieved. But trust can only be built up step by step. Genuinely effective coaching therefore in practice almost always requires the discussions to be held with some regularity over a certain period of time.

- *What is the difference between "coaching" and "supervision"?*
  There is not really any difference between the two. What you happen to call it is ultimately just a matter of semantics. In professions involving health care, education, and social work, this form of further professional development has always been a natural and indispensable means of enhancing one's professionalism – and is known as "supervision." In the management field, however, it is only a recent discovery, which has come to be known by the term "coaching", and the latest fashion is to call it "mentoring".

Conceptual and methodological basis for team coaching

When fundamental processes of change are about to take place in a company, executives at any level who are in particularly exposed positions need to receive appropriate practical support. Team coaching has more than proved its worth in this area. In larger companies, in-house coaching teams can be set up. For executives in medium-sized companies and managers at top levels, only teams with participants from other companies as well can be used. "Joint ventures" with other firms and institutions are required.

In view of the importance of team coaching, we give a brief outline of the methodological approach below:

1 *What is "team coaching"?*
2 *What is special about team coaching?*
3 *What precisely happens during team coaching?*
4 *What happens in a team consultancy meeting?*
5 *What is the benefit of team coaching?*
6 *What are the administrative and organisational essentials?*
7 *What working agreements are needed?*
8 *What are the duties of the facilitator or coach?*
9 *How much time is involved for each individual participant?*
10 *For whom is team coaching suitable?*

1 What is "team coaching"?

It is a particularly effective form of management development. Small teams of participants meet at regular intervals for one and a half days along with a facilitator specially trained for the task, for a systematic exchange of experiences, mutual collegial advice, and personal feedback. The subject of the discussions: current management issues, problems, or conflict situations from each individual's everyday professional life.

2 What is special about team coaching?

Team coaching is a method for exchanging experience on a team-oriented professional basis that is adapted for use in firms and companies.

- *Highly interactive*
  Discussions in a small team
- *On the job*
  Relating to specific questions from everyday professional life
- *With practical follow-up*
  Regular meetings
- *Process-oriented*
  Step-by-step handling of complex processes (managing change) over time

In addition, there are further advantages:

- *No long periods of absence for the participants*
  One and a half days for each meeting
- *Minimal organizational costs*
  Decentralized organization in small teams

3 What precisely happens during team coaching?

The individual participant puts up questions from everyday professional life for discussion:

- *Critical problems of management and communication*
- *Tricky personnel questions*
- *Politically delicate decisions*
- *Complex, conflict-laden projects*
- *Areas of tension in one's own immediate working environment*
- *Acute conflict or crisis situations in the company, or in important external relations*

The team analyzes the problem together, and develops potential approaches to a solution along with the person affected (possible alternative procedures). Based on their own personal experience, colleagues can offer ideas, tips, and food for thought.

An important part of the analysis affects personal attitudes, interests, and motives, as well as the role and behavior of the colleague concerned in his own professional environment.

Difficult projects, longer-term processes of change, and conflict situations that have become ossified can be approached on a process-oriented basis, i. e. worked through step by step with accompanying advice.

A decisive aspect of coaching work is that the problems put up for discussion should not only be analyzed and methodically worked through from purely rational points of view, but that personal attitudes and forms of behavior should also be examined, particularly with regard to the subliminal *emotional dynamics* involved.

In this way, each participant's capacity for self-perception can be sensitized. He can also learn how to observe the mood and feelings of bosses, colleagues, and employees and adapt his behavior appropriately to the human and interpersonal realities in his environment.

---

4 *How does the process run in a team consultancy meeting?*

There are six phases of alternating activity on the part of participants (P) or the team (T):

1   P **Following on from the previous meeting**
- *What was the topic* (situation and problem)?
- *What were your messages* (basic recommendations)?

Function:
Helps refresh memories when starting off. But above all, you need to think and act not in terms of isolated individual situations ("still shots"), but in terms of developmental processes ("movie").

2.1 P **Report on further developments**
- *How did things go on, what happened in detail?*
- *What did I do, how did I behave?*
- *How did I feel about it?*
- *How do I assess the situation today?*
- *What went well as I see it, and what did not?*

Function:
Getting colleagues "on board," familiarizing them with events and the current situation. Recalling developments for oneself once again.

2.2 T *Questions to aid understanding*
- Putting questions (no discussion yet)
- Understanding the situation and background

Function:
Those not directly affected have no "blind spots" and have an undistorted view of the individual background and context – particularly regarding the role and behavior of the colleague concerned. Even just the questions your colleagues put can usually lead to important clarification and fresh perceptions.

3   P   **Specific questions for advice**
  ▪ *What am I particularly concerned about?*
  ▪ *On what points do I need to come clear?*
  ▪ *What are the questions I would like to hear your opinions about?*

Function:
a) Making oneself aware of where things are not clear
   (*basic prerequisites for solving a problem and independently controlling one's own process of perception*).
b) Giving colleagues guidance as to where advice is needed (*learning to involve others in a useful way, getting them active and making use of them properly*).

4   T   **Contributions from colleagues (discussion)**
  ▪ Impressions and perceptions (what did I notice?)
  ▪ Assumptions (hypotheses) about possible connections
  ▪ Personal feedback about the colleague's behavior
  ▪ Specific ideas, tips, suggestions (alternative procedures)

Function:
a) *For P:*
   food for thought regarding specific procedure and his or her own be-havior
   (*prerequisite for experimenting with alternatives to previous procedures and patterns of behavior*).
b) *For the team:*
   learning how to advise others; learning how to give personal feedback (*constructive criticism*).

5   P   **Summary and comments**
  ▪ *What new things have I realized?*
  ▪ *Which suggestions were particularly important for me, and why?*
  ▪ *Which points am I still not really clear about?*
  ▪ *What will I now do specifically?*

Function:
  ▶ Crystallizing the essentials
  ▶ Feedback to colleagues about what has "got through"
  ▶ Making oneself and others aware of any gray areas

▶ Planning specific implementation steps, the results of which can be discussed with colleagues again later
(*the "law of reunion": social pressure that forces one to act, and thus to make specific forms of progress*).

6 T Short mutual stocktaking
  ■ *Is there anything else to contribute to the discussion topic?*
  ■ *How did we experience our process and style of communication during this part of the consultation process?*
  ■ *Are there any other personal questions or perceptions that need to be discussed before we go on to the next contribution?*

---

5 *What is the benefit of team coaching?*

For the *individual participant*:

● *Development of management ability*
  ▶ Solving complex management problems
  ▶ Guiding processes of change
● *Development of personality*
  ▶ Individual managerial, communicative, and cooperative behavior

For the *company*:

● *Enhanced problem-solving capacity*
  ▶ More soundly based decision-making
  ▶ Procedures adapted to the situation when complex problems arise
  ▶ Unblocking of "stalemates"

For managers in prominent positions, the coaching team is usually the only place where the individual has an opportunity to:

● Discuss tricky situations in the field of emotional tension between bosses, colleagues, and employees.
● Study critical situations in the company with regard to all the possible consequences in advance of decisions being taken.
● Discuss one's own uncertainties, doubts, and fears and go over them with others.
● Develop procedural steps and personal forms of behavior during situations of acute conflict and crisis.
● Recognize one's own "blind spots" and analyze personal failures without loss of face.
● Examine one's own attitudes, convictions, and values with regard to their relevance and suitability.
● Carefully examine issues to do with planning one's individual career and life, in advance of important choice points.

6 What are the administrative and organisational essentials?

- **Minimum team size: five people**
  - ▶ Range of ideas and experience (no mental "inbreeding")
  - ▶ Range of personalities (differentiated relationship structure)

- **Maximum team size: six people**
  - ▶ Sufficient time for each individual's questions
  - ▶ Ease of team communications
  - ▶ Continuous active participation by all team members

- **Colleagues who do not have direct relations at work**
  - ▶ Impartiality as advisers ("coaches")
  - ▶ No mutual prejudices or dependencies
  - ▶ No vested interests in other people's issues

- **Colleagues from different functions**
  - ▶ Management experience from various fields in the team
  - ▶ Learning to distinguish between general and situational contexts

- **Colleagues with comparable levels of management responsibility**
  - ▶ Mutual understanding
  - ▶ Balanced give-and-take
  - ▶ No preestablished hierarchy in the team

- **Stable team membership**
  - ▶ Building up mutual personal trust
  - ▶ Close mutual familiarity with individual work situations

- **Regular meetings**
  - ▶ Dealing with specific questions and issues (*relevance*)
  - ▶ Ongoing consultancy of complex processes, step by step measures taken taylored to actual progress (*process-oriented*)

- **Regular review – equal time allowances**
  - ▶ No passive observers, no one dominating the proceedings
  - ▶ Learning how to take good advice, learning how to give others good advice

- **Competent facilitation**
  - ▶ Ensuring professional working methods
  - ▶ Constructive ways of dealing with internal group dynamics

7 What working agreements are needed?

- **Active participation**
  All participants take an active part in the team's work – both as seekers of advice and as advisors.

- *Willingness to be open*
  Openness in giving reports about oneself and in giving personal feedback to colleagues is the most important prerequisite for effective team consultancy.

- *Responsibility for oneself*
  Each member continues to be responsible for himself with regard to what he does or does not do in his own field of work. He decides which arguments to accept and which not to. The other members' contributions are offers, and only the one seeking advice can take decisions about whether to implement them.

- *Obligations and attendance*
  Agreed times for meetings must be consistently observed. No one is here just for his own benefit. Each member of the team is also a fellow learner and "coach" for his colleagues.

- *Individual preparation*
  Competent advice from colleagues is only possible if the individual carries out careful preparation for his own discussion and advice units.

- *Confidentiality of information*
  The information received during team consultancy is strictly confidential and must never be passed on to others.

---

8 *What are the duties of the facilitator or coach?*

1) *Creating an atmosphere of openness and trust*
   - Openness, honesty, spontaneity
   - Responding to one another personally
   - Being aware of one's own sensitivities and feelings
   - Being aware of the sensitivities and feelings of others

2) *Ensuring professional working methods*
   - Observing the rules
   - Observing regular turns for advice
   - Observing the process steps during coaching
   - Ensuring the necessary care during each working step

3) *Ensuring analysis of the emotional dynamics*
   - Open and hidden goals, interests, and needs of the "principal actors"
   - Social dynamics ("sociogram") and power structures
   - Explicit and implicit moods and feelings of those affected
   - Interests and needs, sensitivities and feelings of the participant

4) *Chairmanship of team discussions*
   - Time management
   - Ensuring balanced participation

- Ensuring competent communication in the team
- Summing up and keeping a record of results

5) *Dealing with the team's internal group dynamics*
  - Ensuring regular and open process reviews and "debriefing"
  - Giving the team feedback with regard to its style of communicating and cooperation
  - Adressing emotional tensions and letting them be discussed
  - Advising the team on constructive ways of dealing with any conflicts arising

6) *Active participation ("player/coach model")*
  - Putting questions for clarification
  - Drawing attention to critical points
  - Contributing one's own ideas and experiences
  - Giving the individual team members personal feedback
    (*But: serving the team takes top priority. The facilitator never presents his own problem situations for discussion.*)

---

9 *How much time is involved for the individual participant?*

- *Ideally, one and a half days 5–6 times per year; alternatively, one day 8–10 times a year*
  Distributed as evenly as possible over the year

  One and a half days allow each participant a time slot of about two hours per meeting to work through his questions with the team.
  One evening together per meeting for informal personal contacts is included as an explicit part of the program.

- *Plus: 1–2 hours' individual preparation for each meeting*
  For structured, visual presentation of the topic

  Careful preparation by each individual makes a vital contribution to the effectiveness and time economy of the coaching work.

However, the total time required should not be regarded as a "training" cost, but as work on specific questions in the individual's field of responsibility. Experience shows that the time used for coaching work is later regarded as having been particularly valuable and well spent.

---

10 *For whom is team coaching suitable?*

Team coaching is suitable for executives who ...

▶ Set themselves high standards with regard to the professionalism of their management work.

- ▶ Are willing and ready to reflect on their own professional work together with others, and to question it critically.
- ▶ Enjoy working in a team and wish not only to "benefit," but also have an interest in other people and a willingness to respond to them.
- ▶ Are sensitive, on the one hand, to the *strategic, political and tactical aspects* of management work, and on the other to the *psychosocial dynamics* of the processes that take place in a company (human, interpersonal, group-dynamic, and mass- psychological phenomena interfering with objective corporate and business questions).
- ▶ Are not subject to any taboos, but are willing to talk about questions of personal attitude and forms of behavior within a small circle of close confidantes.
- ▶ Wish to develop themselves further in a consistent fashion with regard to their strategic and social abilities and capacity to deal with conflict.
- ▶ Are willing and ready to invest 8–10 working days each year for closed sessions in the coaching team and consistently keep to agreed meeting times.

Team coaching is not suitable for executives who ...

- ▶ Have disturbed behavior and lack sufficient competence or are out of their depth in their job, and in the view of those around them need to be "put in order."

Criteria for
Successful Management

14

One of the ways of achieving sensitivity to the issues and making a start is to carry out a stocktaking exercise. This can be done either on one's own, or together with colleagues, employees, and selected customers or suppliers. As in a general inspection, what matters is giving one's own company, or the specific area that one has entrepreneurial responsibility for, an expert check-up. And this is exactly the purpose for which we have designed the following checklist. It includes all of the aspects we regard as being essential to up-to-date company management and company design.

A self-assessment inventory

Many roads lead to Rome – and all the different places you can start from are even more numerous. But before you set off on your pleasant trip, today's gods have ordained that careful identification of your current position and some planning work have to be carried out first. The following framework of criteria for success is intended to allow you to comb through your company to identify its strengths and weaknesses. You can then decide in a meaningful way where it is worthwhile for you to start.

My company	Applies …				
	Fully	Largely	Partly	Not really	Not at all
1 A lively sense of mission and clear basic principles create throughout the company a sense of identification with the firm and motivation to contribute to its further development. These provide the foundation for the annual target agreements at every level of the organization.	❏	❏	❏	❏	❏

My company	Applies ...				
	Fully	Largely	Partly	Not really	Not at all
2 Market orientation and customer orientation are at the top of the company's list of priorities. The minds and actions of executives and employees are focused on the customer and his needs. Internal customers for services provided are also regarded and treated as "customers."	❏	❏	❏	❏	❏
3 A lean organizational structure – small head office, short distances to cross and heavily decentralized responsibilities – encourages entrepreneurial thinking and action at the lower levels and ensures that intensive attention is given to the customer on the market as well as the "customer" within the company.	❏	❏	❏	❏	❏
4 There is a strong orientation toward performance and a strong awareness of costs throughout the company. Management is generally based on targets and performance, and even at the lowest non-managerial levels, employees show commitment to reaching targets and give their active assistance in keeping costs down.	❏	❏	❏	❏	❏
5 A modern range of management tools, which is obligatory throughout the company with the extent to which it is applied being regularly checked, ensures effective guidance and the necessary uniformity in management practices.	❏	❏	❏	❏	❏

My company	Applies ...				
	Fully	Largely	Partly	Not really	Not at all
6 Innovation is emphasized. Tailor-made solutions to problems for the customer are the most important goal. Ideas are developed in close contact with the customer – and in-house, every effort is put into transforming these ideas into practical products and services as quickly as possible.	❏	❏	❏	❏	❏
7 Development and change are not regarded as exceptional, but as a constant task. Management, executives, and employees are constantly giving thought to ways of improving things. The organizational structure and working processes are always flexibly adapted to current requirements.	❏	❏	❏	❏	❏
8 The company's internal condition and external image are given regular and systematic check-ups. Careful consultation – not only with employees, but also with customers and suppliers – allows strengths, weaknesses, and problem areas, as well as development trends, to be recognized and realistically assessed.	❏	❏	❏	❏	❏
9 Wholistic thinking is used both when analyzing and when initiating changes. Leadership and collaboration, motivation and competence, working atmosphere and company culture are just as systematically investigated as the product range, productivity, profit performance, and net value added.	❏	❏	❏	❏	❏

My company	Applies …				
	Fully	Largely	Partly	Not really	Not at all
10 At all levels, people work together freely and straightforwardly. Team-work is highly valued. Neither the levels of the hierarchy nor depart-mental boundaries create barriers. People work together on a basis of healthy common sense with regard to the benefit for the customer, and are not primarily concerned with strict areas of formal responsibility.	❏	❏	❏	❏	❏
11 There is an openess of communica-tion. Information is not monopoli-zed, but regarded as an important working resource for all employees. A diverse range of internal company communications tools ensures that all employees are not only kept in-formed about the most important data and facts, but also that the aims, background, and context of current events are understood within the company.	❏	❏	❏	❏	❏
12 Employees' abilities and qualifica-tions are regarded as a central poten-tial for productivity and creativity, and are systematically encouraged through appropriate training and further education programs, as well as through personnel and organiza-tion development measures.	❏	❏	❏	❏	❏
13 Employees' potential is systematically utilised through the delegation of responsibility, the use of semi-auto-nomous groups, and direct participa-tion in the process of opinion forma-tion and decision-making.	❏	❏	❏	❏	❏

My company	Applies …				
	Fully	Largely	Partly	Not really	Not at all
14 Company management gives regular and intensive consideration to the medium-term and long-term future of the company. It develops and implements strategies aimed at securing its own future, which are understood and supported by employees.	❏	❏	❏	❏	❏
15 Members of company management regularly get out into everyday operational work so that they can talk to employees at their own workplaces. They are familiar with the mood at the grass roots and know what employees are concerned about.	❏	❏	❏	❏	❏
16 Management is open to critical feedback and gives constant attention to improving its own abilities and qualifications, particularly with regard to its strategic and social skills.	❏	❏	❏	❏	❏
17 Management has the courage to take clear decisions, as well as unpopular measures. Targets that have been set are consistently pursued. However, great care is taken with specific measures to ensure that they are socially acceptable and that dealings with employees are based on partnership.	❏	❏	❏	❏	❏
18 Company management is a genuine team. Decisions are mutually supported, management initiatives are carried through without dissent. This gives employees orientation and security.	❏	❏	❏	❏	❏

My company	Applies …				
	Fully	Largely	Partly	Not really	Not at all
19 Management cultivates a culture in which people can discuss differing opinions and interests openly. Conflicts are not suppressed, but exposed and constructively resolved.	❏	❏	❏	❏	❏
20 The company as a whole can be described as a "learning organization." It has a sensitive early-warning system, flexible structures, and motivated, capable, and adaptable employees. Whenever changes become necessary, it is recognized quickly, and appropriate adjustments and innovations are carried out without delay.	❏	❏	❏	❏	❏

Score

		++	+	+/-	–	– –
1	Mission and basic values	❏	❏	❏	❏	❏
2	Market orientation and customer orientation	❏	❏	❏	❏	❏
3	Lean organization	❏	❏	❏	❏	❏
4	Results orientation	❏	❏	❏	❏	❏
5	Management tools	❏	❏	❏	❏	❏
6	Innovativeness	❏	❏	❏	❏	❏
7	Flexibility	❏	❏	❏	❏	❏
8	Regular feedback	❏	❏	❏	❏	❏
9	Wholistic management	❏	❏	❏	❏	❏
10	Cooperation	❏	❏	❏	❏	❏
11	Communications	❏	❏	❏	❏	❏
12	Developing employees' potential	❏	❏	❏	❏	❏
13	Utilising employees' potential	❏	❏	❏	❏	❏
14	Strategy development	❏	❏	❏	❏	❏
15	Direct contact with grass roots	❏	❏	❏	❏	❏
16	Competent management	❏	❏	❏	❏	❏
17	Clear, socially acceptable management	❏	❏	❏	❏	❏
18	Management team	❏	❏	❏	❏	❏
19	Ability to deal with conflict	❏	❏	❏	❏	❏
20	Learning organization	❏	❏	❏	❏	❏

Qualifications for
Managing Change

15

As always in life, talents are not equally shared out – and this is not the case in managing change either. There are people with a natural talent who seem to have a feeling for processes of development and change in their very blood. There are others who have to go through systematic education and training to enable them to manage the more demanding projects for change. And then there are those who from the very start are not suitable to direct processes of change, and whom no training course in the world will ever be able to turn into useful "managers of change." The reason is that there are some abilities you can learn, and others that – at least by the adult stage – can simply no longer be acquired. That's just the way things are with many activities. If you are only five foot three inches tall, you are never going to be a successful high-jumper. If you are color-blind, you should not be trying to earn your living as an artist. And if you've got two left hands, you should not be training to become a surgeon, even when it has been a family tradition for generations.

Is there a universally valid job description for managers of change? Fortunately not – just as little as there is a single, universal job description for entrepreneurs, research directors, or sales directors. However, a rough guide can be given, describing the qualifications that are important in the field of managing change. Some people have strengths in one area, others in another. Both can be highly successful. But if some of the important abilities are completely lacking, then failure is bound to ensue. And if there are gaps of this type, a careful examination should be made to see whether they involve abilities that can be learned – or whether they are abilities that can never be acquired.

A self-assessment inventory

We provide here a questionnaire of relevance to the selection or development of training measures, as well as internal personnel decisions – and you can of course use it for self-assessment as well.

It includes the following sections:

A **Personal qualities** – *cannot be learned*
B **Special abilities** – *most people can develop these up to a certain extent*
C **Specific experience** – *depends on previous activities*
D **Specific expertise** – *can be learned*

Inventory
Competence in managing change
++ *Distinct strength*
+ *Well developed*
+/– *Half and half*
– *Less well developed*
– – *Distinct weakness*

		++	+	+/–	–	– –
A	*Personal qualities*					
1	Healthy mental constitution (*self-confident, stable, resilient*)	❏	❏	❏	❏	❏
2	Positive basic attitude (*optimistic, constructive approach*)	❏	❏	❏	❏	❏
3	Openness and honesty (*direct, spontaneous, genuine*)	❏	❏	❏	❏	❏
4	Willingness to take responsibility (*personal commitment*)	❏	❏	❏	❏	❏
5	Basic attitude of partnership (*vs. elitist, hierarchic, authoritarian*)	❏	❏	❏	❏	❏
6	Courage to take a personal stance and decisions (*courage of one's convictions*)	❏	❏	❏	❏	❏
7	Reliability (*keeping to agreements made*)	❏	❏	❏	❏	❏
8	Intuitiveness (*access to the emotional sphere*)	❏	❏	❏	❏	❏
9	Degree of realism (*feeling for what is feasible*)	❏	❏	❏	❏	❏
10	Humor (*ability to relax and put others at ease*)	❏	❏	❏	❏	❏

		++	+	+/–	–	– –
B	*Special abilities*					
1	Ability to create an atmosphere of openness and trust	❏	❏	❏	❏	❏
2	Good ability to listen (*"active listening"*)	❏	❏	❏	❏	❏

		++	+	+/-	–	– –
3	Ability to persuade people and create enthusiasm (*creating motivation and identification with the company*)	❑	❑	❑	❑	❑
4	Ability to integrate people ("*welding" people into a team*)	❑	❑	❑	❑	❑
5	Ability to cope with conflict (*defining one's own position and defending it, and being able to confront others*)	❑	❑	❑	❑	❑
6	Ability to work in processes (*ability to grasp developmental processes and guide them*)	❑	❑	❑	❑	❑
7	Ability to deal with chaos (*ability to remain capable of action in turbulent, extremely complex situations*)	❑	❑	❑	❑	❑
8	Strategic ability (*ability to grasp complex contexts and deduce implications relevant to action*)	❑	❑	❑	❑	❑
9	Intercultural competence (*ability to work in different social fields*)	❑	❑	❑	❑	❑
10	Clarity of expression (*clarity of thinking, succinctness of formulation, simple and generally comprehensible form of expression*)	❑	❑	❑	❑	❑

		++	+	+/-	–	– –
C	*Specific experience*					
1	Self-awareness (*intensive, long-term self-examination of one's own personality, motives, and social behavior*)	❑	❑	❑	❑	❑
2	Individual counselling (*advising, accompanying, "coaching" individuals*)	❑	❑	❑	❑	❑
3	Teamwork and team development (*directing and developing small groups*)	❑	❑	❑	❑	❑
4	Chairing large groups (*designing and directing conferences with large numbers of participants*)	❑	❑	❑	❑	❑
5	Project management (*organizing and directing projects for change*)	❑	❑	❑	❑	❑

	++	+	+/-	-	- -
D Specific expertise					
1 Basic knowledge of psychology	❑	❑	❑	❑	❑
2 Basic business knowledge	❑	❑	❑	❑	❑
3 Systems theory/chaos theory	❑	❑	❑	❑	❑
4 Group dynamics	❑	❑	❑	❑	❑
5 Organizational theory	❑	❑	❑	❑	❑
6 Organizational psychology	❑	❑	❑	❑	❑
7 Organization development approaches (*concepts, strategies*)	❑	❑	❑	❑	❑
8 Organization development interventions (*tools, methods, procedures*)	❑	❑	❑	❑	❑

Outlook and Prospects

There is no sign at all that we are moving into quieter times. There is therefore no prospect of the topic of "change," and the challenges involved in designing necessary changes, losing their significance. Quite the contrary. We are probably facing a revolutionary situation that will dwarf anything seen before. Developments are accelerating, becoming more turbulent, more radical, more global. The chances of building refuges and withdrawing into them to seek peace and quiet away from these developments are getting more and more remote. But fundamental problems require solutions that are just as fundamental. In this context, the slogan "paradigm change" is often heard: the existing ways of looking at things and evaluating them are no longer adequate to grasp what is going on – new categories are needed.

We live in a period of transition. The tools and methods that are on offer may fail us, for two reasons:

- They are being offered *too early.* The time is not yet ripe, and it would take too much effort to start using them so soon. This is what happened with the topic of "de-hierarchization," for example. What some years ago was dismissed by most people as being a provocative slogan, "the twilight of the hierarchy," and was only taken seriously by a few people with foresight, is hastily being put into practice today under the slogan "lean management."
- But they can also be offered *too late.* The patient's condition has changed so much that the treatment is no longer the right one. Damaging developments have progressed so far that only drastic measures are going to be of any use.

This book is intended to provide a set of tools that will allow people to successfully face today's challenges. We have deliberately confined ourselves to describing methods and techniques that can be used to make a start *now.* But what is the destination?

To avoid the risk of making our solutions part of the problem in turn, we can briefly mention here a few of the current aspects and trends that will need to be taken into account – probably in the very near future.

Renaissance of authoritarianism

It seems that many people find the constant uncertainty and incalculability of events today unbearable, and are not willing to face up to the fears these bring with them. People remember the so-called good old times, when things were still in order, when people knew what was going on. This longing for a return to the old days, seen through rose-tinted spectacles, threatens to become an obsession – providing fertile soil for authoritarian approaches. Popper's statement about society in general is applicable here:

"There is no return to a harmonious state of nature. If we turn back, then we must go the whole way – we must return to the beasts ... If we dream of a return to our childhood, if we are tempted to rely on others and so be happy, if we shrink from the task of carrying our cross, the cross of humaneness, of reason, of responsibility, if we lose courage and flinch from the strain, then we must try to fortify ourselves with a clear understanding of the simple decision before us. We can return to the beasts. But if we wish to remain human, then there is only one way, the way into the open society. We must go on into the unknown, the uncertain and insecure, using what reason we may have to plan as well as we can for both security and freedom". (The Open Society and its Enemies, London: Routledge, 1945; 5th edn. 1966, vol. 1, pp. 200–1.)

Those who choose not to abandon their own responsibility and prefer to pull the ground away from under authoritarian temptations have to offer something positive. It can never be the certainty that we will one day reach a "promised land." It would be charlatanism to promise anything of the sort. There remains the possibility of offering to analyze the turbulent developments that are taking place and the fears they create and trying to recognize what possible action one can take, what opportunities one can exploit. This will not banish the fears, but it may shackle them. However, the analysis needs to be carried out carefully. Too much analysis might lead to a sense of paralysis, driving those who have such fears into the arms of authoritarian rabble-rousers.

In authoritarian systems, a lot of time and energy is devoted to defining the one redeeming truth – and fighting to preserve this pure doctrine. Open analysis and discussion will make it possible to advance and possibly break through to rational ways of looking at the problems, where it is not a matter of who has possession of the ultimate truth, but of filtering out what has proved itself in action. We need this open dialogue to develop together the steps that will serve to ensure survival on a fair basis, instead of blindly running into the arms of people who tout themselves as saviors.

A new solidarity instead of "winners making the rules"

Existing ways of planning developments would gradually lead to the creation of more and more losers. Because the concepts that were created to ensure prosperity within a framework of economic growth are just not appropriate to a situation in which what matters is ensuring survival in a stagnating or shrinking market – in a situation of clearly limited resources, where success is usually only achieved by ousting others or by redistributing resources. Elsewhere in this book, we have already pleaded for the creation of socially accepted patterns for downgrading and layoffs that would make the personnel changes that are required both flexible and socially acceptable. But if we assume that economic purchasing power and demand are not going to rise dramatically in the foreseeable future, if we assume that competition will force further rationalization in the production of products and services, and that environmental concerns will require much more sparing use of resources, especially energy resources, then more generalized solutions are going to be needed:

- In the long term, people cannot apply their energies at a consistently high level if they constantly feel their job is not secure – if they are always being threatened with being pushed off to join the hordes of those who, due to current developments, are dismissed as "human trash." Our entire economy is based on the model of "Who has to jump out of the boat next to ensure the survival of the rest?" Insecurity leads to fear, and fear to mistrust. Because the workplace is the center of the social network, as well as of an individual's chances of developing his or her own potential.
- Due to the control mechanisms we have today, there will in future be fewer and fewer people in what by today's standards would count as well-paid jobs. What this means is that *the general standard of living will noticeably sink.* In our affluent society, this will for many people mean reducing things to what is absolutely necessary. But even in today's society, there are already many living below the poverty line.
- And even if layoffs can be regulated in a socially acceptable form: those who have lost their jobs are still liable to become a burden to society as a whole, "hardship cases." Due to general economic developments, however, society will not be able to finance the massive and constantly growing social costs involved. This means that we will have to expect an *alarming impoverishment of wide sections of the population.*
- Last, but not least: the social tensions associated with these developments, and the ways in which the serious social conflict they imply will be expressed – all of this can today only be speculated on.

A genuine solution to all of these problems must basically include the following approaches:

First, the legal framework will have to be designed in such a way that it once again becomes an attractive proposition to maintain jobs, or create new ones, instead of just rationalizing and reducing them. This could be done, for example, by uncoupling social security contributions from pay, and linking them instead to value creation.

Secondly, someone expecting identification with the company and commitment from his or her staff has to offer security in return. Admittedly, this cannot be security in the form of guaranteeing a specific activity or a fixed rate of pay; but it can mean security in belonging to the company and, in consequence, security of employment.

Thirdly, the principle of solidarity has to be built into the business unit. Rewards need to be made so flexible that, depending on the level of economic return, everyone will earn more in good times and make the same sacrifices in bad ones. It has been proved by several companies – among them quite successful ones – that this is basically possible.

At present, we are still light years away from this kind of thinking. Top managers of large companies earn not double, not triple, but ten or twenty times the salaries of the staff whose fates are ultimately in their hands. This relationship alone, seen in the cold light of day, is obscene, and bears no relation whatever to what they actually achieve. But it is even more remarkable that none of these numerous so-called leading business figures has so much as thought aloud about such questions. A lot of swaggering talk about ethics in business is heard from people with remarkably straight faces. In reality, however, what counts for managers is the principle of the market – and the attitude that "everybody's in business for himself." Well, it's not against the law. But it would at least be nice if people would admit the reality and not go spouting about ethics.

Last, but not least: to master the tasks of the future together, the first thing labor union organizations and employers' organizations will have to do is dump their ritualized power struggles in the Museum of Sociology, and get on with creating a new form of collaboration, one which:

- Will approach the problem not from the good old class struggle model, but taking a *general view* and a *common approach.*
- Will allow *the people affected to participate directly* and take their real interests and needs much more strongly into account than has ever been the case in recent decades.
- Will, while establishing guidelines and frameworks, not regulate everything down to the last iota, but leave enough freedom for *solutions adapted to the local situation* to be introduced in individual companies.
- Aim for an *adaptable solution* that can be flexibly adjusted to new developments within a general legal framework.

There is one fundamental prerequisite for all this to be possible: against the background of the current challenges facing society, roles need to be completely redefined. However, this will only be possible to the extent that trust can be built up and modes of social security developed that will prevent abuse and avoid unilateral opting out of the new roles being played.

Speed and consistency in implementation

In almost all organizations, there is already some awareness of what currently needs to be done, and of the requirement for fundamental change – at least in the form of dark forebodings and fears. And the same is true of the treatment that is needed. What is missing in many places is a willingness to accept the consequences and act on this awareness, turning it into programs of action that are then consistently executed:

- There is a character type that can be described as the "inhuman redeveloper" – and in the period we are facing, these people will be as much in demand as ever. But usually it only becomes apparent when it is too late that this type of economic redevelopment is a Pyrrhic victory – once the hidden costs in loss of motivation, and the delayed social consequences, emerge.
- In our view, *radical consistency in the implementation* of therapeutic measures is required – but at the same time, there needs to be just as much consistency in the *attention given to the social needs* of those affected and in the *application of process-oriented procedures* while this is done. We are convinced that these three aspects can be extremely well integrated with each other.

This book is intended to encourage this second type of redeveloper, and provide the tools that are needed.

Acknowledgments

We are grateful to the following colleagues for valuable tips:

Dr. Klaus Hinst in the sections on "*Conflict Management*" and "*Changing a Company's Culture*", Part 3, Chapters 10 and 11 and in preparing the english edition.

Benno Honold and Eckart Müller in the section on "*Criteria for Successful Company Management*", Part 3, Chapter 14.

Printing (Computer to Film): Saladruck, Berlin
Binding: Lüderitz & Bauer, Berlin